Apocalypse and Armada in Kyd's *Spanish Tragedy*

Habent sua fata libelli

Volume XXIX
of
Sixteenth Century Essays & Studies
Charles G. Nauert, Jr., General Editor

ISBN 0-940474-31-X

Composed at Northeast Missouri State University, Kirksville, Missouri
Book design by Tim Rolands, typesetting by Gwen Blotevogel
Cover Art and Title Page by Teresa Wheeler, NMSU Designer
Manufactured by Edwards Brothers, Ann Arbor, Michigan
Text is set in Stone Serif 10/13

APOCALYPSE &ARMADA

IN KYD'S SPANISH TRAGEDY

FRANK
ARDOLINO

Volume XXIX
Sixteenth Century Essays & Studies
Kirksville, MO USA
1995

This book has been brought to publication with the
generous support of
Northeast Missouri State University

Library of Congress Cataloging-in-Publication Data

Apocalypse and Armada in Kyd's Spanish tragedy / Frank Ardolino
    p.   cm. — (Sixteenth century essays & studies : v. 29)
    Includes bibliographical references and index
ISBN 0-940474-31-X
    1. Kyd, Thomas, 1558–1594. Spanish tragedy. 2. Apocalypse in litera-
ture. 3. Protestantism in literature. 4. Reformation in literature.
5. Armada, 1588, in literature. 6. Revenge in literature. 7. Literature and
history—England—History—16th century.
I. Title. II. Series.
PR2654.S63A7 1995   95–25542
822'.3—dc20   CIP

To June as always

THE

SPANISH TRAGE-
die, Containing the lamentable
end of *Don Horatio*, and *Bel-imperia*:
with the pittifull death of
olde *Hieronimo*.

Newly corrected and amended of such grosse faults as
passed in the first impression.

AT LONDON
Printed by *Edward Allde*, for
Edward White.

Contents

Abbreviations

ELH	*Journal of English Literary History*
ELR	*English Literary Renaissance*
JEGP	*Journal of English and German Philology*
JWCI	*Journal of Warburg and Courtauld Institute*
MLR	*Modern Language Review*
MP	*Modern Philology*
RQ	*Renaissance Quarterly*
SEL	*Studies in English Literature*
SP	*Studies in Philology*

Introduction

THREE SCHOOLS OF CRITICAL THOUGHT have developed to explain the nature of Hieronimo's act of vengeance against his son Horatio's murderers. The first school, represented primarily by Fredson Bowers, Eleanor Prosser, and Charles and Elaine Hallet, has argued that Hieronimo must have been condemned by Elizabethans as a homicidal revenger because he violated the Christian injunction to leave vengeance to God (Rom. 12:17–19).[1] However, by judging Hieronimo's action solely according to the New Testament ethos, these critics do not account for the paradox of his being rewarded and his enemies punished in the classical underworld.

The second school of critics vindicates Hieronimo's revenge as the fulfillment of either a classical code of justice or an apocalyptic nationalism. Frank Ardolino, Sacvan Bercovitch, Ernest de Chickera, Herbert Coursen, G. K. Hunter, Ejner Jensen, David Laird, Michael Levin, and John Ratliff[2] have argued that Kyd wants us to evaluate Hieronimo's action according to the classical code of justice, which is set in motion when Proserpine sends Andrea back to earth with Revenge, who gives the doom prophecy at the outset:

[1] Fredson Bowers, *Elizabethan Revenge Tragedy: 1587-1642* (Princeton: Princeton University Press, 1940), 65–85; Charles and Elaine Hallett, *The Revenger's Tragedy: A Study of Revenge Tragedy Motifs* (Lincoln: University of Nebraska Press, 1980), 131–59; Eleanor Prosser, *Hamlet and Revenge*, rev. ed. (Stanford: Stanford University Press, 1971), 44–52.

[2] Frank Ardolino, "*Veritas Filia Temporis*: Time, Perspective, and Justice in *The Spanish Tragedy*," *Studies in Iconography* 3 (1977):57–69; idem, *Thomas Kyd's Mystery Play: Myth and Ritual in The Spanish Tragedy* (New York: Peter Lang, 1985); idem, "The Hangman, the Villain, and the Playwright: Kyd's Ironic Use of Morality and *Commedia* Traditions in *The Spanish Tragedy*," *Allegorica* 13 (1992):53–63; Sacvan Bercovitch, "Love and Strife in Kyd's *Spanish Tragedy*," *SEL* 9 (1969): 215–29; Ernest de Chickera, "Divine Justice and Private Revenge in *The Spanish Tragedy*," *MLR* 57 (1952):228–32; Herbert Coursen, "The Unity of *The Spanish Tragedy*," *SP* 65 (1968):768–82; G. K. Hunter, "Ironies of Justice in *The Spanish Tragedy*," *Renaissance Drama* 9 (1965):89–104; Ejner Jensen, "Kyd's *The Spanish Tragedy*: The Play Explains Itself," *JEGP* 64 (1965):7–16; David Laird, "Hieronimo's Dilemma," *SP* 62 (1965):137–46; Michael Levin, "'Vindicta Mihi!': Meaning, Morality, and Motivation in *The Spanish Tragedy*," *SEL* 4 (1964):307–24; John Ratliff, "Hieronimo Explains Himself," *SP* 54 (1957):112–18.

> thou shalt see the author of thy death,
> Don Balthazar . . . ,
> Depriv'd of life by Bel-imperia:
> Here sit we down to see the mystery,
> And serve for Chorus in this tragedy.[3]

Another group of scholars, including Ardolino, Broude, Hill, Johnson, and Justice, have also justified Hieronimo's revenge from the historical perspective of English nationalism.[4] Instead of viewing *The Spanish Tragedy* as a sensationalist revenge tragedy without any historical context, these critics place the play within the context of the late-sixteenth-century struggle between England and Spain, which along with Rome, was identified by Protestant apologists as the Whore of Babylon doomed to be overthrown by the true followers of Christ.

S. F. Johnson and Ronald Broude have argued that when Hieronimo declares, before the enactment of his revenge playlet, "Now shall I see the fall of Babylon / Wrought by the heavens in this confusion" (4.1.195-96) he becomes the instrument of apocalyptic revenge against Babylon/Spain. Eugene Hill has demonstrated that the nationalistic themes are represented symbolically in the plays-within-the-play devised by Hieronimo in the first and last acts; these celebrate the passage of power from Spain to England. Steven Justice has explained that Kyd's depiction of a corrupt Spain is based on contemporary anti-Spanish tracts. Finally, I have argued, and will develop at greater length in this book, that *The Spanish Tragedy* is a syncretistic play governed by related codes of pagan and apocalyptic justice which endow Hieronimo's act of revenge with a historical

---

[3]Thomas Kyd, *The Spanish Tragedy*, ed.Philip Edwards (London: Methuen, 1959), 1.1.87-91. All quotations of the play will be from this edition.

[4]Frank Ardolino, "Corrida of Blood in *The Spanish Tragedy*: Kyd's Use of Revenge as National Destiny," *Medieval and Renaissance Drama in England* 1 (1983):37-49; idem, "'Now I shall see the Fall of Babylon': *The Spanish Tragedy* as a Reformation Play of Daniel," *Renaissance and Reformation* 14.1 (1990):49-55; idem, "'Now I shall see the Fall of Babylon': *The Spanish Tragedy* as Protestant Apocalypse," *Shakespeare Yearbook* 1 (1990):93-115; idem, "'In Paris? Mass, and Well Remembered!' Kyd's *The Spanish Tragedy* and the English Reaction to the St. Bartholomew's Day Massacre," *Sixteenth Century Journal* 21 (1990):401-9; Ronald Broude, "*Vindicta Filia Temporis:* Three English Forerunners of the Elizabethan Revenge Play," *JEGP* 72 (1973):489-502; Eugene Hill, "Senecan and Vergilian Perspectives in *The Spanish Tragedy*," *ELR* 15 (1985):143-65; S. F. Johnson, "*The Spanish Tragedy*, or Babylon Revisited," in *Essays on Shakespeare and Elizabethan Drama in Honor of Hardin Craig*, ed. Richard Hosley (Columbia: University of Missouri Press, 1962), 23-36; Steven Justice, "Spain, Tragedy, and *The Spanish Tragedy*," *SEL* 25 (1985):271-88.

necessity that raises his personal vengeance to the level of nationalistic retribution.

The third school of criticism denies that Hieronimo's act of revenge can be justified according to a Christian or non-Christian ethos. These critics (Aggeler, Edwards, and Siemon) argue that justice, either human or divine, is absent from the play, which presents only an illusion of justice.[5] For Geoffrey Aggeler and Philip Edwards, there is no providential order in the moral and philosophical sense, but only a cruel and senseless fulfillment of the will of dark gods who dictate the necessity for human hatred and the enactment of revenge. As Edwards says:

> *The Spanish Tragedy* . . . sets up a rather horrifying un-Christian cosmic machinery in which metaphysical control is absolute and 'justice' an irrelevance. . . . [T]he cosmic machinery of the play is a decisive repudiation of the idea of Christian providence.[6]

If Aggeler and Edwards believe that *The Spanish Tragedy* is dominated by meaninglessness, James R. Siemon argues that there are too many meanings created by dialogic complexity in the language and stage action. The plethora of contesting meanings attached to words, objects, and actions undercuts the notion of a stable, unified, and providential ethos and aesthetic. The proliferation of dialogic oppositions in such schemes as rising/falling and vegetal imagery leads to the notion that the contesting meanings cancel each other, producing the inescapable sense that Kyd is interested in creating a macabre joke rather than a providential universe: "Kyd's invocation of an invisible . . . religious backdrop raises [the] irony . . . [that] all this might be but a play, its 'reason' no more than madness, its suffering protagonists driven by infernal powers better resisted than embraced, and its elaborate choric frame . . . an 'odde jest'"[7]

---

[5]Geoffrey Aggeler, "The Eschatological Crux in *The Spanish Tragedy*," *JEGP* 86.3 (1987):319–31; Philip Edwards, "Shakespeare and Kyd," in *Shakespeare, Man of the Theater*, ed. Kenneth Muir, Jay Halio, and D. J. Palmer (Newark, New Jersey: University of Delaware Press, 1983), 148–54; idem, "Thrusting Elysium into Hell: The Originality of *The Spanish Tragedy*," in *Elizabethan Theater XI* (1985), ed. A. L. Magnusson and C. E. McGee (Port Credit, Ontario: P. D. Geary, 1991), 117–32; James R. Siemon, "Dialogical Formalism: Word, Object, and Action in *The Spanish Tragedy*," *Medieval and Renaissance Drama in England* 5 (1991):87–115.

[6]Edwards, "Thrusting Elysium," 131.

[7]Siemon, "Dialogic Formalism," 108.

My response to the third school of criticism is based on the play's syncretistic quality and its historical subtext. What appears to be meaningless from the perspective of Christian mercy and leaving vengeance to God is not meaningless when seen from the combined classical and apocalyptic codes of harsh retribution. Moreover, a seemingly irrational and unjust act like Hieronimo's murder of Castile becomes, as I intend to demonstrate in the final chapter, part of the political subtext—the fall of Spain as represented by its most powerful province of Castile. If only the literal level is considered, then the play can be seen as ambiguous and irrational. But if the play is analyzed as a mystery with a historical subtext based on the Anglo-Spanish conflict, then the apparent contradictions and meaninglessness can, for the most part, be resolved. Siemon's able demonstration of the conflicting meaning of words, objects, and actions as proof of the play's complexity fits the nature of my interpretation of it as a mystery. We are presented with various, sometimes conflicting, schemes as part of the play's process toward the creation of an initiated awareness of the political subtext. My interpretative method, admittedly an old-fashioned one, maintains that among the contesting and multiple interpretations and the seemingly meaningless and ruthless acts of revenge, there is a privileged level of meaning—the allegorical political subtext—which ultimately justifies Hieronimo's act of revenge as the triumph of England over Spain in 1588.

It has been the purpose of my work on *The Spanish Tragedy* to explain how this historical context is present in the subtext. *The Spanish Tragedy* is a mystery play as Kyd establishes through three analogies between a dramatic production and the word *mystery* (1.1.90; 1.4.139; 3.15.29). The primary meaning of *mystery* in the Renaissance refers to a work containing hidden meanings available only to the initiated and concealed from the uninitiated.

Kyd's creation of a subtext available only to the initiated parallels Spenser and Jonson's appeal to a select audience which would be aware of their covert topical meanings. As Leah Marcus explains, covert "local" meanings become available to "those viewers or readers . . . willing to limit the scope of their interpretive activities within boundaries set by the author."[8] In some texts like Shakespeare's *Cymbeline*, authors stimulate the audience's awareness of local meaning through the creation of "a the-

---

[8]Leah Marcus, *Puzzling Shakespeare: Local Reading and Its Discontents* (Berkeley: University of California Press, 1988), 42.

atrical cryptonymy . . . [which] call[s] attention to the play's disjunctions and difficulties to beckon beyond them toward an idealized realm which . . . is at one with itself at the level of deep structure."[9] Similarly, Kyd creates a cryptonymic text whose prophecies, symbolic historical masque, and mysterious playlet followed by Hieronimo's enigmatic hierophantic silence point toward the idealized theme of Elizabethan empire forged by the defeat of Babylon/Spain.

The major problem with the interpretation of cryptic subtexts is that some critics argue that such meanings are outside the text and therefore do not belong in a discussion of it. However, Jonathan Crewe has maintained that schemes of topical reference in which exchanges occur between figures and events within the work and those outside it can effectively erase the distinction between the inside and outside of the text.[10] Dismissing such local meanings, as David Norbrook has asserted, "can itself become a limiting dogma, inhibiting a full understanding of the past."[11]

In my first volume *Thomas Kyd's Mystery Play: Myth and Ritual in The Spanish Tragedy*, I analyzed the play as a mystery ritual based on the pagan mystery rites of Eleusis which celebrated the death and rebirth of Proserpine. Andrea's descent into the underworld and meeting with Proserpine initiates the mystery ritual in the aptly named induction scene. The ritual continues in the earthly play primarily with the death of the "hanged god" Horatio in the violated sacred bower and his subsequent "resurrection" after the revenge playlet during which Hieronimo has effected the fall of Babylon/Spain. In allegiance to "The thing which I have vow'd inviolate" (4.4.188), Hieronimo bites out his tongue, leaving the onstage Iberian audience confused about his revenge plot; however, the theater audience watching the action from a more detached perspective can go beyond his vow of silence to discover the hidden meanings of the mystery play.

The emphasis in my first volume was on the pagan nature of the justice fulfilled by Hieronimo. However, *The Spanish Tragedy* is not only a

[9]Ibid., 145.

[10]Jonathan Crewe, *Hidden Designs: The Critical Profession and Renaissance Literature* (New York: Methuen, 1986), 140–41.

[11]David Norbrook, *Poetry and Politics in the English Renaissance* (London: Routledge and Kegan Paul, 1984), 10.

pagan mystery play; it is also a Christian mystery, showing the working out of the vengeance of God, the unsleeping revenger who appoints the time and ministers of his revenge. In effect, Kyd has created a syncretistic play, joining the classical code of justice with an equally unforgiving Christian ethos of divine vengeance as enunciated in the apocalyptic books of Daniel and Revelation. In this book, I will demonstrate that Kyd has created an apocalyptic revenge play which presents in a mysterious subtext the overthrow of the Antichrist, Babylon/Spain, by England in 1588. It is this actual nationalistic context, the defeat of the Spanish Armada in 1588, that vindicates Hieronimo as the representative of the English nation which has been destined to fulfill the prophecies contained in Daniel and Revelation concerning the fall of Babylon.

I have divided this book into two major parts: the first (chapters 1–4) treats the relationship between *The Spanish Tragedy* and the books of Daniel and Revelation, while the second part (chapters 5–8) analyzes the play as a Tudor history play which culminates in the representation of the destined victory over the Spanish Armada. The first chapter traces the history of sixteenth-century commentaries on the Book of Daniel, analyzes the Reformation tradition of Danielic exegesis, and concludes with the history of dramatizations of scenes from Daniel. The second chapter provides an analysis of *The Spanish Tragedy* as a Reformation Book of Daniel. The structure of the Danielic visions, which are based on the apocalyptic motifs of revelation, lawsuit, and redemption, is paralleled in the play by the rhetorical and dramatic patterns of question/testimony/judgment followed by reward and punishment. These apocalyptic motifs culminate in the "Soliman and Perseda" revenge playlet, which parallels in a number of significant ways Belshazzar's feast. The playlet is couched in four sundry languages which represent the four Danielic empires that will fall and be replaced by the fifth monarchy of Christ. Hieronimo uses the confusion inherent in the tongues as the cover for his revenge against Prince Balthazar, the namesake and counterpart of the doomed King Belshazzar of Babylon. Hieronimo concludes the playlet in the vulgar tongue of English which represents the translation of power from Babylon/Rome/Spain to Protestant England.

Chapters 3 and 4 parallel the first two chapters in that they trace the history of sixteenth-century commentary on the Book of Revelation and analyze *The Spanish Tragedy* as a Protestant Apocalypse. The Book of Revelation was read as a four-act tragicomedy written by Christ, with John and the chorus of angels serving as actors in a divine drama presenting the rise and fall of Antichrist and the triumph of the true church. *The Spanish Tragedy* contains many of the elements found in Revelation, including the four-act structure, the contrast between Fortune and Destiny, and the ongoing byplay between secrecy and revelation.

Chapter 5 discusses *The Spanish Tragedy* as a Tudor history play, belonging to the tradition of "Nemesis" plays, which combine revenge and historical necessity. *Horestes, Gorboduc, The Misfortunes of Arthur, The Battle of Alcazar,* and *Locrine* present a series of revenge motifs which, in effect, lead to the establishment of Elizabeth's rule in a Protestant England that has defeated the forces of chaos and anti-Christian domination. In the second part of chapter 5 and in chapter 6, I discuss how Hieronimo alludes to three historical precedents in the enactment of his revenge play-let: the historical plots against Nero, Lorenzo de' Medici, and the French Huguenots, all of which he will reverse in his revenge against his son's murderers.

The seventh chapter combines the twin foci of this book, the Apocalypse and Armada defeat, in a discussion of the predictions of the *annus mirabilis* of 1588. Apocalyptic prophecies for 1588 were rife in the preceding decades, with Protestant commentators predicting the fall of the Catholic Antichrist, while Spain anticipated that this year would mark its fated triumph over Protestantism. When England defeated the Armada, English writers interpreted the great victory as the destined defeat of Babylon/Spain and celebrated the decisive battle in an outpouring of commentaries, pamphlets, poems, histories, and plays.

In the final chapter, I describe the ways in which Kyd symbolically recreates the struggle with Spain in 1588. English commentators treated the defeat of the Armada as a revenge tragedy in which God exacted vengeance on Babylon/Spain through England. Similarly, Kyd creates a nationalistic revenge tragedy in which Hieronimo serves as the divinely appointed revenger whose marriage playlet destroys Babylon/Spain. With the Armada subtext in the revenge playlet, Kyd completes the delineation of his play as an apocalyptic revenge tragedy celebrating the victory of England over Antichrist Spain in 1588. In sum, *The Spanish Tragedy* is a Reformation play of Daniel, a Protestant Book of Revelation, and a Tudor historical play couched in the mystery rubric, which when interpreted correctly reveals the process of Destiny leading to England's apotheosis as God's favored country under the Virgin Queen Elizabeth, the returned Astraea.

My methods for interpreting *The Spanish Tragedy* have been developed from the principles upon which Kyd has built his play: analogy and adaptation, repetition and reversal of scenes, conflated and plurisignificant imagery, and composite and duplicate characters, many of whom have allegorical and historical names. The major result of Kyd's multiple parallels and hidden meanings is that some scenes can be analyzed on many levels of meaning. The revenge playlet provides the most significant example of a multicontextual scene. The "Soliman and Perseda" playlet can be viewed as the parallel and fulfillment of the historical masque at the end of act 1 and as the culmination of the apocalyptic context in which Hieronimo predicts the fall of Babylon and then enacts it at the wedding celebration of Prince Balthazar, the counterpart to the doomed King Belshazzar of Babylon. Moreover, the revenge playlet also is related to the three historical plots involving Nero, Lorenzo de' Medici, and Catherine de' Medici. Most significantly, the revenge playlet also contains the historical subtext of the English victory over the Armada in 1588. Because of this multileveled characteristic, the critic is required to repeat the analysis of certain key scenes from different perspectives, which may lead to the appearance of redundancy, but which is necessary to isolate the various layers of meaning. Through my analysis of Kyd's methods of creating multiple meanings and subtexts, I believe that I have resurrected the historical context of this mystery play which has been lost over the years. Instead of being merely a sensationalist revenge tragedy which is primarily important as the progenitor of the revenge tragedy genre, *The Spanish Tragedy* contains the mysterious celebration of the great victory of England in 1588. With an awareness of this context, we can date the play for the first time, and we can also account for its tremendous popularity from its first performances in 1592 into the early seventeenth century. Although there is no contemporary testimony about the Elizabethan audience's awareness of the mysterious subtext, there must have been members of the audience who either recognized the play's celebratory nature or responded to the nationalistic context of *The Spanish Tragedy* on a subliminal level. For the Elizabethan audience, the play's mystery would have been more available because it was based on a recent momentous event. However, for succeeding audiences the mystery has indeed been a "closed" one with four hundred years passing before its recovery in this book, which will, no doubt, arouse strong controversy over whether this historical subtext is present in the play.

PART ONE

Apocalypse

THE
Spanish Tragedie,

Containing the lamen-
table ende of Don Horatio, and
Bel-imperia: with the pittifull
death of old Hieronimo.

*Newly corrected and amended of such grosse
faultes as passed in the former impression.*

AT LONDON
Printed by VVilliam VVhite,
dwelling in Cow-lane.
1599.

I

The Exegetical and Dramatic Traditions of the Book of Daniel

*D*URING THE SIXTEENTH CENTURY, the Book of Revelation or the Apocalypse of St. John the Divine served as the primary source for the Protestant Reformation's attack on the Pope as the Antichrist and the Roman Catholic Church as the Whore of Babylon, the tyrannical enslaver of the beleaguered Protestants, who were compared to the Israelites during the Babylonian captivity imposed by King Nebuchadnezzar. Richard Bauckham has calculated that in the sixteenth century nine commentaries on the Apocalypse were published in English, four of them by Englishmen, and that, including second editions, there was a total of eighteen commentaries.[1] Although not as popular a subject for commentary as the Apocalypse, the Book of Daniel was given an important supporting role by Protestant reformers in their creation of a body of apocalyptic exegesis "calling for the divine judgment on the present . . . powers of the world and their overthrow by the heavenly armies that will install on earth the true City of God."[2]

Because of the similarities in the nature and theme of their symbolic and prophetic visions, the Old Testament Book of Daniel was viewed as the proleptic and parallel to the final book of the New Testament. Hugh Broughton, who published commentaries on both books, saw the Book of

[1]Richard Bauckham, *Tudor Apocalypse: Sixteenth-Century Apocalypticism, Millennarianism, and the English Reformation from John Bale to John Foxe and Thomas Brightman* (Appleford, England: Sutton Courtenay Press, 1978), 137.

[2]Florence Sandler, *"The Faerie Queene*: An Elizabethan Apocalypse," in *The Apocalypse in English Renaissance Thought and Literature: Patterns, Antecedents and Repercussions*, ed. C. A. Patrides and Joseph Wittreich (Ithaca: Cornell University Press, 1984), 158.

Daniel as a Jewish Apocalypse and Revelation as a Gentile Book of Daniel.[3]
Walter Raleigh maintained that "the Revelation is wholly an interpretation of Daniel's vision."[4] In his commentary on Daniel, Thomas Brightman, who also wrote commentaries on both books, stated that "these
[books] doe proclaime one and the same thinge"[5] concerning the nature
and ultimate downfall of Babylon/Rome under the Antichrist Pope. A half-
century later, Isaac Newton summarized learned opinion concerning the
similarities between the two prophetic books by declaring that they are
"written in the same style and language . . . and hath the same relation to
. . . one another, so that . . . together [they] make but one complete Prophecy."[6]

   The principal link between Daniel and the Apocalypse is the vision
concerning the Antichrist which both were said to share. Protestant commentators, including Heinrich Bullinger, Lambert Daneau, Laurence
Deios, William Fulke, Rudolph Gualter, John Hooper, Jan van der Noot,
George Sohn, Thomas Tymme, and William Tyndale, treated Daniel as a
prophet of Antichrist.[7] Following Martin Luther's analysis of Dan. 8:23–25
in the *De Antichristo*, they argued that the Antichrist, the archetypal
enemy of the true church identified through the ages as, among others,
Nebuchadnezzar, Antiochus Epiphanes, Nero, the Pope, Rome, the Turkish
Empire, and Spain under Philip II, was represented in Daniel's description
of the little horn which grew out of the ten horns of the fourth beast
(Dan. 7:8), in the tyrant-king in Daniel 8 and 11, and in the composite
symbolic beasts in Revelation 13, 17:19, 19:20, and 20:8. In *A Sermon
Preached at Hampton Court: Wherein is playnly proved Babylon to be Rome*
(1570), William Fulke stated that

> Whoso therefore will compare these things that are written in
> this book [Revelation], concerning the disposition of that
> monstrous beast, with those things that the prophet Daniel in
> the seventh chapter of his prophecy describeth of the four

   [3]Katherine Firth, *The Apocalyptic Tradition in Reformation Britain 1530–1645* (London:
Oxford University Press, 1979), 253.
   [4]Sir Walter Raleigh, *The History of the World, The Works of Sir Walter Raleigh*, 6 vols.
(Oxford, 1829; rpt. New York: Burt Franklin, 1964), vol. 5, bk. 3, chap. 1, p.5.
   [5]Thomas Brightman, *A Most Comfortable Exposition . . . of Daniel . . .* (Amsterdam,
1635), 4.
   [6]William Whitla, ed., *Sir Isaac Newton's Daniel and the Apocalypse . . .* (London: John
Murray, 1922), 308.
   [7]Bauckham, *Tudor Apocalypse*, 111n.

beasts, and specially of the fourth, which all men confess to be the Roman Empire . . . , must needs acknowledge that this beast which John painteth out, is the same that Daniel setteth out.[8]

Throughout the Reformation, the prophecies in Daniel 2 and 5 and in Revelation 14:8, 17:5, 18:2, and chapters 10 and 21 were invoked by Protestant exegetes to predict the fall of Babylon, the city ruled by the Antichrist and most frequently identified as Rome and Spain.

In their commentaries on the Book of Daniel, these explicators concentrate on the meanings of Daniel's original and assumed names, his function as God's chosen prophet, and the nature and themes of the visions he has and interprets. His position as Israelite judge and divinely appointed hero is inherent in his name *Daniel*, which is glossed by William Patten as "God's Doom" and by Broughton as "of God, a judge mercifull and strong."[9] Sheltco à Geveren contrasts the divinely favored nature of Daniel's name with the debasement and confusion inherent in the name and kingdom of Babylon:

> the Prophet Daniel, his name signifying the judgement of the Lorde: because in him the Lorde did shew foorth his singular kindnesse manie waies, and in his secrete judgement concerning the Empires of the world, and their ends. . . . So likewise *Babylon* received a fit name . . . because . . . in her there was made a confusion of tongues. . . . Wherefore it utterly came to naught, and there is become a meere confusion in deed of al beasts and serpents.[10]

Daniel was a judge in Israel who, according to George Joye,[11] was captured in battle by the Babylonians and taken to their court where he rose to a privileged position as court seer because of the prophetic powers given to him by God. Daniel's dual position in Babylon was made more paradoxical when the chief of the Eunuchs, impressed by Daniel's forti-

---

[8]Quoted in ibid., 327.

[9]William Patten, *The Calendar of Scripture* (London, 1575), 57r; Hugh Broughton, *Daniel his Chaldie visions and his Ebrew . . .* (London: Richard Field, 1596), Clv, n.

[10]Sheltco à Geveren, *Of the End of this Worlde, and second comming of Christ . . .* , tr. Thomas Rogers (London, 1589), 36r. Rogers also translated the first edition of this work in 1577.

[11]George, Joye, *The exposicion of Daniel the Prophete . . .* (Geneva, 1545), 12r.

tude, renamed him *Belteshazzar*, a name which angered Daniel because it was given "in honour . . . of the name of his [Nebuchadnezzar's] Idole [Bel]"[12] and was "a signe of servitude."[13] Ironically, Daniel's imposed name was the same as, or the equivalent of, the name of the ill-fated last king of Babylon, whose overthrow was predicted by the mysterious hand-writing on the wall which Daniel was the only one able to interpret.

Renaissance commentators employ much ingenuity in their inter-pretations of the name shared by Daniel and the king. *Belshazzar* (also spelled *Balthazar, Baltassar,* and *Belsasar*) literally means "he that storeth riches,"[14] "paymaster," or "keeper of the treasure,"[15] but when applied to Daniel, the name takes on hidden meanings indicative of Daniel's heroic stature. Henry More provides the clearest and most complete explication of its many secret meanings:

> in Hebrew the name . . . given to Daniel . . . sounds as if they
> would make Daniel *Arcanorum Beli thesaurium*, the Treasurer
> of the Secrets of *Belus*, understanding thereby the God of the
> Babylonians. . . . But . . . there is a variation of the writing . . .
> [to mean] *Latenter ignis hosticus* . . . signifying that what he
> had predicted did suddenly and unexpectedly come to pass
> upon the *Babylonians*. . . . *Belteshazzar* [also] may signify *Homo
> hostis in abscondito* . . . [which] declares himselfe to be
> inwardly a downright enemy to the *Babylonish* Idolatry.[16]

Similarly, when it refers to the king of Babylon, *Belshazzar* has obvious and esoteric meanings. On the one hand, his name indicates his role as ruler of Babylon—"*In Beli potestate sunt opes et imperia*"[17]—but when Daniel spells it *Beleshazzar* it means "Bel is made a fire by God,"[18] indicating the king's imminent demise. Thus, both the imprisoned Jew and the king of Babylon reverse their ostensible roles; Daniel, given the same name as his

---

[12]John Calvin, *Commentaries of that divine John Calvine, upon the Prophet Daniell*, tr. Arthur Golding (London, 1570), 41v. Golding translated only the first six books; for the remainder of Calvin's commentary I have used *Commentaries on the Book of the Prophet Daniel*, tr. Thomas Myers (Edinburgh: Calvin Translation Society, 1852), 2 vols.

[13]Dan. 1:7, *The Geneva Bible: A Facsimile of the 1560 Edition* (Madison: University of Wisconsin Press, 1969), 357 r, n. All quotations of the Bible will be from this edition.

[14]Broughton, *Daniel his Chaldie visions*, F2v, n.

[15]Patten, *Calendar*, 32v.

[16]Henry More, *A Plain and Continued Exposition of. . . Daniel* (London, 1681), 133–34.

[17]Ibid., 133.

[18]Broughton, *Daniel his Chaldie visions*, E2 r, n.

captor, rises to preeminence as the prophet of God's judgment on Babylon, but his master Belshazzar is doomed to become the conquered and last ruler of Babylon.

Daniel achieved his privileged position at the court of Babylon through his ability to interpret the dreams of Nebuchadnezzar. Raleigh maintains that Daniel was named *Belteshazzar "ob honorem explicationes arcanarum rerum*; 'in honour of his expounding secrets.'"[19] The first six of the twelve chapters of the Book of Daniel describe Daniel's interpretations of royal dreams and portents which no one at the court could decipher. In Daniel 2, King Nebuchadnezzar has a dream which he has forgotten, so he demands that his soothsayers reconstruct its contents and give him its interpretation. When they are unable to do this, Daniel is called upon and he prays to God who reveals "this secrete mystery . . . in a vision by night."[20] Daniel describes the king's dream of a composite beast with a golden head, silver breast and arms, brazen belly and thighs, and iron legs ending in iron and clay feet. After the appearance of the beast, a stone cut by no hands smashed its feet and the beast crumbled. The four metals represent four empires, the Babylonian, Persian, Greek, and Roman, which will rule the world and be overturned successively by each other until the last and worst empire, Rome, will be defeated by the fifth monarchy of Christ's kingdom: "And . . . the God of heaven set up a kingdome, which shal never be destroyed: . . . God hathe shewed the King, what shal come to passe hereafter, and the dreame *is* true, and the interpretation thereof *is* sure" (Dan. 2:44-45, 358r). As a result of Daniel's interpretation, the king saluted the Israelite God as "the reveiler of secrets, seing thou [Daniel] couldest open this secret" (Dan. 2:47).

Commentators on Daniel's vision of the four empires praise his ability to interpret these "secrete misteries," as Joye terms them.[21] In his commentary on Daniel, St. Jerome says that in "terming a mystery . . . a revealed dream, Daniel shows that whatever is hidden and unknown by man can . . . be called a 'mystery,'" and that Daniel "could . . . discern the significance of visions and dreams in which things to come are shown forth by means of certain symbols and mysteries."[22] Through his ability

[19]Raleigh, *History*, 2:1,10,368.
[20]Joye, *Daniel*, 25r.
[21]Ibid., 244v.
[22]*Jerome's Commentary on Daniel*, tr. Gleason L. Archer (Grand Rapids, Michigan: Baker Book House, 1958), 22, 29.

as an interpreter of mysterious visions and dreams, Daniel was able to reveal that "the dreame of the kyng was a publication of Gods decree" providing "a certayne and sure revelation of punishments which should . . . come."[23]

Thus, chapter 2 of Daniel presents a political and eschatological prophecy in the context of a mystery. God gives Daniel the dream and the interpretation, which the prophet then reveals to Nebuchadnezzar. The concept of *mystery* as initiation into God's secret wisdom is central here, as Raymond Brown has explained:

> In this chapter *mystērion* is used . . . to refer to both the dream and its contents; for the dream itself is a series of complicated symbols which envelop a further mystery: the future of the kingdom. . . . And so . . . we have *mystērion* as . . . a vision of the future revealed to man by God in figures. . . . [H]ere for the first time *mystērion* has the sense of an eschatological mystery: a veiled announcement of future events predetermined by God. . . . [W]e have . . . the ancient concept of the prophetic introduction into the heavenly assembly and hearing there what God planned to do . . . (symbols are now used as the vehicle of the message).[24]

Daniel's vision of the fourth worldly empire being replaced by Christ's fifth monarchy predicts that the faithful will be resurrected to participate in a transcendental order.[25]

Chapter 5 presents the most dramatic scene in the Book of Daniel, the ill-fated feast of Belshazzar, the last of the Babylonian monarchs. To show his contempt for the attacking Persians and for God's promised deliverance of the Israelites after seventy years, King Belshazzar, identified as the son of Nebuchadnezzar but actually his grandson (Dan. 5:2, 360r, n), holds a drunken feast during which the fingers of a man's hand appear and write on the wall four words which no one can either read or interpret. Once again Daniel is called upon to interpret a mystery, in this instance the enigmatic writing; he reads the inscription and then expli-

---

[23]Calvin, *Daniel* (tr. Golding), 56v, 57v.

[24]Raymond Brown, *The Semitic Background of the Term "Mystery" in the New Testament* (Philadelphia: Fortress Press, 1968), 7–8.

[25]John J. Collins, *The Apocalyptic Vision of the Book of Daniel* (Missoula, Montana: Scholars Press, 1977), 200.

cates each of the four words which predict that Belshazzar and Babylon will fall to the Medes and the Persians (Dan. 5:25-28). That night Daniel's interpretation of the prophecy is fulfilled when Belshazzar is slain and Babylon is conquered by Darius.

The lesson to be learned from Belshazzar's demise and Babylon's fall is that Israel will be freed from bondage after seventy years as Jeremiah had predicted, and that divine vengeance upon Babylon was destined to be exacted: "God hathe appointed a terme for all kingdomes, . . . a miserable end shal come on all that raise them selves against him" (Daniel 360v, n). George Whetstone explains that Belshazzar was contemptuous of God's power "but in the middest of his banquet the vengeance of God, with a visible hand wrote his destruction upon the wal."[26] Because Belshazzar refused to learn from Nebuchadnezzar's chastisement as a beast of the fields (Daniel 4), he was punished and in his death and the defeat of his kingdom, the overthrow of the evil empire of Rome is prefigured: "In this destruccion of the first Monarchye lerne the figure of the destruccion of the . . . last Monarchye . . . for right just causes. This Belsazar . . . is an evident token of his realme shortly to be translated and himselfe destroyed."[27]

Renaissance commentators place the enigmatic handwriting on the wall within the context of mysteries deciphered by the prophet Daniel. Henry More explains that the individual words *were such single incoherent words without any syntax*, that none could tell what they meant but he that writ them, who haply assisted Daniel in unridling the Riddle."[28] Calvin depicts Belshazzar, his court, and his seers as examples of the uninitiated audience, ignorant of the meaning of the warning: "there is a covering cast over their eyes (as Paul sayth) that they should be blinde in the most cleare light." Calvin goes on to explain that the inscription was "an allegorical prophecy . . . [requiring] an interpreter ordayned from heaven" in whom *"the excellency of the spirit was founde* . . . so that he [Daniel] did interpret dreames, and declare secretes, and open doubtfull matters."[29]

The remaining prophecies in the Book of Daniel (chapters 7-12) are eschatological visions Daniel has which are interpreted for him by angels. Chapter 7 contains the complex vision of the four beasts, an image which

[26]George Whetstone, *The English Myrror* . . . (London, 1586), 209.
[27]Joye, *Daniel*, 63v-64r.
[28]More, *Daniel*, viii.
[29]Calvin, *Daniel* (tr. Golding), 79r, 81v.

repeats the composite beast of four different metals in chapter 2. After the appearance of the four beasts, Daniel sees them destroyed by the dazzling Ancient of Days, who gives to Christ "an everlasting dominion" (Dan. 7:14, 361v). Daniel is confused by the strangeness of this vision, and he asks one of the assembled angels to tell him "the interpretacion of these things" (Dan. 7:16). The four beasts respectively represent the four empires of Babylon, Persia, Greece, and Rome, which shall be destroyed and replaced by God's eternal kingdom.

Chapter 7 is a key text in understanding the structure of Danielic visions and apocalyptic visions in general. Susan Niditch and J. J. Collins have classified the structural patterns of the vision in Daniel 7 as the prophetic revelation, lawsuit, and redemption. Niditch argues in *The Symbolic Vision in Biblical Tradition* that the prophetic revelation in Daniel 7 follows a tripartite scheme: (1) indication that a vision has occurred; (2) description of the vision; (3) a request for its interpretation followed by the fulfillment of the request. The legal or lawsuit pattern is implicit in the presentation of wrongdoing by the beasts (Dan. 7:8), followed by the judgment against them (Dan. 7:10) and their punishment (Dan. 7:11).[30] Closely related to the legal scheme, the redemptive pattern, as analyzed by Collins, also contains three parts: "First there is a *threat* posed by a rebellious king or kings. Then that *threat is removed* by some supernatural power. Finally, there follows a *state of salvation*, expressed as a kingdom in Daniel 7."[31] The redemption predicted for the faithful represents the culmination of the promise implicit throughout the Book of Daniel: the Israelites will be released from bondage, their captors are doomed, and, finally, future kingdoms based on evil power will die and be replaced by the divine monarchy.

The remaining visions in the Book of Daniel are strongly eschatological; they insist on the certainty of the triumph of God's kingdom in the fullness of time. Yet, paradoxically, there is a contrapuntal theme of the need for concealing the import of the visions until the time is right for disclosure. In chapter 10, the angel appears to Daniel "to shewe thee what shal come to thy people in the latter dayes" (Dan. 10:14, 363r), and the vision of the struggles leading to the rise and fall of the Roman empire is delivered in chapter 11. In the final chapter, the movement of the Book of

---

[30]Susan Niditch, *The Symbolic Vision in Biblical Tradition* (Chico, California: Scholars Press, 1980), 184, 201–2.
[31]Collins, *Daniel*, 109.

Daniel toward the prophetic revelation of God's coming culminates in the vision of the Last Judgment when "thy people shal be delivered, everie one that shal be founde writen in the boke. And many . . . that slepe in the . . . earth, shal awake, some to everlasting life, and some to shame and perpetual contempt" (Dan. 12:1–2, 364v). After revealing this, the angel tells the prophet to "shut up the wordes, and seale the boke til the end of . . . time" (Dan. 12:4). When Daniel presses for more information because he "understode it not" (Dan. 12:8), the angel replies that "the wordes are closed up, and sealed. . . . [N]one of the wicked shal have understanding: but the wise shal understand" (Dan. 12:10).

Protestant reformers treat the sealing of the prophetic truths in a book after they have been declared as a metaphor for religious mysteries which are revealed to the initiated audience, i.e., the Protestant faithful, and at the same time concealed from the uninitiated or profane audience of Catholics. George Joye is emphatic about the differences in understanding between the two audiences: "To shut up the wordis and seal up the boke is to hyde . . . wordis and secrets from the ungodly filthy swyne and dogges that thei understand them not. . . . To you [the elect] is it geven to know the mysteries but not to them."[32] Thomas Brightman concludes that the command to seal the truths is actually an incentive to the faithful to exercise more diligence in studying and understanding these mysteries:

> this obscuritie shall not take away all understanding of the Saincts, but shall whet only their diligence in searching, to whom the Angell promiseth a further profiting . . . , seeing by their goodly labour and diligence, God doth make over to the godly all his mysteries and secrets.[33]

For the initiated, the pose of secrecy at the conclusion of Daniel can be seen as a literary fiction, because the mysteries have been revealed within the text by means of cryptic symbols, which must be interpreted correctly.[34] However, these same truths remain concealed from the unbelievers: "God doth open his wil to the unbelievers, but not openly, because they seying would not see: and it is as if one should reach unto them a booke that were shut."[35]

---

[32]Joye, *Daniel*, 238r.
[33]Brightman, *Daniel*, 73.
[34]Collins, *Daniel*, 77.
[35]Calvin, *Daniel* (tr. Golding), 8r.

Throughout the Reformation, Daniel's prophecies of the fall of the four worldly empires and their replacement by Christ's monarchy provided beleaguered Protestants with support and consolation in their struggle against the contemporary Babylon—Rome. Daniel was praised as the great historiographer, whose prophecies promised that after bondage, persecution, and tragedy, God would grant the faithful a blessed resurrection. For Calvin, the visions in Daniel reveal "that the world is so governed by the secrete providence of God . . . the author of all thynges," and "the revenger of his people"[36] who "opposes [his] judgement and providence to all notions of chance."[37]

In their remarks on the consolation afforded the faithful by a study of the Book of Daniel, some commentators place the work within a dramatic context. Brightman compares the reading of Daniel to seeing a play in which "the lovelie face of the truth . . . [is] brought upon the stage in open view, with whose bewtie the most heavenlie minded are especially ravished."[38] Calvin and Joye treat Daniel as a tragicomedy in which the tragic period of Israel's captivity and persecution is followed by its release and the promised resurrection of the faithful. Calvin praises "the goodnes of God that shyneth forth in the end of the tragedy . . . [which] is very profitable to arme us with an invincible fayth and constancy."[39] Joye applies the theatrical metaphor to the Book of Daniel in a manner similar to the situation created by Hieronimo's revenge play-within-the-play when the intended victims are killed for real while they imagine they are acting in a marriage playlet:

> cryst is even now preparinge these jugement seatis to destroy these wicked Anticrysten hornes and to cast them into perpetuall fyery torments . . . and to embrace his chosen thus cruelly of these beastis oppressed receiving . . . [them] unto perpetuall joye for this is lo the end of this tragedye, thus go they [the wicked] out [of] their playe even then when thei thinke to be but in . . . middis of their mater.[40]

[36]Ibid., 65r, 75r.
[37]Ibid. (tr. Myers), 2:173.
[38]Brightman, *Daniel*, 10.
[39]Calvin, *Daniel* (tr. Golding), A4r.
[40]Joye, *Daniel*, 109v.

In their comparisons of Daniel to a play, these commentators draw upon the tradition of the dramatic representation of scenes from the Book of Daniel, which originated in the liturgical celebration of the *Ordo Prophetarum*. In the twelfth century two related plays on the Book of Daniel appeared, one by the wandering scholar Hilarius entitled *Historia de Daniel Repraesentanda*, and the other by students at Beauvais entitled *Danielis Ludus*. Both plays concentrate on Belshazzar's feast, which is presented as a royal spectacle and as the illustration of Daniel's prophetic skills.

During the Renaissance, episodes from the Book of Daniel and apocryphal stories of Daniel's act of saving Susanna from the calumny of the elders and outwitting the priests of Bel were dramatized. In Spain two *autos sacramentales* entitled *La Cena de Baltasar* were published, one in 1574, and the other by Calderon de la Barca in 1634.[41] In France, Antoine de la Croix, a member of the king of Navarre's household, published in 1561 a *Tragicomedie: L'Argument pris du troisieme chapitre de Daniel, avec le cantique des trois enfans, chanté en la fornaise*, a Huguenot play which justifies rebellion against the king when his commands defy God. Robert Garnier, whose Roman tragedy *Cornélie* Kyd translated, wrote *Les Juifves, tragedie* (Paris, 1583), which compares the turmoil resulting from Nebuchadnezzar's insane pride to the horrors of the French civil wars caused by the replacement of God with intestine sects.[42]

Dramatizations of the story of Susanna and the elders were especially popular in the sixteenth century. The Latin and vernacular sacred tragicomedies of Sixt Birck (1537), Tibortio Sacco (1537), Nikodemus Frischlin (1578), and Cornelius Schonaeus (1592) inculcated Protestant and humanist themes.[43] Thomas Garter wrote *The Commody of the most vertuous and Godlye Susanna* (1578), in which Susanna's vindication is equated with the divine preservation of Queen Elizabeth, the Privy Council, and the common people:

[41]Alexander Parker, *The Allegorical Drama of Calderon: An Introduction to the Autos Sacramentales* (Oxford, England: Dolphin Book Co., 1968), 160.

[42]J. S. Street, *French Sacred Drama from Bèza to Corneille: Dramatic Forms and Their Purposes in the Early Modern Theatre* (Cambridge: Cambridge University Press, 1983), 69, 80–84.

[43]Marvin T. Herrick, "Susanna and the Elders in Sixteenth-Century Drama," *Studies in Honor of T. W. Baldwin*, ed. Don Cameron Allen (Urbana: University of Illinois Press, 1958), 125–35; and idem, *Tragicomedy: Its Origin and Development in Italy, France, and England* (Urbana: University of Illinois Press, 1955), 46–50.

> Defende her [Elizabeth] Lorde in all affayres, give
>   passage to thy word.
> And cut them short that will her wo. . . .
> And to her noble counsayle Lord, give wisedome and
>   good helth,
> Graunt that they . . . may glory thee, and mende the
>   common welth.
> And for the commons of this realme . . .
> But what thou and the Prince doth will, they judge it
>   for the best.[44]

Thus when Kyd wrote *The Spanish Tragedy*, there existed dual traditions of dramatic representation and biblical exegesis of the Book of Daniel with which at least some segments of his audience would have been familiar. It is my contention that Kyd conceived of *The Spanish Tragedy* as a sixteenth-century play of Daniel intended to represent to English audiences the fall of Babylon/Spain. *The Spanish Tragedy* is a mystery of divine vengeance exacted against Spain in which Hieronimo, the Danielic figure, the judge, bearer of the sacred name (*hieros nym*), anglophile representative of God's will at the court of Babylon/Spain, author, actor, and revenger, causes the "fall of Babylon" in his revenge playlet, ostensibly intended to celebrate the marital and dynastic union of Spain and Portugal. Similarly, in the guise of presenting a play about the Iberian war and subsequent abortive union of Spain and Portugal through the ill-fated marriage of Bel-imperia and Balthazar, Kyd creates a mystery play whose hidden political and eschatological meanings concern the fall of Spain—the Spanish tragedy—and the triumph of England—the English comedy.

The key to understanding the political and eschatological meanings of *The Spanish Tragedy* lies in Kyd's use of the word *mystery* to define the play. As I have demonstrated in *Thomas Kyd's Mystery Play . . .* , Kyd identifies his play as a mystery by having three plays-within-the-play defined as a mystery. The first and most general and inclusive identification occurs at the conclusion of the induction when Revenge announces to Andrea "Here sit we down to see the mystery" (1.1.90). Revenge calls the framed play,

---

[44]Thomas Garter, *The Commody of the most vertuous and Godlye Susanna* (Oxford, England: Malone Society Reprints, 1936), 1,435–40.

the largest of the three plays-within-the-play, a mystery. The second example occurs after Hieronimo has presented the historical masque to celebrate Spain's victory over Portugal. The Spanish king exclaims, "I sound not well the mystery" (1.4.139), and Hieronimo proceeds to explain the contents of the three scenes. Finally, at the conclusion to act 3, Revenge, in response to Andrea's impatient demands for the fulfillment of his prophecy about Balthazar, produces the Hymen dumb show, after which Andrea asks him to "reveal this mystery" (3.15.29).

In the second and third instances, both the contents of the play-within-the-play and its meanings are mysteries. After the presentation of the three historical events, Hieronimo reveals the identities of the characters and the nature of their actions, whereupon the meanings of the scenes are interpreted, albeit wrongly as we shall discuss later, by the Spanish king and the Portuguese ambassador. Similarly, after Andrea declares his confusion about Revenge's dumb show, Revenge identifies the characters and explains their actions. With this information, Andrea is able to interpret its meaning: "Sufficeth me, thy meaning's understood" (3.15.36). By analogy with these two examples, Revenge's first use of *mystery* can be seen as referring to both the play and its meanings.

Thus, *The Spanish Tragedy* can be classified as a mystery and as an allegory, for the words were synonymous in the sixteenth century. In the preface to his translation of *Orlando Furioso* in 1591, an important apologia for allegorical literature and interpretation, Harington equates the profound meanings or "mysteries" found in ancient writings with the figurative meanings present in allegory: "The ancient Poets have indeed wrapped . . . in their writings divers and sundry meanings which they call the sences or mysteries. . . . [T]hese same sences . . . we call the Allegorie."[45] It was a short step from the equation of allegorical and mysterious meanings to the treatment of *mystery* and *allegory* as synonyms for literary works with literal and figurative levels. On a literal level, as I have demonstrated in *Kyd's Mystery Play* (chapter 3), Kyd constructs a prototypical detective mystery story in which Hieronimo, the justice-figure and grieving father, discovers the identities of his son's murderers, whom we have seen hang Horatio in the bower, and executes them in the marriage playlet after abortive attempts to bring them to official justice. On the figurative

---

[45]John Harington, tr., *Ludovico Ariosto's Orlando Furioso*, ed. Robert McNulty (London: Oxford University Press, 1972), 5.

level, the play is a pagan mystery ritual, based on the secret rites enacted at Eleusis, with Hieronimo serving as the hierophantic bearer of the sacred name who fulfills the destiny emanating from the pagan underworld, represented onstage by Revenge (chapters 4–7). However, *The Spanish Tragedy* is not only a pagan mystery; it is also a Christian mystery play.

As used in the Septuagint, where it appears twenty-one times, and in the New Testament, where it occurs twenty-seven times, *mystery* has three related meanings which parallel its usage in *The Spanish Tragedy*. Raymond Brown has traced the development of the Christian concept of *mystery* from the Hebrew word *sōd*, which refers to the secret assembly of the gods where the privileged seer, through an otherworldly journey, receives the esoteric knowledge revealed only at that assembly.[46] The second Christian meaning of *mystery* arises from the recognition that God sometimes reveals his secrets in visions to chosen prophets like Daniel. This meaning originates with the Aramaic word *rāz*, which is translated as *mystērion* in the Septuagint. As previously discussed, *mystērion* appears in Dan. 2:8, where it refers to both Nebuchadnezzar's dream and its secret meanings; Daniel is able to understand these mysteries with the help of a divine vision which reconstructs the king's original dream and reveals the interpretation. In a similar fashion, Daniel reads and interprets the four enigmatic words on the wall predicting Balthazar's doom.[47]

The third Christian meaning of *mystery* in a context similar to its occurrence in *The Spanish Tragedy* is the promise of the resurrection of the faithful, the final state of God's plan of salvation. This type of *mystery* is referred to in Daniel 12, where the final judgment and the resurrection are promised to the faithful, and in 1 Cor. 15:51–52, when Paul announces the mystery of eternal life. As Brown says of these passages: "The mystery here seems to be that all the elect of God, dead or alive, will in the end be transformed so that they may inherit the kingdom of God. . . . The 'mysteries of God' of which the wicked are ignorant . . . are the rewards of the just in the afterlife."[48]

In sum, *mystery*, as used by Kyd in the play, involves pagan and Christian concepts which are similar in that they concern: esoteric religious truths revealed to initiates through a mystery ritual or an otherworldly journey; the interpretation of enigmatic visions, texts, and symbols to

[46]Brown, "*Mystery*," 6.
[47]Ibid., 36.
[48]Ibid., 47.

reach an understanding of their hidden meanings; and the idea of destiny and divine providence governing the universe and leading to a final judgment in which the good are rewarded and the evil punished. Kyd's linking of pagan and Christian concepts of mystery helps to define the syncretistic nature of the universe created in *The Spanish Tragedy*.

The pagan aspects of the play have been said to coexist uneasily with the Christianity of the play's earthly setting—Catholic Iberia. The apparent confusion between these realms is reflected in Hieronimo's impassioned pleas for justice from heaven, hell, and Hades. Finally, despairing of obtaining legal justice, Hieronimo adopts personal vengeance, an act which seems to make him the villain according to the Christian injunction to leave vengeance to God (Rom. 12:17–19). But at the end of the play, Hieronimo is rewarded, as is his accomplice Bel-imperia, with an Elysian resurrection. Thus, for some critics, the play's morality seems hopelessly muddled, an odd mixture of pagan and Christian concepts. However, as Allan Sinfield has argued, there are similarities between the pagan revenge enacted and the divine providence associated with the Calvinist deity of the Reformation:

> The slow but inexorable control exercised by Revenge is just like that which Calvin attributes to God. . . . Those who believe in Christian predestination may see Revenge as a spirit delegated by God to execute his just judgments. . . . [T]he characters live vicious lives in submission to the will of vindictive powers which hover disconcertingly (for the Elizabethan protestant) between pagan fate and the Calvinist God. The play ends with a distribution of the characters which parodies the Christian. . . . It sounds very like the protestant dispensation, despite the admixture of pagan imagery. Is the Reformation God to all intents identifiable with Revenge?[49]

The answer to Sinfield's closing question is that in *The Spanish Tragedy* Kyd creates a syncretism of classical and Christian concepts of destiny and divine providence, respectively, which justify the act of revenge Hieronimo carries out against his son's murderers. This is not a Christian play in the sense that mercy is accorded to one's enemies and vengeance

---

[49]Allan Sinfield, *Literature in Protestant England 1560–1660* (Totowa, New Jersey: Barnes & Noble, 1983), 115–16.

left solely to Judgment Day. The God the play invokes is the vengeful deity Calvin describes in his commentary on Daniel, the apocalyptic and wrathful God who predestines earthly events and appoints certain nations and individuals to effect his will. Through the presence of the underworld observers, Kyd demonstrates that Hieronimo acts *sub specie aeternitatis*; he is the providential revenger who not only predicts the fall of Babylon/ Spain, but also, in effect, brings it about in his playlet when he and Belimperia kill the Iberian heirs.

2

The Spanish Tragedy as Play of Daniel

THE SPANISH TRAGEDY PARALLELS the Book of Daniel in Kyd's use of *mystery* to refer to symbolic representations with hidden political and eschatological meanings; in his employment of the three connected rhetorical and thematic motifs of prophetic revelation, lawsuit or judgment, and redemption, which are characteristic of apocalyptic literature; in the names and roles of Hieronimo and Balthazar, who are counterparts to the biblical Daniel and King Belshazzar; and, finally, in the presentation of two scenes, 4.2. and 4.4., which are analogous, respectively, to Daniel 4 and 5. The parallels between the play and the Book of Daniel as the presenters of mysteries begin in the induction scene when Andrea describes his underworld journey during which he experiences the operation of the justice system that will pass judgment on the characters at the end of the play. For some as yet undetermined reason, Andrea has been allowed to return from the otherworld to reveal to us the nature of underworld justice and to witness an earthly play, called a mystery and a tragedy, in which his slayer will be slain. Revenge, the chthonic emissary from Proserpine's court, serves as the embodiment of the destiny which will be fulfilled onstage. He tells Andrea and us what will take place, and when Andrea becomes impatient with the slowness of revenge, Revenge produces the symbolic Hymen dumb show which assures Andrea that Balthazar will be defeated.

In his role as the presenter of mysteries, Revenge parallels the biblical Wisdom figure who reveals secret truths to chosen prophets. The transmission of secret knowledge from a Wisdom figure to a seer and then to the seer's audience is common to historical apocalypses like Daniel and Revelation and to a number of apocryphal and pseudepigraphical otherworldly journeys known as tour apocalypses. These tours involve a journey to either heaven or hell by a hero or heroine in the company of an angelic guide, a Wisdom figure, who reveals the rewards and punishments awaiting mankind at the Last Judgment. As Martha Himmelfarb states, "The visions . . . take the form of guided tours. Usually the guide is an angel. In many of the texts, the visionary questions his guide about each sight. The interchanges between visionary and guide, or in some cases the guide's unsolicited explanations, provide the structure for the tours."[1] The visions in the tour apocalypses and in the Book of Daniel share "the pattern of vision followed by angelic interpretation [and] . . . are God's means of revealing his secrets to his chosen ones."[2]

The secrets revealed in the tour apocalypses primarily involve the nature and outcome of God's plan for the universe as demonstrated by the operation of otherworld justice. For example, in the Greek Apocalypse of Ezra, the prophet takes a tour of hell during which he sees the joys and splendors of Paradise and the punishments of Tartarus, including those inflicted on the Antichrist.[3] Similarly, in the Book of Enoch the seer journeys to the heavens accompanied by an angel, who has been compared to the mystagogue in the mystery religions[4] and who shows Enoch "all the secrets of the heavens, . . . how the kingdom is divided; and the deeds of men, how they are weighed on the scale."[5] Enoch sees the final judgment and its aftermath: "Enoch swears he knows a mystery (*mēstir/mystērion*) from reading the heavenly tablets: the righteous shall be rewarded, but the evil punished (103:2). Further, the destiny of people who are dead but who have yet to be judged seems to be called a mystery."[6] After reading the heavenly tablets, Enoch writes the divine secrets in a book which promises future joy to the righteous.[7]

In the induction scene Kyd draws upon classical and biblical otherworldly journeys to create Andrea's *descensus ad inferos* in which he experiences the justice system which governs the world. Andrea sees the punishments inflicted on the wicked and is allowed to return to earth

---

[1]Martha Himmelfarb, *Tours of Hell: An Apocalyptic Form in Jewish and Christian Literature* (Philadelphia: University of Pennsylvania Press, 1983), 45.
[2]Ibid., 60.
[3]Ibid., 25.
[4]Brown, "*Mystery*," 15n.
[5]Enoch 41:1, qtd. in ibid., 16n.
[6]Ibid., 17.
[7]Ibid., 18.

with Revenge to watch the unfolding of destiny. As in Enoch, Andrea's fate in the afterworld remains undecided—a mystery—until the final judgment when Revenge, Proserpine's emissary, permits Andrea to become the judge instead of the judged. Further, although Revenge does not conduct Andrea on his underworld journey, Revenge nevertheless serves as an enigmatic Wisdom figure, who presents to Andrea the mystery of the earthly play and the symbolic dumb show, which concern the working out of divine providence.

Kyd's most significant adaptation of the apocalyptic tours and symbolic visions lies in making the interpretation of *The Spanish Tragedy* the means of Andrea's and our initiation into the nature of divine providence. Whereas Eleusinian mystery initiates saw a sacred drama during which Proserpine's descent was reenacted and secret truths were revealed (*Thomas Kyd's Mystery Play*, 59–66), and the biblical prophets took otherworldly journeys and had dream visions which were interpreted for them by a divine intermediary, Andrea and we are expected to interpret the mystery play to achieve comparable enlightenment. As in Daniel, the mystery to be solved occurs within the context of a dream vision. Andrea and Revenge's ascent to earth through the "gates of horn" (82), the passageway of true dreams, indicates that the events to follow constitute, as G. K. Hunter has put it, a dream "allegory of perfect justice."[8] Revenge, who functions as a chorus in a Greek tragedy declaring the destiny of the characters at the outset, also resembles the choruslike nuntius or expositor of a medieval mystery play whose announcement of the events to follow demonstrates, as John Elliott has stated, "that the ultimate control of human destiny lies beyond man himself."[9]

The induction scene is also significant for its introduction of the rhetorical and thematic patterns of the prophetic lawsuit, redemption, and revelation, which are characteristic of the Book of Daniel and other apocalyptic writings. By introducing these apocalyptic motifs within the otherworldly context of the induction, Kyd provides an eschatological framework for their repetition in the earthly framed play. When we see dramatic action built on these motifs, we recognize that they are part of the providential movement controlling the play.

[8]Hunter, "Ironies," 93.
[9]John Elliott, "The Sacrifice of Isaac as Comedy and Tragedy," *Medieval English Drama: Essays Critical and Contextual*, ed. Jerome Taylor and Alan H. Nelson (Chicago: University of Chicago Press, 1972), 165.

As G. K. Hunter has pointed out, the judgment scenes—which comprise the prophetic lawsuit motif—begin with Andrea's appearance before the three infernal judges, who are unable to decide whether to place him with the lovers or the martialists in the underworld.[10] Consequently, Andrea is sent to the court of Pluto and Proserpine, who, instead of determining Andrea's fate, permit him to return to earth with Revenge to attend a play in which Balthazar will be killed by Bel-imperia, Andrea's former secret love. The two judgment scenes in the induction are alike in that the final decisions are deferred. By contrast, in the judgment scenes of the framed play, characters pass judgments which are supposed to be decisive but are in fact wrong or circumscribed, leading to unseen consequences that in turn create the need for further judgments. In other words, the play consists of a series of tightly connected judgments, which create a scheme of causality moving inevitably to the final judgment in the afterworld.

Many of the judgment scenes in the play occur primarily in connection with Hieronimo's dual role as lord marshal and grieving father determined to bring his son's murderers to justice. After murdering Horatio and imprisoning Bel-imperia, Lorenzo attempts to insure secrecy by sending one accomplice, Pedringano, to kill another accomplice, Serberine, while at the same time arranging to have Pedringano apprehended in the act. The subsequent hanging of Pedringano provides important insights into the complex and ironic nature of the judgment scenes, in which, despite appearances, nothing happens because of chance and everything, even misconceptions and erroneous decisions, leads inexorably to the final underworld judgment. When Pedringano is condemned to death, Lorenzo deceitfully promises him a pardon, which supposedly is contained in an empty black box held by a mocking page.[11] On the scaffold, Pedringano scoffs at his imminent demise, still thinking he will be pardoned, and Hieronimo, unaware of Pedringano's role in Horatio's death, laments his inability to bring his son's murderers to the justice that Pedringano has received. However, after the hanging, Hieronimo discov-

[10]Hunter, "Ironies," 92.

[11]For a discussion of the mythic, moral, mysterious, and theatrical aspects of the empty box, see Barbara Baines, "Kyd's Silenus Box and the Limits of Perception," *Journal of Medieval and Renaissance Studies* 10 (1980):41–51; and my "The Hangman's Noose and the Empty Box: Kyd's Use of Dramatic and Mythological Sources in *The Spanish Tragedy* Dramatic and Mythological Sources in *The Spanish Tragedy* (III.iv.viii)," *Renaissance Quarterly* 30 (1977):334-40.

ers their identity by means of the posthumous confession found on Pedringano's body by the hangman, who, ironically, believes the letter to be the pardon Pedringano thought he would receive. This letter, written to Lorenzo, confirms the bloody letter Hieronimo had received from Bel-imperia, but which he refused to believe until the discovery of Pedringano's letter. The two letters propel Hieronimo toward the revenge he inexorably exacts in the playlet.[12] At the end of the play, because of our wider perspective as members of the theater audience, we can see how each judgment has led causally to the next one, creating an unbroken succession culminating in the final otherworld judgment.

The apocalyptic motif of the prophetic redemption is introduced in the induction scene with the return of Andrea's ghost from the underworld to the earth. Describing the quickness of their ascent, Andrea says, "No sooner had she [Proserpine] spoke but we were here, / I wot not how, in 'twinkling of an eye'" (84–85). The expression "twinkling of an eye" comes from St. Paul's First Epistle to the Corinthians (1 Cor. 15:51–52), where Paul speaks of the resurrection of the dead at the Last Judgment:

> Beholde, I shewe you a secret thing [mystery],
> We shal not all slepe, but we shall all be changed,
> In a moment, in the twinkling of an eye at the last
> trumpet: for the trumpet shal blowe, and the dead
> shal be raised up incorruptible, and we shalbe
> changed. (82v)

This is the prophetic resurrection toward which the mystery play moves.

The reasons for Andrea's "resurrection" are enigmatic; we know that he has been allowed to return with Revenge to witness the death of Balthazar, but we do not know why Balthazar's death is required and why we are going to see a play in which Balthazar's death is of major importance. When the play opens we see Balthazar as a captive at the Spanish court, in love with Bel-imperia, and befriended by Lorenzo who is anxious to use him for his dynastic machinations. In the third scene, which takes place at the Portuguese court, Villuppo charges Alexandro with the murder of Balthazar, an accusation we know to be false because we have seen Balthazar alive at the Spanish court.

---

[12]For a comparison of Kyd, Marlowe, and Shakespeare's use of the motif of "dead letters," see my "The Bearing of Deadly Letters: 'Uriah's Letter' in Marlowe, Kyd, and Shakespeare," *Journal of Evolutionary Psychology* 6 (1985): 292–300.

The byplay between death and resurrection culminates in 4.4 when Hieronimo directs the "Soliman and Perseda" playlet to celebrate the marriage between Balthazar and Bel-imperia. During the playlet, Lorenzo and Balthazar actually are murdered by Hieronimo and Bel-imperia, respectively, and she really commits suicide as her character Perseda originally was supposed to until Hieronimo changed the script to save Bel-imperia. The attending Spanish and Portuguese monarchs and lords expect the dead characters to rise to their applause at the conclusion of the playlet, but Hieronimo explains that they are in fact dead. In the ensuing confusion, Hieronimo manages to kill Castile and himself, but the final scene presents all of the dead from the playlet and the play—the three suicides, Bel-imperia, Isabella, and Hieronimo; the murdered, Horatio, Lorenzo, Balthazar, Castile, and Serberine; and the officially executed Pedringano—resurrected in the afterworld. The play ends where it began with infernal justice at work, except that, unlike in the induction scene, here final judgments are delivered as the good are rewarded with a blissful existence in the Elysian Fields and the evil are condemned to "endless tragedy" (4.5.48).

The prophetic revelation motif is introduced in the induction with Revenge's announcement that we are about to see a mystery, but we must wait for the entire play to unfold before we understand its complete nature. The pattern of prophetic revelation occurs primarily in the scenes containing the two plays-within-the-play referred to as mysteries. In 1.4 the Spanish king calls for Hieronimo to produce the "pompous jest" (137) to celebrate the Spanish victory over Portugal. The presentation of the historical masque and the subsequent interpretations of it follow the pattern of the Danielic symbolic vision, as outlined by Susan Niditch: (1) indication that a vision has taken place; (2) the description of it; (3) request for the interpretation followed by the interpretation itself. After the king's call for the "jest," the stage direction provides the bare description of the action in the three masques. Following the king's request for the interpretation of the mysterious or symbolic masque, Hieronimo fleshes out its contents, giving the names and historical incident presented in each scene. Hieronimo's explanation is followed by the interpretations of the Spanish king and Portuguese ambassador concerning the contemporary political import of the masque. The king then salutes Hieronimo for his masque with a toast from Horatio's cup, a dual honor for the lord marshal. This pattern is repeated in 3.15 when, after the stage direction indicates that the Hymen dumb show has occurred, Andrea asks for Revenge's explanation, which is given immediately and is followed by Andrea's implicit interpretation of its meaning.

The effect of presenting scenes built on the apocalyptic schemes of revelation, judgment, and redemption is to show the theater audience, as Barry Adams and Carol Kay have argued, that we are engaged in similar activities in the interpretation of the play and that because of our wider perspective on the action we can avoid the shortsighted and erroneous judgments of the circumscribed onstage characters.[13] Through these scenes, especially in the plays-within-the-play, Kyd instructs, by analogy, the theater audience in the ways that the mystery play should be interpreted. Like Andrea, we are directed to see the play not only as an aesthetic construct but also as a work which has a direct relationship to reality. Just as Andrea learns what happened to himself by watching the murder of Horatio by Balthazar and Lorenzo,[14] so too the Elizabethan audience is encouraged to relate the play to its own contemporary historical situation.

Kyd establishes the play's contemporary political context in the three plays-within-the-play presented at the end of the first, third, and fourth acts. In 1.4 Hieronimo is called upon to provide a courtly entertainment to celebrate Spain's victory over Portugal. He devises an historical masque in which three knights take three kings captive. When the Spanish king requests an explanation of the "mystery," Hieronimo describes three historical scenes showing the past victories of little England over Portugal (twice) and Spain (once). In the first scene, Robert, earl of Gloucester, defeats the Saracen king of Portugal and forces him "[t]o bear the yoke of the English monarchy" (146). After Hieronimo's description, the Spanish king delivers a contemporary interpretation as a mocking consolation to the Portuguese ambassador for his country's recent defeat: "by this you see / That which may comfort both your king and you, / And make your late discomfort seem the less" (147–49).

The second scene of the masque presents the victory of Edmund, earl of Kent, over the Portuguese king in the late fourteenth century. Again the Spanish king places contemporary relevance on the scene by declaring

[13]Barry Adams, "The Audiences of The Spanish Tragedy," JEGP 69 (1969):221–36; Carol Kay, "Deception through Words: A Reading of The Spanish Tragedy," SP 74 (1977):20–38.

[14]Coursen, "Unity," 772–73.

that the past historical situation should make it easier for Portugal to accept its present defeat by Spain. But the third and last historical scene changes the pattern of Portuguese defeat by presenting the victory of England over Spain when John of Gaunt defeated the king of Castile. The Portuguese ambassador now becomes the interpreter, applying the ironic consolation to Spain who "may not insult for her success, / Since English warriors likewise conquer'd Spain" (170). Finally, the king of Spain thanks Hieronimo "for this device, / Which hath pleas'd both the Ambassador and me" (172–73).

Despite the king's effort at harmonizing the Iberian interpretations of the masque, Hieronimo's courtly "device" raises some disturbing questions about his presentation of scenes showing the defeat of both Spain and Portugal by little England. If the masque is intended ostensibly to celebrate Spanish martial prowess and future Iberian unity, why does Hieronimo produce a show in which the Iberian countries are defeated? Is this masque merely a sop to English audiences who would respond favorably to Hieronimo's history lesson or is the device a key to the political meanings of the play? Kyd establishes by means of analogy that just as the Spanish king and Portuguese ambassador relate the past historical scenes to their contemporary reality—the Iberian war and settlement—so too the theater audience is to relate the play it is watching to its own contemporary reality. As John Colley argues,

> A play has mysterious relevance for the political world of international warfare and international peace treaties. The little masque is another gloss upon the events of the real world, and . . . Kyd encourages his audience to connect the various dramatic mysteries it observes within the structure of the play to the truths such mysteries hold for the audience's own nonfictional existence. The characters in *The Spanish Tragedy* observe fictions which can interpret for them the circumstances of their own lives; the audience must likewise be aware that little pageants have special meanings, . . . which are on the surface mysterious, but which ultimately must be interpreted.[15]

---

[15]John Colley, "*The Spanish Tragedy* and the Theatre of God's Judgments," *Papers in Language and Literature* 10 (1974):246.

Although the theater audience is expected to follow the onstage interpreters in the relation of the masque to their contemporary reality, it is also supposed to see that their specific historical applications are short-sighted and therefore erroneous. The king and the ambassador, in their eagerness to apply ironic political consolations to each other, miss the central idea of the three pageants: little England has defeated both countries in the past, and the implication is that England is destined to be victorious over Iberia in the future as well. This is the reality the Elizabethan theater audience is directed to apply to Hieronimo's masque. Eugene Hill has described the process by which Kyd directs his audience to interpret the masque as the symbolic representation of England's domination over its Iberian rivals:

> The illogic of the Spanish King's explanation is patent. . . . The King's fatuous misreading of the dumb show serves as a warning to Kyd's audience. For the Spanish King, 'little England' . . . is peripheral to the meaning of the dumb show; but for the English audience it is the central agent of the dumb show—and of *The Spanish Tragedy* as a whole. The three captive Kings of the dumb show . . . represent two countries (Portugal and Spain), but one fate: submission to English power. Hieronimo with his playlet reminds the onstage audience of past defeats at the hand of . . . the English; Kyd with that same playlet hints at the return of English dominance.[16]

At the end of the first two acts, Andrea expresses dissatisfaction with Revenge's slowness and apparent lack of interest in effecting vengeance. On each occasion, Revenge responds with prophecies of the future defeat of Andrea's enemies: "Be still, and ere I lead thee from this place, / I'll show thee Balthazar in heavy case" (2.6.10–11). This prediction echoes Revenge's announcement at the outset of the framed play that Balthazar will be killed by Bel-imperia. But at the conclusion of act 3 Andrea becomes very importunate in his demands that the sleeping Revenge awaken and punish Horatio's murderers. In order to quiet Andrea's impatience, Revenge—who is the image of God as the sleeping revenger biding his time for the right moment[17]—produces a dumb show which he introduces with this pronouncement:

[16]Hill, "Perspectives," 160.
[17]Johnson, "Babylon," 29.

> Behold, Andrea, for an instance how
> Revenge hath slept, and then imagine thou
> What 'tis to be subject to destiny.   (26–28)

When Andrea asks Revenge to "reveal this mystery," Revenge responds:

> The two first, the nuptial torches bore, . . .
> But after them doth Hymen hie as fast, . . .
> And blows them out and quencheth them with
>   blood,
> As discontent that things continue so.
>
>   (30, 32, 34–35)

Andrea now finally understands what will happen in the play.

This scene resembles Revenge's presentation of the earthly play as a mystery concerning the destiny of Balthazar; Revenge produces the dumb show to remind Andrea and us what is destined for Balthazar. The dumb show also is similar to Hieronimo's historical masque, because in both cases the respective onstage audience calls the presentation a mystery and asks the presenter to provide an explanation, which is then followed by that audience's interpretation. However, unlike the interpreters of the masque, Andrea merely says that he understands the meaning without telling us what it is. By Andrea's silence we are encouraged to proceed with our own interpretation which involves making an analogy between the dumb show and the larger play we have been watching. At this point we know that Balthazar and Bel-imperia's marriage is planned, but we also expect Bel-imperia to murder Balthazar as Revenge has predicted. With this in mind, we see the blood marriage enacted by Hymen as a foreshadowing of the violent disruption of the impending dynastic wedding. In sum, the dumb show is first identified as a mystery, then explained, and finally interpreted as an analogy and proleptic to the planned dynastic wedding.

But in addition to drawing the parallel between the small and large plays, we are also expected, like Andrea, to make the analogy between the play and reality. The dumb show that Andrea interprets is a dramatic production; Hymen symbolically destroys the marriage represented there. But the planned marriage of Balthazar and Bel-imperia represents "reality" for Andrea. Although he is only a stage character in the play entitled *The Spanish Tragedy*, the events that he sits down to watch with Revenge represent Andrea's "reality" within the context of the play world. Thus when he applies the mystery of the dumb show to the larger play for which he serves as chorus, Andrea learns what destiny in his "real world" will be. And we, watching him go through this process, understand by analogy that we are to compare the dumb show and the larger play to our reality—which in the case of the Elizabethan audience would be the rivalry with Spain. Like Hieronimo's masque which placed the play in a real historical context and predicted, by implication, future glory for England, the dumb show points toward Hieronimo's "Soliman and Perseda" playlet which will have "real" consequences for the dramatic characters and the theater audience.

Between Hieronimo's prophecy of the "fall of Babylon" (4.1) and his preparation of a "stage" for the revenge playlet Kyd inserts a scene which is indebted to chapter 4 of the Book of Daniel. As in chapter 2, King Nebuchadnezzar has a troubling dream which none of his seers can interpret, so he calls upon Daniel to decipher it for him. Nebuchadnezzar dreamed of a great tree which was cut down by a watchman and an angel, and its stump, bound with iron and brass, was left among the beasts of the field. Also, the king heard a voice declaring that he would be transformed into a beast and "seven times [would] be passed over him" (Dan. 4:13, 359r). Daniel interprets the destruction of the great tree as the symbol of the coming discomfiture of the king, whose excessive pride would cause God to change him into a beast for seven years. One year later, the dream was fulfilled and for seven years the king roamed as a beast until God restored him to his throne. As a result of his experience, Nebuchadnezzar recognized and extolled Daniel's God as the "King of heaven" (Dan. 4:34, 359v). Commenting on this dream, Calvin emphasizes the equation between the cutting down of the tree and the destined fall of Nebuchadnezzar and Babylon: "the cutting downe of the tree was but a figure of that ruine and fall which he shortly should have."[18]

In the play, Isabella, distraught over her son's murder and her inability to obtain justice, anticipates Hieronimo's actions by "taking revenge" on the place where Horatio was murdered as she chops down the tree from which he was hanged, curses and destroys the garden containing the tree, and then commits suicide:

> I will revenge myself upon this place
> Where thus they murder'd my beloved son.

---

[18]Calvin, *Daniel* (tr. Golding), 52r.

> Down with these branches and these loathsome
>   boughs
> Of this unfortunate and fatal pine. . . .
> I will not leave a root, a stalk, a tree,
> A bough, a branch, a blossom, nor a leaf,
> No, not an herb within this garden plot. (4–7, 10–12)

S. F. Johnson has compared Isabella's description of the wasteland she creates by her devastation of the bower to the biblical accounts of the ruins of Babylon in Jer. 51:37–43, Isa. 13:19–22, and Rev. 18:19–24,[19] but her destruction of the garden and the tree is also directly related to the chopping down of the mighty tree symbolizing Babylon in Daniel 4. As Wineke argues, "Spain has become a modern incarnation of the biblical Babylon, symbol of corruption and injustice. As such it is ripe for destruction. So too is the garden. . . . [B]y reducing it to rubble Isabella converts it from a false mirror to a true one, reflecting the chaos that actually exists in Spain."[20] Thus, Isabella's making the tree and the garden fruitless (14, 35), parallels and prefigures Hieronimo's "cutting off" the line of accession to the thrones of Spain and Portugal in the revenge playlet.

The culmination of the Danielic, mystery, and political contexts of *The Spanish Tragedy* occurs in the "Soliman and Perseda" playlet which Hieronimo devises to celebrate the doomed union of Bel-imperia and Balthazar. In the marriage playlet Hieronimo not only avenges his son's death, but also brings about the fall of Spain–Portugal/Babylon, which he foreshadowed in his historical masque and announced in his prophetic utterance. Just as Daniel prophesied the fall of Babylon when he interpreted Nebuchadnezzar's dream of the metallic beast (Daniel 2) and the enigmatic handwriting at Belshazzar's feast (Daniel 5), so too Hieronimo proclaims the destined fall of England's Catholic rival, Spain. However, unlike Daniel, Hieronimo is the instrument of the Iberian defeat, which is brought about by the deaths of Castile and Lorenzo—the heirs to the Span-

[19]Johnson, "Babylon," 26.

[20]Donald Wineke, "Hieronimo's Garden and the Fall of Babylon: Culture and Anarchy in *The Spanish Tragedy*," *Aeolian Harps: Essays in Literature in Honor of Maurice Browning Cramer*, ed. Donna and Douglas Fricke (Bowling Green: Bowling Green University Press, 1976), 74.

ish throne—and Balthazar, the Portuguese heir, whose death at the hands of Bel-imperia was announced by Revenge at the outset of the framed play. The connection between Balthazar's death in the "Soliman and Perseda" playlet and the apocalyptic overthrow of Spain–Portugal/Babylon is the political and eschatological mystery of *The Spanish Tragedy*. Kyd is revealing to his Elizabethan audiences the mystery of the destined defeat of Catholic Babylon by England, and he parallels that fall to the overthrow of Babylon and Balthazar in the Book of Daniel. As Peter Goodstein has noted, "Prince Balthazar represents Babylon . . . , Hieronimo becomes (4.4), like Daniel, the eventual decipherer of the confusion. Balthazar the Prince, as well as Balthazar the King, is destroyed, both destructions, in fact, being 'wrought by the heavens.'"[21]

To heighten the irony of Hieronimo's role as the divinely appointed enemy of the contemporary Babylon, Spain, Kyd reverses the positions of the prophet and King Belshazzar at the Babylonian court by making Hieronimo the established official at the Spanish court and Balthazar the prisoner of war favored by his ostensible enemy, Lorenzo. Daniel was an Israelite judge captured in the war and taken to Babylon where he was given a slave name *Belteshazzar*, which ironically corresponded to the name of the king of Babylon, Belshazzar. Daniel rose to prominence as a court seer when he interpreted mysteries which, ironically, predicted the demise of the nation that rewarded him for his interpretations. Unlike Daniel, Hieronimo belongs to the official power structure of "Babylon" as the lord marshal of Spain, who also devises courtly entertainment for Spanish victories and dynastic weddings. However, Hieronimo, like Daniel, is actually at odds with the country that honors him for his presentation and interpretation of mysteries. As S. F. Johnson has stated, Hieronimo would have been identified with the English office of lord marshal and seen as a decided enemy to Spain and Portugal because of his courtly masque in which England is the victor and his revenge playlet which causes the fall of Babylon/Spain.[22] Hieronimo, the judge, bearer of the sacred name, presenter and interpreter of political and eschatological mysteries, and the prophet and engineer of Babylonian Spain's fall, is the English Daniel fulfilling pagan justice and divine providence.

---

[21]Peter Goodstein, "Hieronimo's Destruction of Babylon," *English Language Notes* 3 (1966):173.

[22]Johnson, "Babylon," 30.

Like Hieronimo, Prince Balthazar's initial position at the Spanish court is the reverse of that of his biblical analogue at the Babylonian court. Belshazzar was the king of Babylon, Daniel's master, doomed to fall with his country to the Persians as predicted in the handwriting on the wall. In the play, Prince Balthazar of Portugal is, like Daniel, a prisoner of war at a foreign court where he is elevated to prominence by his ostensible enemy, Lorenzo. However, unlike Daniel, Balthazar achieves his position at the court of Spain through the murder of Horatio and his intended marriage to Bel-imperia, the sister of the Machiavellian Lorenzo, who has created the various plots to further his dynastic ambitions. For his depiction of Prince Balthazar as the murderer of his rival, Kyd may be adapting Raleigh's description of King Belshazzar as a violent, headstrong youth who had "in his father's time slain a noble young man that should have married his sister."[23] Finally, in his ignorance of the true nature of his role in the playlet, Prince Balthazar is like King Belshazzar who was killed at a feast "by the hands of those whom he had wronged . . . and was slain as he deserved."[24]

The revenge playlet represents Kyd's adaptation of the most celebrated event in the Book of Daniel, Belshazzar's feast. As Goodstein has pointed out, Prince Balthazar becomes an analogue to King Belshazzar "who saw the incomprehensible handwriting on the wall. Prince Balthazar's calling the play-within-the-play 'a meere confusion' that will hardly be understood is analogous to the Babylonian's reaction to the words 'Mene, Mene, Tekel, Upharsin.'"[25] Kyd also uses the scene to present the Danielic concept of the superseding of the four worldly empires by God's fifth monarchy, represented in the play by England which defeats Spain/Babylon and emerges as God's chosen nation. Further, in the apparent contradictions between the promised sundry languages of the playlet and their translation into English, Kyd alludes to a number of important issues connected with the translation of the Bible into English as the central Reformation act against the hegemony of the Roman Catholic Latin Vulgate. Finally, in Hieronimo's biting out his tongue rather than providing further explanation to his inquisitors, Kyd echoes the Danielic "sealing of the book" and signals to his audience that it must go beyond Hieron-

[23]Raleigh, *History*, 5:3.1.44.
[24]Ibid., 5:3.1.45.
[25]Goodstein, "Destruction," 173.

imo's silence to gain an understanding of the hidden meanings of the mystery text.

The revenge playlet which Hieronimo presents is directly related to the historical masque he devised for the Spanish victory over Portugal. Both productions occur respectively in the penultimate scene of the first and last acts of the play; both are viewed by onstage audiences consisting of Iberian dignitaries, with the addition of the viceroy and his brother Pedro at the marriage playlet, and in both playlets the past exerts an important influence on their meanings and consequences. In the masque, Hieronimo drew upon historical relations between the Iberian countries and little England to show past English dominance and to suggest its future conquest of Babylon/Spain-Portugal. In the marriage playlet, the historical Anglo-Iberian past as delineated in the historical masque and the dramatic past in the form of Horatio's murder create the symbolic and actual context of Hieronimo's presentation; Hieronimo will avenge his son's death and at the same time fulfill Revenge's prophecy concerning the murder of Balthazar by Bel-imperia and his own prediction of the "fall of Babylon." But the intended victims of the playlet, Lorenzo and Balthazar, are unaware of Hieronimo's true intentions in wanting to enact a tragedy instead of a comedy to celebrate the upcoming wedding. In their inability to recognize Hieronimo's purposes from his broad, sardonic hints, these villains parallel the unsuspecting Babylonian King Belshazzar who, as Raleigh said, "was ceaselessly feasting when danger hemmed him in on every side. . . . So the end of him was base and miserable; for he died as a fool taken in unexcusable security."[26]

Although Lorenzo and Balthazar agree to Hieronimo's questionable decision to play a tragedy instead of a comedy for the wedding celebration, when Hieronimo adds the stipulation that the playlet shall be acted in four foreign tongues—Greek, Latin, Italian, and French—Balthazar rightly objects: "But this will be a mere confusion, / And hardly shall we all be understood" (4.1.180–81). Agreeably, Hieronimo promises that he "in an oration, / . . . shall make the matter known" (184, 187). Balthazar's use of the word *confusion* ties the sundry languages of the playlet to Hieronimo's subsequent prediction that "Now shall I see the fall of Babylon, / Wrought by the heavens in this confusion" (195–96). As S. F. Johnson has demonstrated, Kyd conflates the Babel/Babylon reference into a dual image of the fall of the Babylonian empire and toppling of the Tower of Babel, which resulted in the confusion (Babel/babble) of tongues:

> To Protestant interpreters, the symbolic Babylon was of course Rome, the whore of Babylon being equated with the Antichrist, in turn equated with the Pope, . . . one of whose agents . . . was the King of Spain. . . . Hieronimo's couplet equates Spain with Babylon and with Babel, for Babel was thought to mean "confusion" (Genesis, 11.9, gloss).[27]

For Prince Balthazar, as well as Lorenzo and the assembled Iberian royalty, the marriage playlet performed in sundry tongues is the equivalent of the indecipherable handwriting on the wall predicting Belshazzar's downfall. Like his biblical namesake, Balthazar cannot interpret the figurative "handwriting on the wall" of Hieronimo's broad hints concerning the intended tragic consequences of the playlet. For the unaware participants in Hieronimo's presentation and for the equally unaware Iberian audience watching it, confusion is their inescapable condition. But Hieronimo, the Danielic *Vindicta Dei*, is the decipherer of the confusion, the explainer of the mystery playlet with the hidden meanings. Like Kyd, Calvin applies Daniel's prophecy of the fall of Babylon to the contemporary Catholic powers whose legacy will be Babylonian confusion: "they pretende the name of Christianity, and do boast themselves the chief defenders of the Catholicke faith, [but] it may easely bee confuted as a vayne bablyng."[28]

In addition to their analogy to the confusion of Babel/Babylon, the sundry tongues also establish a Danielic sense of the passage of the four empires described in Daniel 2 and 7 as the Babylonian, Medo-Persian, Greek, and Roman. In *The Spanish Tragedy* Spain and Portugal are considered collectively as the contemporary Babylon and are represented by Lorenzo, Balthazar, and Castile, who are killed during and after the playlet. Within the playlet, Hieronimo speaks Greek, and the Roman empire and Roman Catholic Church under the Pope are represented by Lorenzo and Balthazar, who perform double duty, so to speak, by speaking Latin and Italian, respectively. In addition, Bel-imperia speaks French, the lan-

---

[27]Johnson, "Babylon," 24–25.
[28]Calvin, *Daniel* (tr. Golding), B1r.

guage of the Catholic country that carried out the infamous massacre in Paris on St. Bartholomew's day in 1572.

The only Danielic empire missing from the playlet is the Persian, which Kyd replaces with its contemporary equivalent, the Turkish empire. Balthazar plays Soliman, a character based on the Turkish historical figure of Suleiman I (1494–1566), who seized the island of Rhodes from the Knights of St. John in 1522. In the playlet, Soliman has his Bashaw slay Erasto, the knight of Rhodes, and then Perseda (Bel-imperia) kills the emperor for murdering her husband. When Bel-imperia kills Balthazar as Soliman, Kyd is representing the "death" of the "scourge of Europe," the Turkish empire. Geveren's description of the Danielic rise and fall of Turkey fits the context of Hieronimo's playlet: "the state of these tymes marveilously . . . aunsweare[s] unto the Prophesie of *Daniel*. . . . [I]t appeareth . . . that the Turke . . . wyl subdue al kingdomes. But I trust the Lord God . . . wyll bryng to nought, these endevours of Turke and Pope."[29]

On the symbolic politico-religious level of the revenge playlet, Kyd equates the Danielic passage of empire with the contemporary Protestant notion of the imminent and destined overthrow of the Babylonian Catholic countries by God's fifth monarchy. Calvin's description of God's allowing the appearance of bestial and evil nations to provide a spectacle for believers who know he will soon destroy these countries parallels Hieronimo's presentation of these same ill-fated empires in his playlet: "For God hath brought forth certayne monsters, that we might be astonished with such a sight and spectacle, both greekes, and of partes of the East, and Spaniardes, and Italians, and Frenchmen."[30] And Joye's depiction of the efforts of these Babylonian countries to join in marriage to create one powerful empire coincides with the intended dynastic union of Spain and Portugal which Hieronimo destroys through his "marriage" playlet:

> kynges have joyned together in maryages with theyr daughters and sonnes . . . and with holy sacred others in lege. . . . They shal be consedered to make a newe and all one Monarchye, but all in vayne, for this is the last empire to be destroyed at the last daye . . . for persecutynge Gods worde. . . . For in the

---

[29]Geveren, *End of World* (1577 ed.), 16v.
[30]Calvin, *Daniel* (tr. Golding), 48r.

tyme of these kynges the God of heven shal set up a kyngdom
which shall never be destroyed.[31]

Kyd indicates that England is the nation which has succeeded the
Babylonian empires through the note appearing directly before the enactment of the playlet that "this play of Hieronimo in sundry languages, was
thought good to be set down in English more largely, for the easier understanding to every public reader." The translation of the foreign languages
into English signifies the passage from the Babylonian confusion of the
sundry tongues to the clarity of English, from the fall of Catholic Babylon
to the emergence of England, a process effected by God, "the most just
translatour and changer of realmes."[32] As Eugene Hill has remarked: "The
playlet is an enacted pun on translation in different senses and different
media. The real 'passing' involved is the *translatio imperii*—to England, to
English."[33]

There has been much critical speculation concerning the discrep-
ancy between the promised sundry tongues of the playlet, the note to the
reader announcing the translation of the playlet into English, and Hieronimo's statement at the conclusion of the playlet, "Here break we off our
sundry languages" (74). Philip Edwards has developed an explanation for
the apparent contradiction based on textual corruption resulting from the
printer's use of divergent texts.[34] However, it can be argued that Kyd pur-
posefully creates the apparent contradiction between the sundry tongues
and the English translation as an essential part of the mystery, Danielic,
and politico-religious contexts of *The Spanish Tragedy*. To begin with, as I
have already argued (*Kyd's Mystery Play*, 151–56), the paradox can be
explained by the pagan mystery rubric which demands that the secrets
revealed to the initiates at the mystery rites be kept hidden from the uninitiated. Kyd uses this inherent tension between revelation and secrecy and
between the initiated and the uninitiated audiences in the marriage playlet
where the onstage assembly of Iberian royalty constitutes the unaware,
ignorant audience that knows nothing of the hidden meanings—i.e., the
real consequences—of Hieronimo's play-within-the-play. For this audi-

---

[31]Joye, *Daniel*, 29v–30r.
[32]Ibid., 64r.
[33]Hill, "Perspectives," 163.
[34]Edwards, *The Spanish Tragedy*, xxxvii–xxxix.

ence, the playlet remains in sundry tongues, causing them confusion. But for the theater audience, the initiated into the secrets of the mystery, the playlet is translated into English, that is, its hidden meanings are made known to us because of our wider aesthetic perspective on the action. Thus, the playlet can be said to be performed in sundry tongues *and* at the same time translated into English for the respective audiences.

The apparent contradiction can be explained in terms of Christian mystery as well. As we have seen, commentators on the Book of Daniel use the metaphors of sundry tongues and a closed book to express the inability of the unbelievers to understand the mysteries of Daniel's prophecies. Calvin declares that God's enemies can look at the truth but cannot actually see or understand God's word, which for them remains a "booke . . . in a straunge . . . toung."[35] But to the faithful, "God doth make over . . . all his mysteries and secrets."[36] In a similar fashion, a number of related New Testament passages concern the contrast between the confusion of unbelievers as represented by sundry tongues and the clarity of the believers' understanding of God's word as represented by synonymous acts of prophecy, interpretation, and revelation. In the First Epistle to the Corinthians (1 Cor. 14:21-22), St. Paul declares that God speaks to his enemies in sundry tongues, but he prophesies to His followers:

> In the Law it is written, By men of other tongues, and by other languages wil I speake unto this people: yet so shall they not heare me, saith the Lord. Wherefore *strange* tongues are for a signe, not to them that beleve, but to them that beleve not: but prophecying serveth not for them that beleve not, but for them which beleve.   (81v)

Throughout this chapter, St. Paul distinguishes between the confusion inherent in sundry or divers tongues and the illumination produced by prophesying, which is synonymous with interpretation and revelation: "If anie man speake a *strange* tongue, *let it* be by two, or . . . thre, and that by course, and let one interpret. . . . For God is not the *autor* of confusion, but of peace . . ." (27, 33). In Hieronimo's playlet, the promised sundry tongues represent the confusion of the unbelievers, but the translation into English and Hieronimo's subsequent explanation of the playlet are the interpretation and revelation to the faithful demanded by God.

[35]Calvin, *Daniel* (tr. Golding), 8r.
[36]Brightman, *Daniel*, 73.

Three passages in the synoptic Gospels (Matt. 13:10-15; Mark 4:10-12; Luke 8:9-10) present the contrast between the incomprehension of unbelievers and the understanding of Christ's followers in the context of the parable of the "Sower and the Seed." The parable concerns the ways in which God's word is rejected by those unable to understand it and received and nurtured by those who can. Moreover, Christ's delivery of the parable to uncomprehending crowds and to his disciples reinforces the theme concerning divergent audiences. Thus the parable serves as the *mystērion*, which, as in Daniel, is closed to the uninitiated but revealed to the initiated. As Raymond Brown has explained, "the Synoptic use of *mystērion* is like that of Daniel and the apocalypses . . . [in the] revealing [of] divine secrets through enigmatic symbols."[37]

In the three accounts, Christ delivers the parable, glossed in Luke 8:10 as "an obscure or darke saying" (31v, n), to a crowd of people who have followed him to receive his instruction. After he finishes preaching, Christ's disciples question him concerning the purpose and meaning of the parable. In Matt. 13:10, they ask him why he preaches in parables if he intends to have the crowd understand him. In Mark and Luke, the disciples question Christ about the meaning of the parable itself. Christ's answer is the same in Matthew and Luke; he teaches in parables because they, the stubborn unbelievers, cannot understand him: "Because it is given unto you, to know the secrets of the kingdome, but to them it is not given. . . . Therefore speake I to them in parables, because they seing, do not se: and hearing, they heare not, nether understand" (Matt. 13:11-13, 8r; cf. Luke 8:10).

However in Mark(Mark 4:11-12), Christ first reproves his followers for their ignorance of the meaning of the parable and then explains that he uses parables so that the unbelievers will not be able to understand his truths, in other words, to exclude them from the possibility of accepting these truths:

> To you it is given to knowe the mysterie of the kingdom of God: but unto them that are without, all things be done in parables, That they seing, may se, and not discerne: and they hearing, may heare, and not understand, lest at any time they shulde turne, and their sinnes shulde turne, and their sinnes shulde be forgiven them. (18v)

[37]Brown, "*Mystery*," 34.

Frank Kermode has explained that Matthew and Mark's versions involve "two kindred but different secrecy theories. . . . One says the stories are obscure on purpose to damn the outsiders; the other . . . says that they are not necessarily impenetrable, but that the outsiders, being what they are, will misunderstand them anyway."[38] Christ's concealment of the meaning from the uninitiated and his clear explanation of it to his followers represent the paradoxical actions inherent in mystery texts: "Parable . . . may proclaim a truth like an oracle. This double function . . . [is] simultaneous proclamation and concealment."[39]

Kyd's contrasting of the sundry tongues to the English translation of the playlet provides a striking parallel to the synoptic contexts for the parable of "The Sower and the Seed." As the playlet is about to begin, the Spanish king hands the playbook to his brother Castile: "Here brother, you shall be the bookkeeper: / This is the argument of that they show" (4.4.9–10). The playlet and its playbook are the mystery text, the parable whose true meaning the uninitiated can never understand. To them it remains the "closed" book in sundry tongues, even though the note of the English translation follows. The onstage Iberian audience reads the playbook and hears the playlet in English, but the real meanings of the text remain closed to them. What Calvin says about Belshazzar and his guests' inability to understand the handwriting on the wall fits the uncomprehending Iberian audience: "they were so blinded, that in seeing they should not see. . . . If any man say, read thys, he will say the booke is sealed, I can not: or let the booke be opened and all . . . shal be as it were blynde."[40]

After the playlet, Hieronimo "breaks off our sundry languages" and explains in English to the onstage audience the real nature of the stage deaths and his reasons for the murders. But even after his lengthy explanation and the showing of his dead son Horatio, the uncomprehending king demands further explanation:

> Speak, traitor: damned, bloody murderer, speak:
> For now I have thee I will make thee speak:
> Why hast thou done this undeserving deed?
>
> (163–65)

---

[38]Frank Kermode, *The Genesis of Secrecy: On the Interpretation of Narrative* (Cambridge: Harvard University Press, 1979), 32.

[39]Ibid., 47.

[40]Calvin, *Daniel* (tr. Golding), 78v.

Hieronimo's captors press for more information until he refuses to speak
further, citing his allegiance to a vow of secrecy: "But never shalt thou
force me to reveal / The thing which I have vow'd inviolate" (187–88).
Hieronimo then seals his vow of silence by biting out his tongue and by
using the knife with which he is supposed to "mend his pen" to kill
Castile and himself.

In their insistence that Hieronimo reveal more about the playlet even
after he has explained its hidden meanings to them, the Iberian audience
members serve as graphic examples of the uninitiated blocked by their
confusion and ignorance from understanding the mystery. Hieronimo is
the Danielic prophet who declares that the hidden meanings of the mystery are concealed from the unbelievers in a book written in sundry languages and at the same time revealed to those who have the knowledge to
understand the English translation, as we do in the theater audience. Thus,
to the theater audience, Hieronimo's vow and subsequent "closing of the
book" is a signal that we should go beyond the ignorant onstage audience
to a deeper understanding of the entire play's hidden meanings which
already have been revealed to us within the symbolic plays-within-the-
play.

The final and most comprehensive context for the apparent contra-
diction between sundry tongues and the English translation is that of the
English Reformation's attack against the hegemony of the Roman Catholic
Latin Bible. The most important intellectual and religious accomplishment of the English Reformation was the translation of the Vulgate into
English, which enabled the literate English believer to read and understand the Scriptures without the intervention of Catholic authorities.[41]
Analogously, Hieronimo's playlet is translated from the sundry tongues
into English "for the easier understanding to every public reader"; Greek
and Latin, the languages of the Septuagint and the Vulgate, respectively,
and Italian and French, the languages of England's Roman Catholic enemies, are replaced by English, the new sacred tongue. Significantly at the
grisly conclusion of the playlet, Hieronimo breaks off the sundry lan-

[41]For analyses of the importance of Bible translation into English to the English Reformation, see, among many others: Ronald B. Bond, "The 1559 Revisions in *Certayne Sermons
or Homilies*: 'For the better Understanding of the Simple People,'" *English Literary Renaissance*
9 (1978): 239–55; William Haller, *Foxe's Book of Martyrs and the Elect Nation* (London:
Jonathan Cape, 1963), esp. 52, 90–96; John King, *English Reformation Literature: The Tudor
Origins of the Protestant Tradition* (Princeton: Princeton University Press, 1982), esp. 16–17,
55, 211–21.

guages and speaks "in our vulgar tongue." Like his namesake St. Hierony-mus (Jerome),[42] Hieronimo translates the Catholic languages into the vulgate, but instead of Latin, English is now the common tongue.

Hieronimo's translation of the sundry tongues of the playlet into the English vernacular reenacts and at the same time changes the biblical account of the Pentecostal gift of tongues. On Pentecost Sunday, the Apostles "began to speake with other tongues, as the Spirit gave them utterance.... [T]he multitude ... were astonied, because that everie man heard them speake his owne langage" (Acts 2:4, 6, 54v). The gloss further explains that "they coulde speake all languages" and thus were able to communicate with the different nationalities gathered to hear the Apostles preach. However, Hieronimo reverses the Pentecostal gift of tongues by translating the foreign tongues into one language, English, which will be understood by his auditors, the Elizabethan theater audiences watching *The Spanish Tragedy*. Hieronimo's translation of the many into the one parallels John Mirk's description of the Apostle's gift of tongues in *Festial* (1483): "sodenly they were the wysest and the best clerkes in al the world and spake al manes language under one."[43] Thus, in Kyd's recreation of Pentecostal inspiration, English serves as the sacred language used by Hieronimo—and by extension the English nation—to overcome the confounding of language associated with Babel/Babylon and the Roman Catholic Church and its Latin Bible.

[42]For a discussion of Hieronimo as an analogue to St. Jerome, see my "Hieronimo as St. Jerome in *The Spanish Tragedy*," *Études Anglaises* 36 (1983): 435–37.
[43]John Mirk, *Festial* (Westminister, 1483), unpaged entry under "Pentecost."

3

The Exegetical and Dramatic
Traditions of the Book
of Revelation

THE SYMBOLIC VISIONS IN the books of Daniel and Revelation were interpreted by sixteenth-century Protestant commentators as signs that the fall
of Catholic Babylon, that is, Rome and Spain, was imminent. The images
and terms common to both books—the composite beasts, the Antichrist,
the time prophecies, the prophetic books sealed and unsealed, and the
depictions of the fall of Babylon—became essential parts of the scriptural
attack upon the Pope, Rome, and Spain.

In their attack on Catholic Babylon, the Protestant apologists interpret the Book of Revelation as the prophecies contained in Daniel. This
complementary relationship is expressed primarily by the unsealing of the
prophetic book closed at the end of Daniel when the angel ordered the
prophet to "shut up the wordes, and seale the book til the end of the
time . . ." (Dan. 12:4, 364v). The gloss to this passage states that the truths
will be sealed "Til the time that God hathe appointed for the ful revelation
. . . of these mysteries." In Rev. 22:10, the angel tells John to "seale not the
wordes of the prophecie of this boke: for the time is at hand" (122r), and
the gloss explains that "this is not then as the other Prophecies . . . in
Daniel 12, 4, because . . . these thinges shulde be quickly accomplished,
and did now begin." The revelation of these secrets tells the faithful that
God's justice will prevail, for, as Heinrich Bullinger asserts, "the opening
of the booke . . . is . . . the revalying of Gods judgements and the

declaryng . . . of his most secret determinations, and . . . the most holy and just execution of his will."[1]

In a more expansive and emphatic manner, John Bale argues that the secrets unveiled in the Apocalypse reveal the nature of the struggle between the true church and the Antichrist. Anyone who wants to understand the past, present, and future course of this conflict must read the Apocalypse, because it reveals not only the history of the church, but also the causes of historical events:

> It is full clerenes to all the cronicles and most notable hystories . . . , openynge the true nature of their ages. . . . He that . . . shall diligently serche them [Revelation and history] conferrying the one with the other . . . shall perceyve most wonderful causes. For in the text are they only proponed in effecte, . . . but in the cronicles they are . . . sene . . . fulfilled.[2]

Similarly, George Gifford maintains that the prophecies of Daniel and Revelation are now being revealed and fulfilled by the events of the Reformation: "this revelation hath many thinges in it, which . . . were *Aenigmata*, darke riddles, and ambiguitie, . . . because they lived before the times in which they should be fulfilled, which now unto us that have seene them come to passe, have a cleare and an undoubted position."[3] Thus, a reciprocal relationship is established in which the prophecies in Daniel and the Apocalypse help to predict and elucidate contemporary events, while the latter assist in the clarification of the biblical mysteries. As Carol Stillman has remarked, "In the sixteenth century, the Apocalypse acquired national and party interpretations that could dominate religious meanings. The Book of Revelation affected Protestant politics, and politics in turn changed the reading of Revelation."[4]

The number of full-length commentaries on the Apocalypse published in English attest to its religious and political importance in sixteenth-century England. Between 1548 and 1603 nine commentaries were published by: John Bale (1548, 1550, 1555, 1570); Heinrich Bullinger (1561,

---

[1]Heinrich Bullinger, *A Hundred Sermons Upon the Apocalipse of Jesu Christ*, tr. John Day (London, 1573), 72v.

[2]John Bale, *The Image of Bothe Churches after the moste wonderfull and heavenly Revelacion of Sainct John* . . . (Antwerp?, 1548), "Preface," Pt. 1:A4v.

[3]George Gifford, *Sermons Upon the Whole Book of Revelation* (London, 1596), 2–3.

[4]Carol Stillman, "Spenser's Elect England: Political and Apocalyptic Dimensions of *The Faerie Queene*" (Ph.D. diss., University of Pennsylvania, 1979), 51–52.

1573, tr. John Day); William Fulke (1573, tr. George Gifford); Augustin Marlorat (1574, tr. Arthur Golding); Jacobus Brocardus (1582, tr. James Sanford); François Du Jon (Junius) (1592, 1594, 1600, shorter ed.; 1596, longer ed.); John Napier (1593, 1594, 1600, 1603); George Gifford (1596), and Arthur Dent (1603). The most influential commentaries were Bullinger's, which is the source of the Geneva Bible's (1560) annotations, and Du Jon's shorter edition, which was added to the notes on Revelation in the Geneva Bible of 1598 and 1601.[5]

A number of these commentaries were issued in answer to political crises. For example, in 1569 William Fulke was serving as the chaplain to the Earl of Leicester when news of the Northern Rebellion reached him. Fulke expounded upon the pertinent parts of Revelation from chapter 12 to the end; then in 1570 when Pius V excommunicated Queen Elizabeth, he completed the commentary on the first eleven books and lectured on the entire Apocalypse at Cambridge. Finally, after the massacre in Paris on St. Bartholomew's day in 1572, the Latin and English editions of Fulke's *Praelections upon the Sacred and holy Revelation of S John* were published, so that, as the English translator Gifford said, "the Romish monster . . . [should know] that in the ende he [God] will revenge the bloud of his Sainctes."[6] Moreover, some commentators fit their annotations on passages of Revelation to suit recent historical events, as is the case with John Napier, who relates the sea imagery connected with the fall of Babylon (Rev. 18:7) to the defeat of the Spanish Armada in 1588.[7] In sum, the ways in which the commentaries are used reveal, as Richard Tresley asserts, that "the Apocalypse, as the vehicle for interpreting the troubled times in which Protestants found themselves, . . . became a source of moral and intellectual strength. By means of prophecy the faithful are taken behind the scenes of history and assured that God reigns supreme, in command of events past, present, and future which he directs toward the fulfillment of his final purposes."[8]

---

[5]Bauckham, *Tudor Apocalypse*, 137–38.

[6]Qtd. in ibid., 133.

[7]John Napier, *A Plaine Discovery of the whole Revelation of Saint John . . .* (Edinburgh, 1593), 223n.

[8]Richard Tresley, "Renaissance Commentaries on The Book of Revelation and Their Influence on Spenser's *Faerie Queene* and d'Aubigné's *Les Tragiques*," (Ph.D. diss., University of Chicago, 1980), 36.

In the Renaissance, the Book of Revelation, like the Book of Daniel, was interpreted as a mystery writing containing many symbolic prophecies concerning God's final purposes. Bale maintains that it "hath so many mysteries as it hath wordes," with John, like "Ezechiell, Daniell, Zacharye . . . , uttering Gods mind in misteries."[9] David Pareus emphasizes the obscurity of the Apocalypse which keeps the secrets hidden from the profane and forces the godly to search diligently for understanding: "the mysteries of the Visions, although he [God] revealed them to his servants and Prophets, yet hee kept them secret from . . . prophane men. . . . [B]ut the godly even by the obscurity thereof be the more stirred up to the searching out of divine mysteries."[10] But, as is traditional with mystery writings, at the same time that the obscurity of the Apocalypse is maintained, there is an equal emphasis on its revelation of God's mysteries. Commentators note that the dual titles, the Apocalypse and Book of Revelation, which derive from their respective Greek and Latin equivalents meaning to *unveil* or *uncover*, indicate its function as the "very complete summe and whole knitting up . . . of the universall veritees of the Bible."[11] John Napier explains that the "*Apocalyps* . . . is a Revelation, and therefore, is this book intituled; for that by the will . . . of God, Christ hath reveiled the same . . . to . . . *John*, and now doth . . . reveile . . . the meaning . . . to us in this our age."[12] Marlorat defines mysteries, visions, and dreams as things discovered that were hidden before which "God . . . reveale[s] . . . by peculiar Revelations to the better sorte of men whome he has appointed to the greatest matters. . . . [A] Revelation happeneth oftentimes by dreame. . . . [A] vision is . . . never given but with a Revelation, that is to say . . . the Lord discloseth what his meaning is by it."[13]

The reader's interpretation of the mysteries of the Apocalypse becomes the means of knowing God's secret plans. This knowledge is transmitted from God to Christ, who, through his angel, shows John the

[9]Bale, *Image*, Pt. 2: Aiiir; Pt. 3 Qqiiir.

[10]David Pareus, *A Commentary upon the Divine Revelation of the Apostle and Evangelist John*, tr. Elias Arnold (Amsterdam, 1644), 9.

[11]Bale, *Image*, Pt. 1: Aiiir.

[12]Napier, *Discovery*, 75.

[13]Augustin Marlorat, *A Catholike exposition upon the Revelation of St. John*, tr. Arthur Golding (London, 1574), 3v.

enigmatic visions which the latter then reveals to the faithful. Pareus traces the series of revelations: "it [Revelation] is . . . called a prophesie, . . . a prediction of future things revealed by God to Christ . . . our mediator, that hee might reveal the same to . . . the faithful of all ages."[14] As a result of the reception of the "knowledge of heavenly mysteries,"[15] the faithful are endowed with prophetic wisdom: "Not only shalt thou be by the . . . manifestacion of thys prophecie an Aungel, but also by an excellent prerogatyve of singuler grace . . . a Prophete."[16]

The specific nature of the prophetic knowledge received by the faithful is established by the contexts of the word *mystery* in the Apocalypse. *Mystery* is used four times—Rev. 1:20; 10:7; 17:5, 7—and means generally, as it does in Daniel, a symbolic vision which reveals some aspect of the purpose of God's kingdom. In the first chapter Christ interprets "the mysterie of the seven starres . . . and the seven candlesticks . . . [as] the Angels . . . [and their] seven churches" (115r); in a similar context at Rev. 17:5, 7, the Whore of Babylon is described as wearing on "her forehead . . . a name . . . , A Mysterie, great Babylon. . . . Then the Angel said . . . I will shewe thee the mysterie of the woman, and of the beast that . . . hathe seven heads, and ten hornes" (120r). Raymond Brown compares these usages with that in Daniel 2 because both the form and the content of the visions "are mysteries. . . . [T]he form . . . is a mystery because it is a communication from God in a supernatural manner, and contains a complicated series of symbols. In turn, the content . . . , i.e., what is signified . . . , is a mystery because it refers to something which has a special role in God's mysterious providence."[17]

The nature of God's mysterious providence is revealed at Rev. 10:7 when "the seventh Angel . . . shall beginne to blowe the trumpet, . . . [and] the mysterie of God shalbe finished . . ." (117v). The gloss explains that "the faithful shal understand and se this mysterie of the last judgement, the damnacion of Antichrist and . . . the glorie of the just at the resurrection" (117v, n). In commenting on this passage, Bullinger elucidates the mystery of the Last Judgment by citing Paul's prediction of the resurrection of the faithful in 1 Cor. 15:52, which Andrea echoes, as we have seen in chapter 2, in the induction:

---

[14]Pareus, *Commentary*, 3–4.
[15]Gifford, *Sermons*, 19.
[16]Bale, *Image*, Pt. 3:Feiiiv–ivr.
[17]Brown, "*Mystery*," 36.

at the last judgement the misterie of God should be made
consummate. . . . What this secret or misterie of God is the
Apostle expoundeth . . . [in] 1 Corinth 15. . . . [T]he end of all
corruptible thynges is at hand, and the happy and everlastyng
world shall succeede. . . . Christ shall then come to
judgement. . . . Antichrist by him shallbe abolished: . . . the
wicked to everlasting perdition, the godly to eternall lyfe. . . .
[T]he misterie of God shall . . . be fulfilled.[18]

Commentators emphasize the necessity and harsh justice of the Last
Judgment at which God emerges as the "revenger of the church [who]
slepeth not."[19] When that time comes, Gifford asserts, "the unchangeable
God declareth himselfe to bee just by taking vengeance."[20] Identifying
Rome as the political object of God's wrath, Gifford, like Bale, emphasizes
the inevitability of its demise in the unfolding of time: "This bloudie
Romane Empire both former and latter which . . . hath drawne infinite
thousands into everlasting captivitie, shall also it selfe bee cast downe,
and . . . because . . . he appoyneth the times . . . , we must patiently waite
for the same."[21]

The certainty of the execution of divine vengeance as revealed in the
Apocalypse results in two perspectives on history, one from above which
views all events as predetermined, and the other from the earth which sees
everything as the result of Fortune. Augustine Marlorat distinguishes
between these two perspectives:

[When] he [John] sayth that these thynges must come to passe,
he doeth us to understand howe greate the stablenesse and
assurednesse of Gods determination is. For . . . things . . . fore-
appoynted by Gods determinate purpose . . . are utterly
unchaungeable. . . . The worldlings surmyse all thyngs to be
doone by Fortune, bycause they are not privie to the reason
why moste of them bee done.[22]

[18]Bullinger, *Sermons*, 134v–35r.
[19]Ibid., 262v.
[20]Gifford, *Sermons*, 310.
[21]Ibid., 254.
[22]Marlorat, *Exposition*, 4r–v.

Similarly, Bartholomew Traheron declares that by reading the Apocalypse the faithful can perceive that "they [earthly events] fal not in my chaunce, but be governed, and ordred by his wisedome and fore knowledge."[23]

This dualistic perspective on the course of earthly events lies at the heart of the apocalyptic interpretation of history. Protestant exegetes are convinced that the history of the true church and, analogously, of the world follows a tripartite temporal structure of the past leading to the present with both resulting in an inevitable end which gives meaning to the tightly ordered progression. In this way, apocalypticism endows each of the time periods with a special significance, showing how the past anticipates and influences the present, how the present reflects and repeats the past, and how the determined future reveals the inevitability of the process leading to it. As C. A. Patrides argues, the apocalyptic view of time

> delineates the future not at the expense of the past but in terms of the past. . . . [T]he fundamental presupposition is that the course of history can be accurately perceived solely from Heaven, for . . . it will be recognized not only that the past and present are anticipatory of the future but that the future is inherent in the past and that both are present in the present. In this respect the numerous allusions within the Apocalypse to times past as if they are times present or time future . . . proclaim . . . the concurrence of all events in the eyes of God.[24]

Exegetes explain that the tightly ordered temporal progression of the Apocalypse is paralleled by its narrative structure. Just as the reader becomes aware of the inevitability of God's judgment through an understanding of how the time periods reflect, repeat, and elucidate each other, so too by seeing how prophecies, scenes, and symbols are repeated and at the same time expanded to include new information, the faithful perceive the destined process leading to the fall of Babylon and the defeat of the Antichrist. David Pareus explains that the repetition in various contexts of the apocalyptic visions of the seven vials, thunders, trumpets, and seals occurs because "it pleased the Lord to shew a thing . . . againe and againe

[23]Bartholomew Traheron, *An Exposition of the 4. Chapter of S. Johns Revelation* (Wesel, Germany, 1557), A3r.
[24]C. A. Patrides, "'something like Prophetick strain': Apocalyptic Configurations in Milton," in *The Apocalypse in English Renaissance Thought and Literature*, ed. Patrides and Wittreich (Ithaca: Cornell University Press, 1984), 229.

in diverse Visions . . . in such a manner, that by a certaine gradation, the latter doe always adde somewhat more cleare and waighty to the former."[25]

Through the perception of the pattern of variety in similitude, the reader achieves a cumulative awareness of the unfolding of divine providence. As Wittreich has remarked, "We are thus made each time to confront the same episode; yet the newly added materials provide a fuller articulation, . . . ensure that each new vision will be a greate unfolding of revelation, bringing us each time one step closer to total understanding."[26] Finally, when the reader finishes the Apocalypse, he will understand fully, through retrospection, the coherence of the worldview conveyed by the temporal and narrative structures. Thomas Brightman applies this method of retrospection to the apocalyptic reading of contemporary history:

> Nowe it (the Historye) is reserved for this time because there could not be a full understanding of these things before the last trumpet. The events came forth by little and little, and point by point, to the knowledge of which the world attained severally and by leasure-like, as when hangings are unfolded, but nowe when al things were at last accomplished, it was a fit time to see the whole garment displaied at once.[27]

In sum, Protestant apologists view the images and prophecies in the Book of Daniel and the Apocalypse as mysteries with eschatological and political significance. To understand these mysteries, the commentators develop exegetical theories and methods which reveal the repetitive, accretive, and providential nature of the apocalyptic narrative and temporal structures. Armed with these insights, they interpret contemporary history as having an apocalyptic context and identify the Catholic Pope and rulers as the forces of Antichrist, the Whore of Babylon, the seven-headed dragon, and the beast from the sea. Thus, by learning to read Daniel and Revelation correctly, the faithful also are able to open the "sealed book" of history.

[25]Pareus, *Commentary*, 22.

[26]Joseph Wittreich, "The Poetry of the Rainbow: Milton and Newton among the Prophets," in *Poetic Prophecy in Western Literature*, ed. Jan Wojcik and Raymond-Jean Frontain (Rutherford, New Jersey: Fairleigh Dickinson University Press, 1984), 98.

[27]Thomas Brightman, *A Revelation of the Revelation . . . of St. John opened clearly . . .* (Amsterdam, 1615), 367.

Protestant commentators encourage readers to see the Book of Revelation as a play created and directed by God, with Christ, John, and the angels serving as actors who show the faithful the unfolding conflict between the Antichrist and the true church. The scenes, presented on a cosmic scale in heaven, on earth, and in the netherworld; the opposing characters, vividly described in horrific and supernatural images, and the mysterious prophecies slowly unveiled—all of these elements contribute to the depiction of the Apocalypse as a cosmic drama being enacted before the eyes of the attentive reader. In the most detailed and influential analysis of the Apocalypse as a drama, Pareus spells out the generic properties of the "Propheticall Drama":

> in this Heavenly Interlude . . . are represented diverse . . . things touching the Church . . . and . . . [the] diverse *Acts* are renewed by diverse *Chores* . . . to infuse holy meditations into the mindes of the Readers. . . . [I]t is an Heavenly *Dramma* . . . not onely of foure, but of diverse persons and things, by Typicall Speeches and Actions exhibiting to Johns sight or hearing those things in the Heavenly Theater, which God would have him to understand . . . touching the future state of the Church.[28]

Pareus divides the book into seven visions, each of which constitutes a four-act play introduced by angelic presenters, who, along with other figures, serve also as "*Chores* or Companies beginning, or comming in between, or ending the . . . Action."[29] Christ is the author of Revelation, maker of its prologue, and John is the main actor and interlocutor. At the Last Judgment, God appears on his throne to put an end to the drama.[30]

In *The Key of the Revelation*, Joseph Mede describes the setting of the Apocalypse as a Theater: "Endeavouring to finde out the meaning of the visions in the Revelation, I must first handle that heavenly Theater, whereupon John is called to behold them as upon a Stage . . . [of] The Apocalyptique Theater."[31] On this stage, God presents, through his angel, the sealed

---

[28]Pareus, *Commentary*, 20.
[29]Ibid., 26.
[30]Ibid., 30, 32.
[31]Joseph Mede, *The Key of the Revelation* . . . (London, 1643), 30.

book to anyone able to open it and interpret the mysterious visions. However, John cannot see into the book, and thus its visions are performed as a drama so that he and the faithful can visualize the scenes and come to understand its secrets. In this way, as Michael Murrin argues, the sealed book becomes the equivalent of a prompter's text.[32]

After defining its dramatic properties, the commentators go on to classify the Apocalypse as a tragedy or a tragicomedy, depending on whether they emphasize the defeat of Antichrist or the victory of the faithful and the establishment of the divine monarchy. Arthur Dent says that "Jesus . . . play[s] his part in this tragedie . . . against the Dragon,"[33] and George Gifford applies the apocalyptic tragedy to the contemporary religious conflict, identifying the hierarchy of the Catholic Church with the Antichrist: "The Pope, . . . Cardinals, . . . great prelates, and Doctors of all sorts, studie and read these scriptures. They speak much of the comming of this monster. They play all the parts in this tragedie, and fulfill al that is written of him."[34] Pareus maintains that "the forme of this Prophesie is truely Tragicall. For it representeth Tragicall motions and tumults of the adversaries against the Church of Christ, and at length the Tragicall end also of the wicked themselves."[35] However, when he describes the contents of the four-act play present in each of the visions, Pareus includes both tragic and tragicomic elements:

> The *first* act . . . [shows] the calamities, with which the Church shall bee assaulted by Pagans and Heretickes untill Antichrists rising. The *second* . . . prefigureth comforts opposite to the calamities of the Godly. The *third* shadoweth out an amplification of calamities, or new and more glorious Combats of the Church under Antichrist. Lastly, the *fourth* . . . sheweth the *Catastrophe* of all evils, viz. the declining of Antichrists Kingdom, and the casting of all adversaries in the lake of fire: and on the contrary the Churchs Victory, and Eternall Glory.[36]

[32]Michael Murrin, "Revelation and Two Seventeenth-Century Commentators," *The Apocalypse in English Renaissance Thought and Literature*, ed. Patrides and Wittreich (Ithaca: Cornell University Press, 1984), 134.

[33]Arthur Dent, *The Ruine of Rome or An Exposition upon the whole Revelation . . .* (London, 1603), 196.

[34]Gifford, *Sermons*, 4.

[35]Pareus, *Commentary*, 26.

[36]Ibid., 27.

In his analysis of Revelation as a "tragicall Comedie" in which "the principall thing to be marked . . . is the [victory of the] Church of Jesus Christ . . . over all . . . enemies," Richard Bernard enunciates an important principle of interpretation, cautioning the faithful "not [to] sticke in the letter, but search out an historicall sense, which is the truth intended, and so take the words typically, and not literally."[37] Bernard maintains that reading the Apocalypse provides the faithful with not only an aesthetic and religious experience, but also an historical one, which reveals truths about the drama of the earthly world:

> the Lord by certain . . . Images and pictures, did lively repre-
> sent the whole . . . tragicall Comedie, . . . the revealing of the
> Revelation, to be acted upon the stage of this world, by the
> Church militant unto his Apostle, and Prophet *John*; who was
> an eare-witness of all that was spoken, and a beholder of these
> shadowes and resemblances of what was truly to be done upon
> the earth, being played . . . before him . . . in the words it is
> written. . . . [W]e must learne by these visions, things done,
> things in doing, or hereafter still to bee don, till the world
> come to an end.[38]

Like Bernard, Thomas Brightman fuses drama, eschatology, and history, declaring that the faithful are witnessing now "the Last Act . . . of a most longe and dolefull Tragedy, which shall wholy overflowe with scourges, slaughters, destruction, but after this Theater is . . . removed, there shall come a most delightful spectacle of perpetuall peace."[39]

The effect of the treatment of the revelation as a tragedy and tragicomedy is to make its readers feel that it is unfolding before them both on the stage of their minds and the world stage. The dramatic rubric established for reading the Apocalypse is extended to the interpretation of history, which supplies the particular conflict and characters for the symbolic and mysterious visions of Revelation. Perceiving the relationship between prophecy and history as dramatic experiences, the reader, as Michael Fixler has argued, becomes "a spectator . . . and even a participating wor-

[37]Richard Bernard, *A Key of Knowledge for the Opening of the Secret Mysteries of St. Johns Mysticall Revelation* (London, 1617), 109, 131.
[38]Ibid., 130.
[39]Brightman, *A Revelation*, A3v.

shipper,"[40] in a prophetic national drama which places the struggle with Catholic Babylon in an apocalyptic context and thus provides the solace that it will result in the triumph of the faithful in this world or the next.

In their analysis of the Apocalypse as a drama, Protestant apologists draw upon medieval and Renaissance dramatic traditions. The medieval dramatizations of the Apocalypse emphasize the traditional eschatological features of the Antichrist legend, including the details of his deceitful career as a pseudo-Christ who falsely raises people from the dead; his debate with the prophets Enoch and Elias whom he puts to death but who are truly resurrected by Christ; and the replacement of his tyrannical reign with the divine monarchy of Christ ushered in by the Last Judgment, which rewards the faithful and sends Antichrist and his followers to hell. The tradition begins with the twelfth-century *Ludus de Antichristo* (1150–60), which is heavily influenced by Abbot Adso's *Libellus de Antichristo* (ca. 954), one of the most important sources of Antichrist lore. Although it supports German nationalism and the Emperor Frederick Barbarossa in his power struggle with the Pope, the play emphasizes the eschatological theme of the Last World Emperor and his war against Babylon, which represents the Saracens and ultimately the Antichrist.

Reformation dramatists politicize the apocalyptic drama, equating the papacy with the Antichrist.[41] In the medieval plays, some popes appear as evil figures, but in the Protestant attack against Catholicism, the papacy as an institution is condemned as the Whore of Babylon which must be defeated if the true church is to be established. The Reformation dramatizations of the Apocalypse, more insistently than the medieval versions, join the eschatological with the political to create a dual view: the faithful watch the unfolding of the Antichrist legend as it is represented in the contemporary historical context. Thus, the plays are both generalized and particular; specific historical figures and conflicts are visible behind the allegorical figures drawn from the Antichrist legend.

[40]Michael Fixler, "The Apocalypse within *Paradise Lost*," *New Essays on Paradise Lost*, ed. Thomas Kranidas (Berkeley: University of California Press, 1969), 149.

[41]Richard Emmerson, *Antichrist in the Middle Ages: A Study of Medieval Apocalypticism, Art, and Literature* (Seattle: University of Washington Press, 1981), 205. I am indebted to Emmerson's fine analysis of the medieval and Renaissance iconographic and dramatic traditions of the Apocalypse, 108-237.

Two plays by continental Protestants, both composed in Latin and translated into English in the 1540s convey the belief that the reformers will effect the overthrow of Catholic Babylon. *Pammachius* (1538), written by the German polemicist Thomas Kirchmeyer (1511–63), has been termed "the representative drama of the Reformation era,"[42] combining eschatological allegory with political satire and Reformation optimism concerning the eventual overthrow of Babylon. Pope Pammachius, through his pact with the devil, conquers the world and banishes Veritas. But Christ sends Veritas to the reformer Theophilus (Martin Luther), who foments a revolt against Pammachius in Wittenberg. The play ends after four acts with Pammachius determined to destroy the reformers; the unwritten fifth act represents the promised Second Coming of Christ: "*Pammachius* thus draws upon the apocalyptic expectations of the sixteenth century to emphasize the Protestant belief that, although the Reformation has wounded the papacy, only Christ can bring the final downfall of the papal Antichrist."[43]

The second important continental apocalyptic play is the *Tragedie or Dialoge of the Unjuste Usurped Primacie of the Bishop of Rome and . . . the Just Abolishinge of the Same* (tr. John Ponet 1549), which consists of nine dialogues that parallel the rise of the evil Papists with the emerging power of the Antichrist. Written by the Italian reformer Bernardino Ochino (1487–1564) when he was in England, the play ends with the promise of the English king, Edward VI, to defeat Antichrist by the power of God's word which, according to the Protestant explication of Eph. 6:17, Heb. 4:12, and Rev. 1:11, 2:16, 19:15, is the two-edged sword issuing from the mouth of Christ. With the rise of Edward comes the fall of the Pope; the play's structure is built on the providential pattern of Christian tragicomedy.[44]

In England John Bale (1495–1563) and John Foxe (1516-87) wrote polemical dramas which, like those of Kirchmeyer and Ochino, present the Reformation as the cure for the diseased and anti-Christian Catholic Church. Both Bale and Foxe were Protestant exiles and both commented on the Apocalypse. They read English history and politics within an apocalyptic context, tracing the struggle of the English church and nation

---

[42]Charles Herford, *Studies in the Literary Relations of England and Germany in the Sixteenth Century* (Cambridge: Cambridge University Press, 1886), 124.

[43]Emmerson, *Antichrist*, 229.

[44]King, *Reformation Literature*, 204.

against the Catholic papacy, which is identified as the Antichrist. Both writers adapt the techniques of morality and mystery plays for their Protestant polemical dramas which portray England as the elect nation that will defeat the Catholic Whore of Babylon. John King's description of the providential design in Bale's plays also fits Foxe's intentions in his *comoedia apocalyptica Christus Triumphans*:

> Bale distinguishes between the two genres in terms of the apocalyptic pattern of salvation and damnation, thus differentiating characters into the comic elect or the tragic reprobate. . . . Inherent in Bale's eschatological framework is the assumption that the Reformation provides an essentially comic resolution to the otherwise tragic course of human history, a resolution that looks forward to the final victory over Antichrist at . . . the Last Judgment.[45]

In Bale's *A Comedy concerning Three Laws of Nature, Moses, and Christ*, which has been called the first English Protestant morality play,[46] the character Vindicta Dei, the representative of divine providence, vehemently upbraids Infidelitas with apocalyptic threats:

> Why dost thou rejoice in cruelty and malice?
> Thinkest thou that God sleepeth, and will not His
>   defend. . . .
>
> The blood of innocents to Him for vengeance call;
> And, therefore, this hour must I fiercely upon thee
>   fall. . . .
> I am . . . in punishment most fierce,
> With water, with sword, and with fire.[47]

After Vindicta Dei defeats Infidelitas with the sword of Christ's word as contained in the Gospel, Deus Pater announces the coming of the apocalyptic "new heaven, and a new earth . . . [created] by our most secret working" (5.72), which results in the fall of Babylon in the bottomless pit,

---

[45]Ibid., 276–77.

[46]F. P. Wilson, *The English Drama 1485–1585*, ed. George K. Hunter (Oxford: Oxford University Press, 1969), 35.

[47]John Bale, *A Comedy concerning Three Laws of Nature, Moses, and Christ*, in *The Dramatic Writings of John Bale Bishop of Ossory*, ed. John S. Farmer (1907; rpt. Guildford, England: Charles W. Traylen, 1966), act 5, 68.

and the restoration of "the true . . . religion / In the Christian church" (75).

In *King Johan* Bale establishes the English chronicle history play by joining the morality with an apocalyptic interpretation of English history. Bale presents King John as the saintly representative of English nationalism beset by the attacks of the anti-Christian Pope Innocent III (Usurped Power), who destroys John and attempts to control England, until Imperial Majesty (Henry VIII) restores order and stability. Bale views John's battle against Catholicism as parallel to Henry VIII's conflict with the Pope, but unlike John, Henry succeeds in defying the Catholic Church, and the Reformation, which was caused in part by Henry's defiance, provides the necessary means for the defeat of the Antichrist as depicted in the Apocalypse. In the epilogue, added after Elizabeth's accession, Nobility and Clergy praise Henry's daughter for her success against the "Papists":

> Nobility: She is that Angell, as saynt Johan doth hym call,
> That with the lordes seale doth marke out . . . hys
> . . . servauntes. . . .

> Clergy: In Danyels sprete she hath subdued the Papistes,
> With all the ofsprynge of Antichristes genera-
> cyon.[48]

Published in Basel in 1556 and acted at Trinity College, Cambridge, in 1562–63, John Foxe's *Christus Triumphans* uses the themes, methods, and motifs in Bale and Kirchmeyer's Reformation plays to create a syncretistic *comoedia apocalyptica*, which Emmerson praises as "the most effective treatment of Apocalyptic imagery . . . to trace the historical pattern of the rise and decline of papal power."[49] In the prologue, Foxe announces that he is a "new poet . . . [bringing] new spectators . . . something new . . . to see," and he compares presence at his play to church attendance: "Our matter is totally sacred and totally apocalyptic, what has been heard of by many but never seen before. Therefore indulge us with

---

[48]*John Bale's King Johan*, ed. Barry Adams (San Marino, Calif.: Huntington Library, 1969), 2675–76, 78–79.
[49]Emmerson, *Antichrist*, 232.

sacred silence, as you are wont to do in holy churches. For why is it less fitting for the eyes than for the ears to be trained in sacred subjects?"[50]

The loosely constructed and rambling plot moves quickly from Satan's fall to the resurrection of Christ in act 1; from there Foxe passes through fifteen hundred years of generalized European history to the Reformation during which Hierologus (Luther) reveals the true identity of Pope Pseudamnus as the Antichrist and propels the rescue of Ecclesia from the subjugation of Pseudamnus and Pornapolis, and the Whore of Babylon. The *comoedia sacra* ends with Ecclesia and her two sons, Europus and Africus, joining with the chorus of five virgins to announce the fall of Babylon (5.5.144) and the coming marriage between the lamb and the bride which is presented at the conclusion of the Apocalypse. In its combination of mystery, morality, and chronicle; of classical, medieval, and Renaissance forms; of world, biblical, church, and English history; and of historical, fictional, and allegorical characters, Foxe's *drama novum* exerts a direct influence on the syncretistic nature of *The Spanish Tragedy*.

[50]*Two Latin Comedies by John Foxe the Martyrologist: Titus et Gesippus [and] Christus Triumphans*, ed. and tr. John H. Smith (Ithaca: Cornell University Press, 1973), 229.

4

The Spanish Tragedy as Apocalypse

LIKE FOXE'S *CHRISTUS TRIUMPHANS*, *The Spanish Tragedy* is a providential tragicomedy, a *comoedia apocalyptica*, presenting the tragedy of Babylon/ Spain's fall and the comedy of the English defeat of the Catholic Antichrist. Like Foxe, Kyd fuses classical, medieval, and Renaissance dramatic forms and techniques with biblical themes and motifs to create a syncretistic playworld. *The Spanish Tragedy* has biblical characters like Balthazar, the namesake of the doomed last king of Babylon, and Hieronimo, the bearer of the sacred name, whose role as the judge/revenger makes him like Daniel. The play also contains allegorically named characters like Revenge, Bel-imperia ("beautiful power"), Serberine ("serpentine"), Villuppo ("confusion"), the ironically named Christophil ("love of Christ)" and Pedringano (the "errant one"); and historical characters like Don Pedro, named after the Portuguese and Castilian Don Pedros the Cruel; and Cyprian, the duke of Castile, associated with the most dominant Spanish province in the sixteenth century. Moreover, the induction scene, which parallels the tour and historical apocalypses; the rhetorical and dramatic patterns of the prophetic revelation and lawsuit schemes; the sense of inevitable doom as personified by Revenge; the temporal scheme of retrospection/anticipation/fulfillment; the apocalyptic iconography; and the four-act structure—all of these characteristics indicate that *The Spanish Tragedy* is modelled on the Apocalypse and its Renaissance commentaries and dramatizations.

The induction scene, as we have already seen in chapter 2, fits the context of the tour apocalypse, during which a select person or prophet undertakes a journey into the otherworld justice system, sees its operation, and returns to earth to deliver his visions to the uninitiated. Similarly, Andrea descends to the underworld, experiences the justice system, and returns to earth. However, the major difference is that Andrea is sent back to earth not to reveal the mystery, but to serve, with Revenge, as the chorus for the earthly mystery play.

The induction sets up a line of transmission of the knowledge of mysteries similar to the one announced at the outset of the Book of Revelation:

> The revelation of Jesus Christ, which God gave unto him, to shewe unto his servants things which must shortely be done: which he sent, and shewed by his Angel unto his servant John, Who bare recorde of the worde of God, and of the testimonie of Jesus Christ, and of all things that he sawe. Blessed is he that readeth, and they that heare the wordes of this prophecie, and kepe those things which are written therein: for the time is at hand.   (Rev. 1:3, 114v)

Similarly, Kyd, the author of *The Spanish Tragedy*, has created the apocalyptic mystery play in which Proserpine, Kyd's surrogate in her role as queen of the underworld, knows what destiny will be and sends her delegate Revenge back to earth with the ghost of Andrea, to whom Revenge presents the prophecy of what "must shortely be done." The play becomes the mystery vision which Andrea and the theater audience will come to understand through seeing it unfold in dramatic form; the interpretation of the play provides their initiation into the mystery of divine providence and the destined fall of Babylon/Spain. As Richard Emmerson has said:

> the purpose of the apocalyptic is primarily to reveal secret knowledge to the initiated few. Apocalyptic language and imagery is thus often obscure, esoteric, and secretive. . . . [I]ts . . . mythical imagery is intended to inform the initiated about the divine secrets, the rise and fall of empires, the working of God in history.[1]

Like the Apocalypse, which is a revelation of divine secrets, *The Spanish Tragedy* contains a continuing byplay between secrecy and revelation. In *Thomas Kyd's Mystery Play* . . . I discussed this scheme in connection with the pagan mystery rubric of the play, and in the second chapter of this work, I discussed the Danielic "shutting of the book" as the meta-

---

[1]Richard Emmerson, "The Prophetic, the Apocalyptic, and the Study of Medieval Literature," *Poetic Prophecy in Western Literature*, ed. Jan Wojcik and Raymond-Jean Frontain (Rutherford, N.J.: Fairleigh Dickinson University Press, 1984), 46.

phor for keeping the secret truths hidden from the uninitiated and revealing them to the initiated. Now I would like to analyze the scheme of
secrecy/revelation to establish the concept of *The Spanish Tragedy* as an
apocalypse, a prophetic revelation of God's secret truths concerning the
providential nature of the universe.

The induction provides us with an introduction into the secrets of
the otherworld justice system. It is as if Andrea's posthumous testimony
about Hades is already inducting us into a mystery, providing information
about a world ordinarily hidden from us which remains concealed from
the stage characters until the final judgment scene. The secrecy/revelation
motif specifically begins with Proserpine's "rounding" Revenge in the ear,
telling him to return to earth with Andrea. We never learn what she says,
but it is obviously connected with the destiny which will be fulfilled
during the mystery play. Revenge announces that Balthazar will be killed
by Bel-imperia, the destiny toward which the play moves, but the connection of Balthazar's demise with Andrea and with the religio-political context is not revealed at the outset. We need to watch and interpret the play
before the full significance and symbolic import of Balthazar's death is
revealed. The knowledge given by Proserpine to Revenge is delivered by
him as an apocalyptic prophecy of what is to come, and the earthly play,
which provides the dramatic action leading to its fulfillment, is the revelation of the mystery of divine providence.

The secrecy/revelation/concealment scheme continues in the scenes
concerning Bel-imperia and Horatio's declaration of love and their ill-
fated attempt to consummate their passion. When Horatio ironically says
to Bel-imperia, "Now Madam, since by favour of your love / Our hidden
smoke is turn'd to open flame" (2.2.1–2), Pedringano "showeth all to the
Prince and Lorenzo, placing them in secret [above]." Pedringano, the
ostensible guarder of his mistress' secrets, reveals the private meeting of
the lovers, who are declaring their "open" love to each other and to
Lorenzo and Balthazar, whom he conceals from detection; the scene contains opposed schemes as the lovers attempt to hide their growing love
from others, while Pedringano reveals it to the concealed villains, who
will use their privy knowledge to commit a crime for which they will
attempt to keep their identities secret. When the lovers meet in the bower
for their tryst, they ironically praise the darkness of the night as a cover for
their actions and set Pedringano as a guard to protect their secrecy; however, he admits the murderers into the bower to kill Horatio and "stop her
[Bel-imperia's] mouth" (4.63).

Hieronimo's efforts to discover his son's murderers are thwarted by Lorenzo's attempts to ensure secrecy by having his subordinates eliminate each other. He sets up Pedringano to murder Serberine while he is being observed by the three members of the Watch whom Lorenzo has placed there in secret to view the "hidden" crime: "I know my secret fault, / And so do they, but I have dealt for them" (3.2.111–12). Later, as he arranges to have his page deliver the bogus pardon to the condemned Pedringano on the gallows, Lorenzo exults

> 'Tis hard to trust unto a multitude,
> Or anyone, in mine opinion,
> When men themselves their secrets will reveal.
> (3.4.47–49)

Ironically, despite his attempts to ensure secrecy, Lorenzo's murder of Horatio is revealed in the posthumous letter found on Pedringano's body after he has been "turned off" by the hangman. When Hieronimo reads this letter, he connects its confession with the revelations in the letter written in blood which dropped almost magically from the heavens as he implored God for justice (3.2.24–52). At that time Hieronimo did not trust the disclosure of Lorenzo and Balthazar's guilt by Bel-imperia who had dropped the letter out of the window of her prison, because he believed it might be a trap. But now with the second letter, Hieronimo connects the two and knows the true identities of his son's murderers:

> O sacred heavens, may it come to pass
> That such a monstrous and detested deed,
> So closely smother'd, and so long conceal'd,
> Shall thus by this be venged or reveal'd?
> (3.7.45–48)

After this discovery, Hieronimo tries to obtain justice at court, but he is thwarted by Lorenzo and thus decides to pursue private vengeance "As by a secret, yet a certain mean, / Which under kindship will be cloaked best" (3.13.23–24). Finally, when he and Bel-imperia join together to exact revenge, they express their plans in the secrecy/revelation/concealment pattern:

> Hier: And here I vow (so you but give consent,
>   And will conceal my resolution)
>   I will ere long determine of their deaths. . . .
> Bel: Hieronimo, I will . . . conceal.   (4.1.42–44, 46)

Hieronimo will reveal his secret plans to her as long as she agrees to conceal them from others.

The secrecy/revelation/concealment motif culminates in the revenge playlet during which Lorenzo and Balthazar are killed and Bel-imperia commits suicide. Hieronimo reveals to the uncomprehending audience of Spanish and Portuguese royalty that the onstage deaths are real, not feigned, and he explains that he has taken this revenge because their sons killed his son. The grief-stricken fathers demand that Hieronimo reveal more about his revenge motives, but he refuses to speak, declaring that "never shalt thou force me to reveal / The thing which I have vow'd inviolate" (4.4.187–88). To seal his silence, Hieronimo bites out his tongue "[r]ather than to reveal what we [the king and viceroy] requir'd" (193–94). When Hieronimo is given a knife to sharpen his pen, so that he might write his confession, he enforces the final silence of killing himself after murdering Castile.

As I discussed in chapter 2, Hieronimo's vow of silence is related to his role as mystagogue and bearer of the sacred name who conceals the secret truths from the uninitiated audience, but at the same time encourages the theater audience, the initiated, to go beyond the silence to discover the ritual truths. In Danielic terms Hieronimo's silence and the sundry languages of the playlet represent the sealed book closed to the ignorant who are unable to understand Daniel's prophecies. Now in reference to the Apocalypse, it is possible to relate the playbook, the sundry languages, and the silence to the seven-sealed book which is opened, that is, revealed, to the audience able to comprehend God's secret truths, but which remains closed to the ignorant audience.

The nature of the mystery revelation to the elect audience of *The Spanish Tragedy* concerns the theme of the Apocalypse that the world which appears to be ruled by Fortune is predetermined, directed toward the destined fall of Antichrist. As Traheron says, "what so ever is don in the world by Antichrist and his members is not tossed at aventure by hap, but governed by the hand and certaine providence of God."[2] At the conclusion of the induction, Revenge delivers the prophecy toward which the earthly play inexorably moves. The events on earth are directed to the fulfillment of Revenge's prophecy; he is the personification of the apocalyptic ethos of the playworld. However, the characters directly involved in the

---

[2]Traheron, *Exposition*, A3r.

dramatic action do not know that they are being viewed *sub specie aeterni-tatis*, although at times Hieronimo and Isabella express their belief that truth must come to light. Unaware of the onstage presence of Revenge and Andrea, the characters attribute the cause of earthly events variously to God, Fortune, heaven, hell, and Hades, but we and Andrea learn that the play is moving inevitably toward the destiny announced by Revenge.

The sense of apocalyptic doom is expressed in the last scenes of the first three acts and is consummated in the final two scenes of the play. At the conclusion of act 1, when Andrea expresses impatience with the "pleasant sights" and the appearance of "league, and love, and banquet-ing!" (1.5.3–4), Revenge declares that these "pleasant sights" soon will be turned into horrors. Similarly, at the end of act 2 Andrea is confused and outraged about the murder of Horatio and Bel-imperia's captivity, and demands that Revenge effect his vengeance faster. Revenge replies with vegetal imagery about waiting for harvest time:

> Thou talk'st of harvest when the corn is green:
> The end is crown of every work well done:
> The sickle comes not till the corn be ripe. (2.6.7–9)

In chapter 14 of the Apocalypse, in which the angel announces the fall of Babylon, the certainty of that punishment is expressed in similar agricul-tural terms as angels are depicted as harvesters ready to reap with sharp sickles: "And the Angel thrust in his sharpe sickle . . . and cutte downe the . . . vineyarde of the earth . . ." (14:19,119r). The gloss explains that "the overthrowe of the people is compared to an harvest, . . . also to a vintage," and goes on to say that the metaphor is used to satisfy human understand-ing concerning the certainty of divine judgment because God does not "nede to be tolde when he shulde come to judgement" (119v). Heinrich Bullinger also uses this passage to insist on the inevitability of God's prov-idence: "the Corne was now ripe. . . . [A]nd . . . it is tyme to be reaped. . . . [W]e understand that a certeine houre of judgment is appointed, at the comming whereof, the godly without delay shall be delivered and the ungodly condemned."[3]

At the conclusion of act 3 when Andrea adjures him to awake and punish the murderers, Revenge replies that

---

[3]Bullinger, *Sermons*, 212v.

> though I sleep,
> Yet is my mood soliciting their souls: . . .
> Nor dies Revenge although he sleep awhile,
> For in unquiet, quietness is feign'd,
> And slumb'ring is a common worldly wile.
> Behold, Andrea, for an instance how
> Revenge hath slept, and imagine thou
> What 'tis to be subject to destiny.   (3.15.19–28)

Bullinger uses the image of God as the sleeping revenger when he comments upon the destined fall of Babylon in the Apocalypse:

> But where as the punishment is not by and by executed upon the impenitent persons; you shall have them exclaime, that God is a slepe, and that he seeth or heareth nothing, Therfore the Lord . . . aunswereth them . . . : And all congregations shall doubtles at the last execute my vengeance in due season. For then shall all men learne, that I neither sleepe, nor neglect my servantes at any tyme, nor will suffer those that deserve evill of me and of my church to escape unpunished. . . . For God is a most just rewarder of good and revenger of evill.[4]

After Andrea understands what is to come, as the Hymen dumb show has revealed, the fourth act shows how Hieronimo becomes the instrument of that fate. Throughout the play, Hieronimo has fulfilled two roles. On the one hand, he is the grief-stricken father and impotent lord marshal vainly searching for justice to be enacted against his son's murderers. On the other hand, Hieronimo serves as Kyd, Proserpine, and Revenge's surrogate in his role as creator of courtly masques and playlets. Through these dramas, he transcends his role as vengeful father to fulfill the apocalyptic ethos of just revenge and to effect the fall of Babylon/Spain. In announcing his intentions to stage a tragedy for the marriage feast, Hieronimo begins to prophesy, using the future tense to make veiled threats to the doomed members of his cast:

> I mean each one of you to play a part—
> Assure you it will prove most passing strange
> And wondrous plausible to that assembly.
>
> . . . .

[4]Ibid., 44r–v.

> I'll play the murderer, . . .
> For I already have conceited that.
>
> (4.1.83–84, 133–34)

Following this oblique but assured prediction, Hieronimo, left alone onstage, delivers the apocalyptic prophecy concerning the fall of Babylon, which he will effect and which will fulfill Revenge's prediction that Balthazar will die.

With this prediction, Hieronimo parallels the angel in Rev. 14:8 and 18:2, who announces "It is fallen, it is fallen, Babylon the great citie" (119r). Bullinger calls this angel the "Maister of execution, and captayne of vengeaunce," who utters a prophecy of what is shortly to come: "And the Aungell . . . sayth she is fallen, which is yet to fall . . . by a propheticall manner of speaking, wherein that which shall . . . come to passe is uttered, as though it were now done. . . . For the Saintes . . . long for the destruction . . . of Antichrist." Bullinger also explains that when prophets like Jeremiah predicted the fall of Babylon, people thought "them to be mad. Notwithstanding . . . so came it to passe."[5] At the end of the play, Andrea and Revenge complete the fall of Babylon by assigning Tartarean punishments to Lorenzo, Balthazar, Castile, Serberine, and Pedringano.

The temporal pattern which emerges from the fulfillment of this destiny demonstrates that the past is repeated in the present, which in turn reveals more about the significance of the past and anticipates a future which is the inevitable result and sum of the past and present. This type of temporal progression requires synchronous scenes that create, through retrospection and anticipation, a cumulative vision leading to the awareness of how divine providence works in the universe. In his *Exposition on the Revelation* (Lausanne, Switzerland, 1584), Nicholas Collado analyzes the ways in which the successive visions in the Apocalypse are both repeated and augmented:

> in this Booke are gathered together seven Visions of three sorts touching the same things, viz. of Seales, Trumpets, and Vials, so as every latter kinde is more full than the former, (which belongs also unto the Narration of things) and propounds the things themselves more neerly to the view of the eye, denot-

[5]Ibid., 213v, 206v, 242v.

ing, and more certainly defining the same with more circumstances.[6]

By watching the scenes in the play repeat and amplify each other, we
learn through a retrospective and cumulative act of interpretation how
destiny is taking place. This process seems to be the normal method for
interpreting a literary work, but through self-reflexive methods like the
plays-within-the-play and verbal and visual patterns which involve making
judgments, Kyd shows that we are to see ourselves as not just passive
watchers but as critical evaluators, that our status as members of the elect
audience aware of the mysteries depends on our ability to interpret the
play correctly.

In the induction scene, Andrea provides an account of his past life at
the court of Spain, his secret love affair with Bel-imperia, his death in the
war, his passage through the underworld, and his return to earth with
Revenge. As the earthly play begins, we are supposed to ask how Andrea's
past and his suspended underworld sentence are related to the present
events shown onstage and the future predicted by Revenge. As he sits on
the stage with Revenge observing the dramatic action, Andrea represents
the past, whose influence on the present is delineated throughout the play.
The earthly drama begins with the victorious Spanish general's testimony
to the king about the recent decisive battle with Portugal in which Andrea
was killed and Balthazar captured by Horatio. Following the general's
account, the three returning soldiers debate their roles in the past struggle, and the king makes his present judgment about the immediate past,
declaring that this decision will end the strife arising from the war and the
subsequent debate. In a sense, the king intends to end the divisive influence of the past on the present with his temperate judgment, but as we
learn in subsequent scenes the awarding of Balthazar as prisoner to
Lorenzo directly aids Lorenzo's Machiavellian plans.

The king's judgment is followed by the Portuguese subplot, which
involves another judgment about the war based on eyewitness testimony
of the past battle. But this time we know immediately that the viceroy is
wrong and Villuppo is lying because we have just seen Balthazar alive at
the Spanish court. The Portuguese subplot provides retrospective insight
into the previous scene as the Spanish king's judgment is rendered suspect
by our seeing an obviously wrong decision made in the present about the

[6]Qtd. in Pareus, *Commentary*, 22.

past. In the fourth scene, Horatio provides another testimony about the battle, describing Balthazar as ruthless in the killing of his outnumbered and helpless foe. On the basis of Horatio's testimony, Bel-imperia concludes that Andrea was murdered:

> For what was't else but murd'rous cowardice,
> So many to oppress one valiant knight,
> Without respect of honour in the fight? (1.4.73–75)

Are we meant to see her judgment as wrong like the two previous ones of the king and the viceroy? The implication at this point is that Bel-imperia's judgment about the past is more valid because it would explain why Andrea has been allowed to return to earth with Revenge to see his murderer's death.

The effect of the five testimonies is to show, as Scott McMillin has pointed out, that the characters are attempting to shape the influence of the past on the present through their use of language:

> Act 1 implies that the past can be controlled and brought into present meanings through acts of speech. . . . [A]s Villuppo's words turn that event into a fabrication for self-gain, as Horatio's words turn that event into a slow overture for Bel-imperia to quicken, the impression forms that the past . . . can through language be modified into essential parts of present relationships.[7]

However, the characters do not control the temporal process represented by Revenge, although their actions, without their knowing it, do contribute to its accomplishment. Lorenzo tries to silence the past, but everything he does ironically brings it into the open. The autonomous influence of the past on the present is exemplified by the discovery of the posthumous letter on Pedringano's corpse which implicates Lorenzo and Balthazar in the murder of Horatio. The past, as represented by the letter from the dead, cannot be suspended or silenced but combines with the present to move toward an inexorable future judgment. As McMillin has stated:

> He [Revenge] knows that the . . . past . . . will have one necessary effect upon the human society of the play—the effect of retribution . . . —and that . . . Lorenzo's manipulations of

[7]Scott McMillin, "The Figure of Silence in *The Spanish Tragedy*," *ELH* 39 (1972):31.

objects and language . . . will be precisely destroyed by that retribution. . . . Revenge knows that these events at the courts of Spain and Portugal are a scheme in time, . . . which can not be affected . . . by . . . Lorenzo's ironic strategy. . . . The time of Revenge is autonomous, making victims of all who speak . . . as though the future is open to their own intentions.[8]

Hieronimo serves as the significant exception to McMillin's final sentence. In his role as court dramatist, Hieronimo acts in concert with Revenge's time scheme by predicting and then effecting the deaths of Horatio's murderers and the fall of Babylon/Spain. When the royal Iberian audience demands that Hieronimo reveal his reason for the murders, the lord marshal displays the body of his son Horatio, whose death in the past has caused this present retribution:

> Behold the reason urging me to this:
> See here my show, look on this spectacle:
> Here lay my hope, and here my hope hath end.
>
> . . . .
>
> He [Horatio] shrieks, I heard, and yet methinks I
>   hear,
> His dismal outcry echo in the air . . .
> Where hanging on a tree I found my son,
> Through-girt with wounds, and slaughtered as you
>   see. . . .
> Speak Portuguese, whose loss resembles mine:
> If thou canst weep upon thy Balthazar,
> 'Tis like I wail'd for my Horatio.
>   (4.4.88–90,108–9,111–13,115–16)

It is as if Hieronimo has resurrected the past in the form of his dead son and verbally reconstructed the night of the murder with Horatio hanging in the tree. The tenses keep sliding from the past to the present, and the distinction between these periods is erased as Hieronimo implores the grief-stricken fathers to imagine his pain upon discovering his dead son, while he displays Horatio to them in the present.

Further, in two ways he has both recreated and adapted the past to fit the present circumstances. First, by killing the two sons before their

---

[8]Ibid., 35.

fathers, Hieronimo almost has reversed his situation on the night of Horatio's murder. Secondly, he has adapted the actual circumstances of the past—the rivalry between Balthazar and Horatio for the love of Bel-imperia—in his "Soliman and Perseda" playlet to produce the opposite results of having the killers murdered.[9]

In the final scene of the play, Revenge and Andrea exercise control over the future when they assign rewards and punishments in the afterworld:

> Then haste we down to meet thy friends and foes,
> To place thy friends in ease, the rest in woes:
> For here though death hath end their misery,
> I'll there begin their endless tragedy.   (45–48)

Ironically, Revenge's pronouncement of the beginning of their "endless tragedy" occurs in the final line of the play. The apocalyptic temporal scheme has moved from earthly time to eternity; the past has been repeated and amplified in the present and both have led to an inevitable and endless future of Elysian reward and Tartarean punishment. The mysterious dream vision has ended with a judgment combining classical and apocalyptic justice. All in all, the temporal structure of *The Spanish Tragedy* can be summarized best by Angus Fletcher's analysis of the providential nature of *The Faerie Queene*:

> the larger mythos of the poem . . . acquires the providential form of an historicist dream. . . . *The Faerie Queene*, like all legitimate prophecy, is a . . . "constitutive" vision. It builds "the constant incorporation of past, present, and future events into that which claims to be a word of the everlasting God." The constitutive aim of prophecy amounts to . . . an assimilation of the poetic narrative to a steadily emerging vision of a final, guiding Logos. Each episode of knight errantry adds its material substance to the accumulated argument of a higher truth, the revelation of a providential will. Because Spenser is a Christian poet, writing in the tradition laid down by the Old and New Testaments, this higher revelation usually ends up as a vision of justice.[10]

[9]Ibid., 46–47.
[10]Angus Fletcher, *The Prophetic Moment: An Essay On Spenser* (Chicago: University of Chicago Press, 1971), 43–44. Fletcher quotes from H. W. Robinson, *Inspiration and Revelation in the Old Testament* (London: Oxford University Press, 1962), 126.

In addition to the apocalyptic structural, verbal, and temporal patterns in *The Spanish Tragedy*, the play also contains a series of props and references drawn from the Book of Revelation: the fall of Babylon in one hour; the extinction of the candle and the wedding ceremony as the symbol of Babylon's destruction; the key of David; the sealed mystery text; the word of God symbolized as a terrible sword; and the "second death." Through the use of these objects, references, and allusions, Kyd economically signals large areas of convergence between the play and the last book of the Bible.

The recognition of these motifs as apocalyptic is directly related to the question concerning the moral nature of Hieronimo's decision to pursue personal vengeance, which is the central crux of the play. At the beginning of 3.13, Hieronimo enters holding an edition of Seneca's works and proceeds to weigh the respective merits of Christian patience and Senecan revenge. He begins by paraphrasing Rom. 12:17–19, which reads: "Recompense to no man evil for evil. . . . [A]venge not your selves, but give place unto wrathe: for it is written, Vengeance is mine: I wil repaye, saith the Lord" (75r). At first, Hieronimo appears to accept the injunction that "mortal men may not appoint their time" (5), but then he quotes a speech of Clytemnestra's from Seneca's *Agamemnon* to the effect that the safe way to prevent crime is always through more crime. This realization impels him to decide that he must strike against those who have murdered his son before they move against him. However, rather than act hastily, he decides to wait, feigning ignorance, before finding the right time to obtain vengeance (10–40).

For some critics, Hieronimo's choice of Seneca over Christianity is proof of his villainy. In *Elizabethan Revenge Tragedy: 1587–1642*, Fredson Bowers charged that Hieronimo's murderous playlet and his subsequent killing of Castile would have earned him the condemnation of Elizabethan audiences.[11] Similarly, Richard Ide has argued that Hieronimo usurps "God's just government of the world stage [as] . . . actor, director, and . . . author of the final, bloody play-within-a-play. . . . There is no choric testimony to the justice of Hieronimo's revenge, no sense that Providence is directing him as its 'scourge and minister,' no appeal to heaven for a bless-

---

[11]Bowers, *Revenge Tragedy*, 65–85.

ing."[12] However, Martha Rozett asserts that Hieronimo "takes God's role upon himself employing the concealed stratagem, the sudden unveiling of purpose behind events, the patient biding of time, and the well-chosen punishments that typify God's control of human events."[13] Further, Ronald Broude maintains that Hieronimo emerges as a martyr-figure who fulfills a harsh Protestant retribution:

> The vengeance personified by the choral figure who presides over the play's action is . . . the providentially directed retribution so central to the Protestant tradition. . . . Granted, . . . the blood-for-blood ethic . . . to which Hieronimo pledges allegiance . . . may not seem "Christian." . . . Nevertheless, it has its basis in the Bible, and was an integral part of the Renaissance Protestant concept of Justice.[14]

Although Hieronimo does choose Senecan vengeance over Christian forbearance, the audience is meant to see that in so doing he follows an apocalyptic justice which is the equivalent of the pagan ethos represented by Revenge. Consequently, the opposition between Hieronimo's alternatives disappears once we recognize that Kyd creates a syncretistic play world which unites pagan justice and a harsh Christian justice in the revenge of the aggrieved father and lord marshal, who acts for himself, his country (England), and God and Hades in the accomplishment of the destined fall of Babylon/Spain.

After Bel-imperia denounces his apparent reconciliation with Balthazar and Lorenzo, Hieronimo now realizes that she will join with him in his plot to avenge Horatio's death. Echoing Vindicta Dei in Bale's *Three Laws* . . . (5.68), he exclaims

> that heaven applies our drift,
> And all the saints do sit soliciting
> For vengeance on those cursed murderers.
>
>   (4.1.32–34)

[12]Richard Ide, "Elizabethan Revenge and the Providential Play-Within-A-Play," *Iowa State Journal of Research* 56 (1981): 91.

[13]Martha Rozett, *The Doctrine of Election and the Emergence of Elizabethan Tragedy* (Princeton: Princeton University Press, 1984), 180.

[14]Broude, "Three English Forerunners," 498–99.

Charles Stein argues that Hieronimo's reference to "saints" at this point is decidedly ironic, because he and Bel-imperia have dedicated themselves to revenge.[15] However, in his exclamation to Bel-imperia, Hieronimo alludes to the heart of the fifth unsealing vision in which from

> under the altar the soules of them, that were killed for the worde of God, and for the testimonie which they mainteined . . . cryed with a lowde voyce, saying, How long, Lord . . . doest not thou judge and avenge our blood on them that dwell on the earth? . . .[A]nd it was said unto them, that they shulde rest for a litel ceason until their . . . brethren that shulde be killed even as they were, were fulfilled.   (Rev. 6:9–11,116v)

When Hieronimo discusses the roles his intended victims will take in the "Soliman and Perseda" playlet, he uses apocalyptic imagery in his ominous hints about their coming fate:

> My lords, all this must be performed
> As fitting for the first night's revelling.
> The Italian tragedians were so sharp of wit,
> That in one hour's meditation
> They would perform anything in action.
>   (4.1.162–66)

As Edwards has noted, the reference to the "Italian tragedians" may allude to the *commedia dell'arte*,[16] but the specifying of "one hour" sounds an apocalyptic note, which is echoed a little later when Hieronimo promises that "all shall be concluded in one scene" (188). The allusion is to the angel's declaration in Rev. 18:10, 17, 19 that "the great citie Babylon . . . in one houre is thy judgment come. . . . For in one houre so great riches are comme to desolation. . . . [I]n one houre she is made desolate" (120v). As S. F. Johnson asserts, "the reiterated phrase, 'in one hour' . . . , emphasizing as it does the suddenness of the destruction of Babylon, is to be recalled in connection with Hieronimo's promise that 'all shall be concluded in one scene.'"[17]

---

[15]Charles H. Stein, "Justice and Revenge in *The Spanish Tragedy*," *Iowa State Journal of Research* 56 (1981): 102.

[16]Edwards, *Spanish Tragedy*, 106n.

[17]Johnson, "Babylon," 25.

Hieronimo's destruction of the intended marriage between Balthazar and Bel-imperia "in one hour" has been foreshadowed by Revenge's marriage masque in which

> [t]he two first, the nuptial torches bore,
> As brightly burning as the mid-day's sun:
> But after them doth Hymen hie as fast, . . .
> And blows them out and quencheth them with
>   blood.   (3.15.30–32,34)

The extinction of the torches as the symbol of the destroyed marriage parallels the description of the aftermath of the fall of Babylon: "And the light of the candle shall shine no more in thee: and the . . . bridegrome and . . . the bride shalbe heard no more in thee" (Rev. 18:23,120v).

Hieronimo is able to accomplish the destruction of the marriage by using the key given him by the duke of Castile (4.3.12–13) to lock in the actors on the stage of death, thus making his victims enact their deaths before their fathers, who watch, unaware and helpless, from the gallery above. The staging of this climactic scene ironically echoes three earlier scenes involving the lovers Horatio and Bel-imperia and Pedringano. In 2.2, Bel-imperia and Horatio met to plan their tryst, but Pedringano, the suborned servant, placed Balthazar and Lorenzo secretly in the gallery above to spy upon them. The villains were in control of the situation as they looked down upon the ill-fated lovers who imagined they were safe from detection. In scene 4, the lovers' tryst in Hieronimo's enclosed bower was violated by the masked murderers who rushed in to kill Horatio and imprison Bel-imperia. Finally, in 3.6 Pedringano, having been set up by Lorenzo to be executed for his murder of Serberine, stood on the scaffold, expecting his pardon to arrive in the black box. Pedringano emerged as the doomed actor in a plot designed by Lorenzo which was performed before an audience that did not grasp the full significance of the execution. However, Hieronimo learned the identities of his son's murderers from the posthumous letter that was discovered on Pedringano's body.

Now in the revenge playlet, Hieronimo holds the key, symbolic of his control over the staging, the lives of the doomed actors, and the mysterious text which remains sealed to the onstage audience. Like Lorenzo in the Pedringano scenes, Hieronimo places his victims onstage, gives them their roles, and causes their deaths to occur before the audience of Iberian royalty. He locks the doors to the stage area and in effect creates an enclosed arena of death, similar to the bower, but which cannot be opened until the

deaths of the murderers, who earlier had invaded the enclosed bower. Like
Pedringano, the villains perform on a stage unaware that they are doomed;
however, unlike Hieronimo who later discovered the relationship of
Pedringano's death to Horatio's murder, the onstage audience members,
although they demand an explanation from Hieronimo about the deaths,
never learn the nature of the mysterious vow he invokes. Even though
they "breake ope the doors . . . and hold Hieronimo" (4.4.155–56), they
can never grasp the meaning of what they have seen. They try to force
Hieronimo to speak, but he bites out his tongue and then commits a final
murder and suicide using the knife with which he was to write his confession.

The key used by Hieronimo to lock in the doomed actors has apocalyptic significance. In the Book of Revelation, the key of David has three
closely related meanings: the power of God over physical and spiritual life
and death; the authority of God to admit or exclude people from his
church and kingdom; and knowledge of divine mysteries as the means of
gaining salvation. In Rev. 1:18, Christ announces to the bedazzled John
that "I have the keyes of hel and of death" (115r), which is glossed as
meaning power over life and death. At Rev. 20:1–3, the angel has the key,
and "he toke . . . Satan, and. . . bounde him a thousand yeres . . . into the
bottomles pit, . . . and sealed the door upon him . . ." (121r). The gloss
states that the victorious angel represents the Apostles or Christ who wield
the key of the Gospel which saves the faithful but shuts the wicked in hell.

The second meaning of the keys as the instrument to open or shut
the door of God's church and kingdom occurs at Rev. 3:7–8, when the
angel says that God "hathe the keye of David, which openeth and no man
shutteth, and shutteth and no man openeth" (115v). The holder of the key
to the House of David, the church, is Christ who "may ether receive or put
out whome he wil" through the door of the kingdom of God (115v, n).
Commenting upon this passage in *A Hundred Sermons Upon the Apocalypse*, Bullinger refers to Isa. 22:20–22, in which the prophet talks about
Eliachim promotion to chief steward at the court of Hezekiah and being
given "the keye of the house of David . . . so he shal open and no man shall
shut: and he shall shut, and no man shall open" (290r). Bullinger explains
that Eliachim's key means that he "shall governe all things in the Court of
Ezechias uprightly. Whatsoever he determineth no man shall infringe it;
and whatsoever he abrogatheth, no man shall restore it."[18] Like Eliachim,

[18]Bullinger, *Sermons*, 20r.

the chief steward, Hieronimo, as lord marshal[19] at the court of Spain, holds the key to the execution of justice, which is symbolized by his shutting the doors leading to the stage on which he causes the deaths of his son's murderers.

The key also represents Hieronimo's knowledge of the divine mysteries which he refuses to divulge to the uninitiated audience, who cannot understand, but at the same time reveals to the initiated, who can comprehend the secret truths of the mystery text. As Bale explains:

> Evident wyll those secrete mysteryes be unto hym whyche are prevylie hidde unto others undre darke . . . parables. Though, this heavenlye treasure of helth be under locke and keye of unknowne similitudes, and to be shutt up from the untowarde and wycked generacion . . . , yet whyl it be playne enough to the faithfull belevers instantly cailinge upon him which hath the keye of David to open unto them the dore of his infallyble verytees.[20]

The text of the playlet is translated into English for those who can understand its true meanings, but it remains couched in sundry tongues, emblematic of the Babylonian confusion of the Iberian audience. Kyd parallels the playbook, the playlet, and, analogously, the entire play as mystery texts to the Book of Revelation as a sealed and unsealed text, and thus anticipates Mede's interpretation of the Apocalypse as a promptbook in an academic play.

The next prop which has dramatic and apocalyptic significance is the knife Hieronimo uses to kill Castile and commit suicide. At the conclusion of the playlet, the Iberian audience demands that Hieronimo reveal more information about his reasons for effecting the deaths of Balthazar and Lorenzo, but in allegiance to "[t]he thing which I have vow'd inviolate" (188), he bites out his tongue. In an effort to make him confess in writing, his captors give him a pen, but he indicates that he needs a knife to sharpen it. However, instead of writing more, he stabs Castile and him-

[19]Giles Quispel, *The Secret Book of Revelation: The Last Book of the Bible*, tr. Peter Staples (Maidenhead, England: McGraw-Hill, 1979), 45–46n, states that the "key of David . . . is an allusion to a prophecy of Isaiah in which it is said that the function of the Marshal of the Court (who naturally keeps the key of the royal palace, the "House of David") will be handed over to a certain Eliakim."

[20]Bale, *Image*, Pt. 1:Biiir–v.

self. Critics have noted the irony of Hieronimo's actions which signal that words are no longer needed, that only violence will suffice. Jonas Barish remarks that

> the final lunatic gesture betrays the final despair at the useless-ness of talk, the beserk resolve to have done with language for-ever. And not spoken language only—the knife he is given to mend his pen he plunges into his heart; the last instrument available to facilitate expression he uses savagely to annul all further possibility of expression.[21]

Similarly, Scott McMillin remarks that the "old man knows how to turn their objects of writing to his own end. With a knife meant to sharpen a pen, the poet-revenger is free to die."[22] However, Barish and McMillin miss the apocalyptic import of Kyd's equation of the knife with the pen as weapons against the representatives of Babylon.

Kyd's equation of the knife and pen derives from the Reformation topos of the "sword and the book," which, as John King explains, concerns the apocalyptic warrior on the white horse who has coming "out of his mouth . . . a sharpe sworde, that with it he shulde smite the heathen: for he shal rule with a rodde of yron . . ." (Rev. 19:15, 121r).[23] In commenting on this passage, Bale describes the rider on the white horse as "the eternal attourneye of God,"[24] and Bullinger places the image within a similar judi-cial context:

> By this is signified the judiciall power full of equitie and jus-tice, and also the deliveraunce of the good, and the punish-ment of the evill. For the sword is geven to the Magistrate, as an authoritie to punish the evill, and defend the good. . . . The sword is the very word of God most sharpe. . . . Christ there-fore governeth his church as Judge and defendour most . . . just.[25]

[21]Jonas Barish, "*The Spanish Tragedy,* or The Pleasures and Perils of Rhetoric," *Elizabe-than Theatre* (*Stratford-Upon-Avon-Studies 9*), ed. J. R. Brown and Bernard Harris (New York: St. Martins, 1966), 82.

[22]Scott McMillin, "The Book of Seneca in *The Spanish Tragedy,*" *SEL* 15 (1974):208.

[23]King, *Reformation Literature,* 190–91.

[24]Bale, *Image,* Pt. 3: fff2r.

[25]Bullinger, *Sermons,* 33v.

Rudolph Gualter calls the image a "mysterie," which he applies to "Antichrist [who] hathe lost both his lyfe and his royaltie, through the sweorde of Goddes worde."[26]

The biblical passages depict the Word of God as a sword issuing from his mouth, but Hieronimo bites out his tongue, ensuring his muteness. However, his use of the knife as the murder weapon during and after the playlet establishes the written word as the sharp sword of divine vengeance. In this case, the pen becomes as mighty as a sword; Hieronimo, the justice figure, has used his pen to write the revenge playlet in which his enemies are stabbed to death and the fall of Babylon is effected, just as Kyd has written a mystery and revenge tragedy in which Spain/Babylon is defeated.

As the representative of divine vengeance, Hieronimo exercises control over life and death in the revenge playlet. He kills Lorenzo and Castile, arranges to have Bel-imperia stab Balthazar, and he and Bel-imperia commit suicide. However, immediately after these deaths, all the characters, including those killed earlier in the play, are resurrected for the final judgment which grants them eternal life or death. The motif of the "second death," symbolic of everlasting punishment in the otherworld, is derived from the Book of Revelation, which refers to it four times. The first reference announces that "he that overcometh, shall not be hurt of the seconde death" (Rev. 2:11, 115r), and the second explains further that "holie is he, that hathe parte in the first resurrection: *for* on suche the seconde death hath no power: but they shalbe the Priests of God and of Christ, and shal reigne with him a thousand yere" (Rev. 20:6, 121v). Immediately following this passage, the Last Judgment is delivered: "And death and hell were cast into the lake of fyre: this is the seconde death. And whosoever was not founde written in the boke of life, was cast into the lake of fyre" (Rev. 20:14–15). The final reference enumerates those who will be punished with the second death in the fiery lake: "the fearful and unbelieving, and the abominable and murderers, and whoremongers, and sorcerers, and idolaters, and all liars shal have their parte in the lake, which . . . is the seconde death" (Rev. 21:8, 121v).

In commenting on these passages, George Gifford explains that everyone undergoes the first death of the body, but that the faithful expe-

[26]Rudolph Gualter, *Antichrist, That is to saye: A true reporte, that Antichriste is come . . .* (London, 1556), 169v, 170v.

rience the first and second resurrection while the sinners are punished
with the second death:

> there is the first and the second resurrection, so is there the
> first and second death. The first death is the separation of the
> soule and bodie, which the elect doe passe through: the second
> death is in the torments of hell, into which all doe enter that
> doe dye in their sinnes. . . . And he [John] teacheth that all that
> have their part in the first resurrection, that second death shall
> have no power over them. . . . Saint John sheweth how these
> that rise in the first resurrection are priestes to God . . . and . . .
> shall raigne with him.[27]

Bale explains the second death as the vengeance exacted upon sinners by
the divine judge: "This terryble apoyntment of the judge . . . is the seconde
death, or perpetuall deprivacion of the syght of God. . . . This death is the
whole vengeance of al innocent bloud which hath bene shed on earth
from . . . Abel to the last faythfull witnesse."[28]

As I have already argued in chapter 2 in connection with the motif
of the prophetic resurrection, *The Spanish Tragedy* contains a series of res-
urrections and near and quasi-resurrections beginning with Andrea's
death and resurrection at the outset and continuing with Balthazar's supposed murder by Alexandro, who narrowly averts execution for the bogus
crime; with Pedringano's expected pardon replaced by his execution,
which leads indirectly to the deaths in Hieronimo's playlet of Balthazar
and Lorenzo, who are expected to rise for applause but actually are killed;
with Horatio's death in the garden and Hieronimo's "resurrection" of his
body in the playlet; and, finally, with Bel-imperia's suicide after Hieronimo had intended to save her by changing the original role, which called
for her death. The resurrection motif culminates in the judgments meted
out by Andrea and Revenge who assign their "friends" an Elysian apotheosis and their "foes" endless Tartarean death.

Andrea's final role as judge helps to resolve the dilemma of his afterworld status when the judges were unable to place him with the lovers or
the martialists. In Empedoclean terms, as Sacvan Bercovitch has pointed
out, Andrea's situation resembles that of the "one [who has] followed

[27] Gifford, *Sermons*, 394.
[28] Bale, *Image*, Pt. 3: Kkir–v.

strife, . . . [and] must wander from the abodes of the blessed [until through the contest of Love and Strife, he has become purified]. One of these I now am, an exile and a wanderer from the gods, for that I put my trust in insensate strife."[29] Although the denouement has been bloody, those who follow love, which in this case means the harsh underworld and apocalyptic justice, have defeated the adherents of war. The victory of love over war is signalled when Andrea becomes the judge, not the judged, as he assigns his friends to "fields of love" and his enemies to their "endless tragedy."

The switch in Andrea's roles also can be explained in apocalyptic terms. At the Last Judgment, the souls of those who suffered for Christ's sake are given the right to pass judgment: "And I sawe seates; and they sate upon them and judgement was given unto them . . ." (Rev. 20:4,121r-v). This passage recalls Dan. 7:22, which describes how the little horn or the Antichrist prevailed against the faithful, "until the Ancient of daies came, and judgement was given to the Sainctes of the most high: and the time approached, that the Sainctes possessed the kingdome" (361v). The saints enthroned are given the right to pass judgment, and in this way, as Austin Farrar points out,[30] the promise of justice for the martyred souls of Rev. 6:9, who cried from under the altar for vengeance, is fulfilled. They receive justice by having justice put into their hands. Similarly, the apocalyptic promise inherent in Hieronimo's exclamation to Bel-imperia that "the saints . . . sit soliciting / For vengeance on those cursed murderers" (4.1.31–32) is completed by Andrea's meting out justice in the final scene. The privilege of judgment granted him by Revenge as surrogate for Proserpine is tantamount to placing Andrea among the elect. Like the saints in the Apocalypse and Daniel, he has become the judge:

> Now will I beg at lovely Proserpine,
> That by virtue of her princely doom
> I may consort my friends in pleasing sort,
> And on my foes work just and sharp revenge.
>
> (4.5.13–16)

[29]*Fragments*, tr. John Burnet, *Early Greek Philosophers*, ed. William L. Lorimer (New York, 1963), 204–26; qtd. in Bercovitch, "Love and Strife," 215.
[30]Austin Farrar, *The Revelation of St. John The Divine* (Oxford: Clarendon Press, 1964), 205.

The last two scenes in *The Spanish Tragedy* combine apocalypse and eschatology in a manner similar to the "*Last Judgment*" play at the end of the mystery cycles."[31] The Chester cycle prefaces the *Last Judgment* play with two related plays, the *Prophets of Antichrist* and *The Coming of Antichrist*, which introduce eschatological prophecies and recount the legend of Antichrist. In the final play, the Last Judgment occurs as "Christ descends from the heavens to judge mankind in a lower place. . . . The entry to heaven on Christ's right is an architecturally designed doorway, and . . . near it are the saved. On Christ's left hand the entry to hell is symbolised by a cauldron or the mouth of Leviathan, and near or around it are a group of devils about to drag off the damned."[32] In *The Spanish Tragedy*, Revenge and Andrea pass judgment in the classical underworld, but the "damned are sentenced to 'deepest hell'" (27), and Balthazar is damned to hang "about Chimaera's neck, / . . . Repining at our joys that are above" (36, 38).

As Woolf has argued, the practice of ending the cycles with the Last Judgment demonstrates the completion of God's work, but at the same time introduces an ambiguity concerning the overall classification of that work as either a tragedy or a comedy or both.[33] For the damned, the final judgment is a tragedy, but for the saved it is a comedy. Similarly, at the conclusion of *The Spanish Tragedy*, the endless tragedy is established for the followers of Babylon/Spain, the Spanish tragedy, and the Elysian resurrection is declared for the heroes, the English comedy. Serving as the representative of underworld destiny and as the surrogate author-figure for Kyd, Revenge announces the movement from earthly time to otherworld timelessness.[34] *The Spanish Tragedy* has, like the Chester mystery cycle and the Apocalypse, presented "this mysterie of the last judgement, the damnacion of Antichrist and infidels, and also the glorie of the just at the resurrection" (Rev. 117v, n).

Unlike most Renaissance dramas, *The Spanish Tragedy* ends after four acts. Bercovitch explains its structure in Empedoclean terms with "the play's . . . acts . . . [representing] four successive rotations of the fixed

---

[31]Hunter, "Ironies," 104.
[32]Rosemary Woolf, *The English Mystery Plays* (Los Angeles: University of California Press, 1972), 295–96.
[33]Ibid., 298–99.
[34]David Leigh, "The Doomsday Mystery Play: An Eschatological Morality," *MP* 67 (1970):223.

'wheel of Time, Justice, and Destiny [which] must turn and bring its revenges.'"[35] Alternating between love and strife, the play ends with a balanced judgment that resolves the strife and places Andrea and his friends in the sphere of love. But the four-act structure can also be explained in apocalyptic terms. As has already been discussed in chapter 2, Kyd uses the four sundry languages of the playlet as an allusion to the Danielic fall of the four empires. Similarly, the four acts of the play may be seen as a parallel to the Danielic empires, ending with the overthrow of Babylon/ Spain and the institution of Christ's kingdom.

Further, the structure of The Spanish Tragedy may also be indebted to the Renaissance analysis of the Apocalypse as a four-act play. Although Pareus' popular commentary appeared some twenty years after Kyd's drama, his commentary certainly reflects the Renaissance consensus on the quadripartite structure of the Book of Revelation. Pareus sees each of the seven visions as a four-act play which presents the struggle between Antichrist and the true church. Like the end of the fourth act of The Spanish Tragedy, the final act of the Apocalypse "sheweth the Catastrophe of . . . Antichrists Kingdom, and the casting of all adversaries into the lake of fire: and on the contrary the Churchs Victory, and Eternall Glory."[36]

Thomas Kirchmeyer's apocalyptic four-act drama Pammachius provides another important parallel to Kyd's play. Unlike The Spanish Tragedy, Pammachius ends with the triumph of evil, but Satan and Pammachius are warned that Luther has begun the Protestant Reformation, which will topple Babylon and lead to the establishment of Christ's kingdom in the unwritten fifth act. Herrick concludes that "counting the postponed fifth act, Pammachius is either a tragedy with a happy ending or tragicomedy."[37] Although The Spanish Tragedy presents the fall of Babylon in four acts, Revenge's announcement that he will "begin their endless tragedy" indicates an eternal tragic fifth act for the villains who have experienced the "second death."

In the second part of this book, I will establish and analyze the historical context of The Spanish Tragedy, which is a nationalistic history play depicting the inevitable victory of England over Antichrist Spain in 1588. To create this context, Kyd borrows from the revenge or "Nemesis" play tradition in which English nationalism is celebrated as the destined tri-

---

[35]Bercovitch, "Love and Strife," 221.
[36]Pareus, Commentary, 27.
[37]Herrick, Tragicomedy, 57.

umph of good over evil. Further, Kyd includes three terse allusions to historical events which Hieronimo will reverse in his revenge playlet. Kyd uses these three analogies as the continuing historical apocalyptic context which the lord marshal's actions will complete. The major effect of Kyd's historical methods is to establish that Hieronimo's revenge playlet has "real" consequences, that Kyd is presenting symbolically the actual victory of England over the Spanish Armada.

PART TWO

History

THE

Spanish Tragedie:

Containing the lamen-
table end of *Don Horatio*, and *Bel-imperia*
with the pittifull death of old
Hieronimo.

Newly corrected, amended, and enlarged with
new additions of the Painters part, and
others, as it hath of late been
diuers times acted.

Imprinted at London by W. White.
1610.

5

The Spanish Tragedy as History Play: Nemesis, Nero, and Lorenzo de' Medici

KYD USES THE APOCALYPTIC elements in *The Spanish Tragedy* to establish the Reformation theme of the fall of Babylon, the Antichrist Rome/Spain. The play is dominated by a providential ethos of justice coming to fruition and, concomitantly, by the historical movement toward the inevitable victory of Protestant England over Catholic Spain. In his use of biblical, morality, chronicle, and Senecan elements to endow Hieronimo's revenge with political, religious, and historical rightness, Kyd draws upon a number of Tudor plays in which the achievement of revenge by a character represents divine retribution enacted on earth. The effect of these "Nemesis" plays, as Broude has termed them, is to change the audience's perception of revenge as an immoral act to a justified strike against God's enemies. The accomplishment of revenge becomes associated with the Reformation as the means of bringing about a divinely sanctioned national order:

> The age of Reformation was understood to be the time
> appointed by God for the Antichrist's downfall, the reformers
> being the agents of the divine vengeance by which the infernal
> powers were to be routed. . . . Regeneration through divine
> retribution, the theme of the Reformation in England, thus
> emerged as a key motif in sixteenth-century English thought
> seemingly explaining to English Protestants what their era was
> "all about."[1]

[1]Broude, "Three Forerunners," 490–91.

John Bale's *A Comedy Concerning Three Laws of Nature, Moses, and Christ* (1538) presents the successive victories of Infidelity and his cohorts until Vindicta Dei, who represents the Protestant Reformation, expels the vices and restores the rule of the three laws. In *Kynge Johan* the Pope is revealed to be the Antichrist who defeats King John and imposes a Catholic tyranny upon England, but Imperial Majesty—Henry VIII as the instigator of the English Reformation—brings in Verity who unmasks the evil forces and creates the new order. At the conclusion, Queen Elizabeth is hailed as another Daniel who has continued to subdue the always dangerous Catholics. Although in the Counter-Reformation morality play *Respublica* (1553) the Catholic and Protestant roles are reversed, the pattern of a justified Nemesis overthrowing the evil order remains the same. Queen Mary serves as the Nemesis figure restoring the rightful Catholic rule to England after the vicious Protestants have been turned out. The Prologue states that

> We . . . thank God . . .
> That he hath sent Mary our sovereign and Queen
> To reform the abuses which hitherto hath been,
> And that ills which long time have reigned incorrect
> Shall now forever be redressed with effect.
> She is our most wise and . . . worthy Nemesis,
> Of whom our play meaneth to amend that is amiss.[2]

As in Bale's plays, the theme of regeneration through retribution is combined with the *topos* of "Truth, the daughter of Time," to produce a sense of the inevitability of the Catholic restoration.

John Pickering's *A New Interlude of Vice (Horestes)* (1567), the first Elizabethan revenge play, continues the morality emphasis on regeneration through retribution in the course of time, but it places the act of vengeance in the hands of a character who is neither an abstraction nor the allegorical representation of the monarch. Horestes debates whether he should revenge his father's murder by killing his mother and her lover. Pickering complicates the situation by introducing the abstract character Revenge, who is both the typical Vice and, by his own claim, a messenger of the god named Courage, who sanctions Horestes' revenge. When the

---

[2]*Respublica*, in *English Morality Plays and Moral Interludes*, ed. Edgar T. Schell and J. D. Schuchter (New York: Holt, Rinehart and Winston, 1969), 48–54.

council of King Idumeus concurs, Horestes is free to carry out the necessary act of vengeance. But after he does so, Revenge incites Menelaus to object to Horestes' act. Finally, the Greek council affirms Horestes' revenge as the will of the gods, Menelaus allows his daughter Hermione to marry Horestes, Revenge is banished, and Horestes is crowned king and surrounded by Truth and Duty who sanction the new reign.

Horestes ends with a celebration of Greek unity which becomes an encomium of English harmony as Elizabeth is saluted and all the parts of her government praised for their loyalty and continuing virtue. Thus, Horestes' act of vengeance is presented as the means of achieving a beneficent national order. Moreover, as Broude has pointed out, the play delivers a specific Reformation message concerning the Catholic queen, Mary Stuart who was deposed after marriage to Lord Bothwell: "Defending the Scottish Protestants, Pickeryng uses *Horestes* to explain the overthrow of Mary and Bothwell as the visitation of divine vengeance on murderers."[3] Although the moral nature of Revenge remains "a mystery . . . [of] the use of an ambiguous 'Vice' in a terrible punishment that Truth and Duty applaud,"[4] the dismissal of Revenge when Horestes is crowned demonstrates that the evil aspects of revenge are now expelled in favor of its beneficial qualities as the creator of national prosperity.

In *Gorboduc, or The Tragedy of Ferrex and Porrex* (1561), *The Misfortunes of Arthur* (1587), *The Lamentable Tragedie of Locrine* (1594), and *The Battle of Alcazar* (1594), there is an increased use of Senecan motifs such as choral summaries and prophecies of violence to come and the presence of ghosts or underworld abstractions seeking revenge. Instead of the concern with the single act of beneficial vengeance, emphasis is placed on interlocking acts of revenge which represent the chaos unleashed by the initial disruption of the moral order. However, the outcome remains the same; the country achieves regeneration through the successive acts of retribution. These plays establish the theme that divine providence is operating on earth to produce ultimately, despite the intermediate divisiveness and violence, a just society.

In Sackville and Norton's *Gorboduc*, the sons of Gorboduc, the king of Great Britain, engage in civil war after their father divides his kingdom between them. When Porrex slays Ferrex, his mother Videna kills him,

---

[3]Broude, "Three Forerunners," 496.
[4]Robert Knapp, "*Horestes*: The Uses of Revenge," *ELH* 40 (1973):219.

and the people rebel and slay both Videna and Gorboduc. This violence results in the punishment of the rebels by the nobility, who then fall into another civil war because of the absence of a capable ruler. This proliferating cycle of doom is summarized by the Chorus:

> When bloud thus shed, doth staine the heavens
>   face,
> Crying to *Jove* for vengeance . . . ,
> The mightie God . . . then sendes forth . . .
> The dreadfull furies. . . .
> These for revenge of wretched murder done,
> Do make the mother kill her onely sonne.
> Blood asketh blood, and death must death requite.[5]

Nevertheless, after enumerating the ills that will afflict an ungoverned England, Eubulus, the king's prescient secretary, declares his faith in the restoration of justice;

> Of justice, yet must God in fine restore
> This noble crowne unto the lawfull heire:
> For right will alwayes live, and rise at length,
> But wrong can never take deepe roote to last.
>   (5.2.276-79)

As Irving Ribner states, these final lines "assert the ultimate goodness of God's providence, and they make it clear that the authors of *Gorboduc* saw history . . . as the record on earth of God's ruling of human affairs, his rewarding of the good and his punishment of the wicked."[6]

The *Misfortunes of Arthur* by Thomas Hughes provides the most striking parallel to *The Spanish Tragedy* with its Senecan ghost Gorlois who is allowed to return to earth to watch the play unfold and with the satisfaction of the ghost's desire for revenge which ushers in a peaceful order that anticipates and parallels the golden age of England ruled by Elizabeth. The play, a Senecan tragedy written by a lawyer in Gray's Inn, emphasizes its concern with the achievement of justice by being addressed to Elizabeth as the goddess Astraea. In the first dumb show three furies appear repre-

---

[5]Thomas Norton and Thomas Sackville, *Gorboduc, or Ferrex and Porrex*, in *Early English Classical Tragedies*, ed. John Cunliffe (Oxford: Clarendon Press, 1912), 4.2.7-11, 15-17.

[6]Irving Ribner, *The English History Play in the Age of Shakespeare*, rev. ed. (London: Methuen, 1965), 49.

senting Uther's lustful crime of killing Gorlois, duke of Cornwall, and stealing his wife Igerna. Then the ghost of Gorlois describes his return from Hades and prophesies the calamities that will befall King Arthur's house as the result of Pendragon's initial crime. In an alternate opening speech written by the law student William Fulbecke, Gorlois' ghost speaks more fully of his passage into the underworld where, like Andrea, he was excluded from the Elysian fields and allowed by Proserpine to return to earth to watch the vengeance visited upon Pendragon's line.

When Arthur's kingdom has been devastated and his desire for revenge satisfied, Gorlois depicts the golden age which is destined to come during the reign of Elizabeth:

> Let *Virgo* come from Heaven, . . .
> That vertuous *Virgo* borne for *Brytaines* blisse:
> That pierelesse braunch of *Brute*: . . .
> Let her reduce the golden age againe, . . .
> A Rule, that else no Realme shall ever finde, . . .
> The sole example that the world affordes.[7]

The Misfortunes of Arthur was performed in February of 1588 for the queen at Greenwich, a few months before the attempted invasion of England by the Spanish Armada, and the play was intended, as Ribner has written, "as a warning against civil war and the annihilation of England which would inevitably follow the joining of Englishmen with foreign powers against their queen."[8]

Like *Gorboduc* and *The Misfortunes of Arthur*, *Locrine* is set in the mythical British past, and it conveys the same warning against the evils of civil war and vulnerability to foreign invasion as *The Misfortunes of Arthur*. Atey or Ate, the goddess of discord, introduces a dumb show about an archer killing a lion, an act which, as she explains, symbolically foreshadows the death of Brute, the mythical founder of Britain. Close to death, Brute divides his kingdom among his children, making Locrine king and giving Albanact the north and Cumber the south. Locrine is married to Gwendoline at Concordia, but the peace is disrupted when Humber and his son Hubba invade England. Albanact is killed, but his ghost appears to

---

[7]Thomas Hughes, *The Misfortunes of Arthur*, in *Early English Classical Tragedies*, ed. John Cunliffe (Oxford: Clarendon Press, 1912), 5.2.14,18–19, 23, 27, 29.

[8]Ribner, *History Play*, 234.

haunt Humber, crying "Revenge, revenge for blood."[9] Locrine defeats
Humber, who commits suicide and earns the condemnation of replacing
the mythological sufferers in the underworld, a punishment similar to
those meted out by Andrea:

> Now maist thou reach thy apples *Tantalus*, . . .
> Now *Sisiphus* leave tumbling of thy rock, . . .
> And laie proud *Humber* on the whirling wheele.
>
> (4.5.1,760; 62; 64–65)

However, Locrine becomes enamored of Humber's widow, Estrild,
and their love produces a daughter, Sabren, and a civil war. Locrine,
Estrild, and Sabren commit suicide, and the play ends with Atey's prophecy of the peaceful reign of Elizabeth:

> [A]s a woman was the onely cause
> That civill discord was then stirred up,
> So let us pray for that renowned mayd,
> That eight and thirtie yeares the scepter swayd,
> In quiet peace and sweet felicitie.   (5.7.2, 274–78)

George Peele's *The Battle of Alcazar* is set not in the mythical past of
Britain, but in the Europe and Africa of the late 1570s when Portugal's
headstrong King Sebastian led a doomed expedition to Barbary to defend
the claims of Muly Mahomet to the much-contested throne. The events
recounted in this play, which was written around 1588–89, serve, in a
sense, as an introduction to *The Spanish Tragedy*, because Sebastian's death
in 1578 and the subsequent struggle for the Portuguese crown led to
Spain's conquest of Portugal in 1580 and the installation of the viceroy in
1582. Peele employs dramatic methods similar to Kyd's in the use of a
choral presenter, who, like Andrea, recounts the past, and, like Revenge,
predicts what will happen. Three furies and Nemesis appear to signify the
retribution to be exacted upon the villainous Muly Mahomet, who

> Murthering his unkle and his brethern
> Triumphs in his ambitious tyrannie,
> Till Nemisis high mistres of revenge,
> That with her scourge keepes all the world in awe,

---

[9]*The Tragedy of Locrine*, ed. Ronald B. McKerrow (London: Malone Society Reprints,
1908), 3.6.1,336.

With thundering drums awakes the God of warre,
... to inflict
Vengeance on this accursed Moore for sinne.[10]

The Battle of Alcazar also parallels *The Spanish Tragedy* in its anti-Spanish sentiments. Philip II encourages Sebastian to indulge in a futile war which will weaken Portugal and make it vulnerable to Spanish conquest. Stukeley, the English adventurer, declares that Philip is treacherous, and Stukeley's interlocutor asserts that lying kings will be punished in the course of time:

The heavens will right the wrongs that they sus-
    taine.
Philip if these forgeries be in thee,
Assure thee king, twill light on thee at last,
And when proud Spaine hopes soundly to prevaile,
The time may come that thou and thine shall faile.
                    (3.1.822–26)

The prediction of doom for Spanish ambition echoes Sebastian's description of the imperviousness of England to invasion:

To invade the Iland where her highnes raignes,
Twere all in vaine, for heavens and destinies
Attend and wait upon her Majestie,
Sacred, imperiall, and holy is her seate, ...
The wallowing Ocean hems her round about
Whose raging flouds do swallow up her foes,
And on the rockes their ships in peeces split.
                    (2.4.675–77, 686–88)

The play thus chronicles the fatal posturing of King Sebastian and the treachery of Spain, and it salutes the power and majesty of England, the destined victor over the Spanish Armada.

The Spanish Tragedy developed out of the matrix created by these Senecan "Nemesis" and revenge plays. Kyd uses Andrea as the returning Senecan ghost, who, like the ghosts of Gorlois and Albanact, sits as an onstage audience to watch the fulfillment of Revenge's prophecy in the

---

[10]George Peele, *The Battle of Alcazar,* in *The Dramatic Works of George Peele,* ed. John Yoklavich. 2 vols. (New Haven: Yale University Press, 1969), 1:1, 32–40.

course of time. Like the presenter in the *Battle of Alcazar*, Andrea also serves as chorus to the earthly play, accompanied by the abstract character Revenge, the representative of the underworld ethos that controls the play. Like Atey in *Locrine*, Revenge predicts the violence to come and, like Revenge in *Horestes*, he sanctions the individual act of vengeance which results in the defeat of evil and the regeneration of the just order. Kyd joins the Senecan motif of interlocked acts of revenge with the idea of the justified revenger, Hieronimo, who kills his son's murderers, topples Babylon/ Spain, and thus serves as a Vindicta Dei ushering in the English golden age under Elizabeth which is celebrated in all of these plays.

In *The Spanish Tragedy* Kyd presents the passage of imperial power from Babylon/Spain to Protestant England under Elizabeth. He sets the play within the context of Spanish–Portuguese conflict about ten years before the defeat of the Armada, and he symbolically exalts England as the destined victor over Spain in the historical pageant and the "Soliman and Perseda" playlet. However, some critics have denied that Kyd is interested in giving his play historical authenticity. Philip Edwards has declared that the play's historical setting is "sheer fantasy" and that Kyd was intent on avoiding verisimilitude. Further, Hieronimo's historical pageant is based on a "vague and inaccurate past" catering to the patriotism of the Elizabethan audiences and "keeping his play at a distance from contemporary events and preserving the unhistorical flavour."[11]

In contrast to Edwards' dismissal of Kyd's historical accuracy, Arthur Freeman argues that Kyd is concerned with paralleling the play with Spanish–Portuguese rivalry in the late sixteenth century. Freeman also cites a "tradition of popular or oral history" which supports the accounts of England's brave victories over Spain and Portugal presented in Hieronimo's historical pageants.[12] Kyd is adapting past and contemporary history to place the specific plot incidents and characters within a larger historical context. The slandered Alexandro parallels Antonio, the Portuguese claimant to the throne, who was defeated by Spain and supported by

[11] Edwards, *Spanish Tragedy*, xxv.
[12] Arthur Freeman, *Thomas Kyd, Facts and Problems* (Oxford: Oxford University Press, 1967), 52, 55.

England,[13] and Lorenzo's duping his murderous factotum into expecting a pardon can be traced to the Leicester/Gates incident in *A Copie of a Leter* (1584).[14] However, beyond these overt historical contexts and references, there exists an historical subtext, which, in keeping with the mystery rubric of the play, contains a network of covert parallels that Kyd is drawing upon for his delineation of Catholic–Protestant hostility. The historical allusion appears in a word or a phrase which, when investigated, reveals the magnitude of the parallel Kyd is drawing. Through the short and unobtrusive allusions, we are encouraged to explore the extent to which the events and characters in the play parallel the historical incidents and analogues.

Three examples of Kyd's covert methodology occur during the preparations for Hieronimo's revenge playlet and are directly related to it. Hieronimo refers first to Nero's enjoyment of dramatic tragedies (4.1.87–89); then to the "Italian tragedians . . . / That in one hour's meditation / . . . would perform anything in action" (164–66); and finally to "Paris . . . mass, and well remembered!" (169), after Lorenzo remarked that he had seen the "French tragedians" (168) perform there. Hieronimo's comments allude to past and contemporary historical plots in which the representatives of Antichrist triumph, twice by avenging plots against their lives and once by massacring unsuspecting victims. Hieronimo alludes to these events as preparation for his enactment of the revenge playlet because by means of that plot he will reverse the past victories of the collective forces of Babylon. The playlet itself serves as the final and most complete example of Kyd's historical allusiveness.

Kyd creates these multiple allusions by giving his characters unfixed references in historical contexts which are united by the theme of the struggle against Antichrist. Thus, in the reference to Nero's espousal of state dramas, Lorenzo, Balthazar, and by extension, Castile, and the Spanish king can be grouped as Nero-like representatives of Antichrist who are

[13]See the following accounts of Antonio's career and claim to the Portuguese crown: Anthony, Prior of Crato, *The Explanation of the True and Lawfull Right and Tytle, of the Most Excellent Prince, Anthonie* . . . (Leyden, Holland: Christopher Plantyn, 1585); Alvaro de Bacan, *Relation of the expongable attempt and conquest of the Ylande of Tercera* (London: T. Purfoote, 1584); Geronimo Conestaggio, *The Historie of the Uniting of the Kingdom of Portugall to the Crowne of Castill* . . . (London: Edward Blount, 1600); Whetstone, George, *The English Myrror* (London: G. Seton, 1586), chap.1.

[14]Fredson Bowers, "Kyd's Pedringano: Sources and Parallels," *Harvard Studies and Notes in Philology and Literature* 13 (1931):241–49.

destroyed by means of Hieronimo's tragedy of state. In the reference to the "Italian tragedians," Lorenzo serves as the dramatic representative of Lorenzo de' Medici, the object of the Pazzi conspiracy to which Hieronimo alludes. Further, the Spanish royal family can be paralleled to the Valois rulers of France, especially Catherine de' Medici, who were responsible for the Paris massacre of St. Bartholomew's day in 1572. Finally, the evil characters killed in the playlet represent the Babylon/Turkey/Spain nexus defeated by Hieronimo, the sanctified revenger and English champion. Kyd's method of shifting the historical identities of his characters within the various historical contexts resembles Spenser's use of unfixed allegorical references: "Allegory allows not just for the continuous possibility, but for the inescapability, pleasure, and profit of unfixed reference; it allows, moreover, for referential schemas to be set up in which those . . . identified change places or names as the game continues, or in which exchanges can occur between figures in the work and those outside it."[15]

The reference to Nero as a proponent of dramatic spectacle on state occasions occurs when Hieronimo suggests that a tragedy be performed to celebrate Bel-imperia and Balthazar's wedding. Balthazar is perplexed by the choice of a tragedy for a festive occasion, but Hieronimo responds,

> Why, Nero thought it no disparagement,
> And kings and emperors have ta'en delight
> To make experience of their wits in plays!   (87–89)

These are famous lines because they were cited by Thomas Heywood in his *Apology For Actors* (1612) as being from Kyd's *The Spanish Tragedy* and provide the only proof of his authorship. But, as Freeman notes, the lines also reveal that "Heywood knew . . . [that] what Hieronimo is actually talking about is the on-stage carnage which Nero sponsored for his own amusement, and which Hieronimo is about to duplicate."[16] Heywood explains that Roman emperors officially made it a practice to kill enemies and accused criminals during state dramas:

> It was in the manner of their Emperours, in those dayes, in their publicke Tragedies to choose out the fittest amongst such, as for capital offences were condemned to dye, and to imploy them in such parts as were to be killed in the Tragedy, who of

---

[15] Crewe, *Hidden Designs*, 140–41.
[16] Freeman, *Kyd*, 97.

themselves would make suit rather so to dye with resolution, and by the hands of such princely *Actors*, then otherwise to suffer a shameful and most detestable end. And these were Tragedies naturally performed. And such *Caius Caligula, Claudius Nero, Vitellus, Domitianus, Comodus,* and other Emperours of *Rome,* upon their festivals and holy daies of greatest consecration, used to act.[17]

Hieronimo is following the practices of the Roman emperors as outlined by Heywood when he plans to kill his enemies in a playlet on a festival day. However, although Hieronimo cites Nero as the prototype for his murderous intentions, this does not mean that in carrying out his plan he becomes a villain like Nero. Rather, Hieronimo is hinting that he will reverse the historical situation by turning Nero's own methods against his representatives at the court of Babylon/Spain, who, unlike the Roman criminals, do not know that they are condemned to die in the play.

Nero is cited as the precedent for Hieronimo's revenge because his career as writer, actor, homicidal emperor, crusher of the Pisonian conspiracy, and figure of Antichrist provides the necessary ironies and themes Kyd wants to create. During the Renaissance, Nero was viewed within a dramatic context as a murderous author and director able to create actual tragic deaths in real life and onstage as well: "It was one of his exercises to translate Greek tragedies into Latine, who made true tragedies in bloud, such as even the Greekes never feigned."[18] In the anonymous play *The Tragedy of Nero* (1624), the emperor is presented as the stage manager of the tragic pageants he creates for the Roman government and stage. When he burns Rome, Nero becomes in effect the director of the tragedy which involves all the people of Rome: "We see Nero in his role of stage-manager . . . [of] a full pageant with the burning city as a backdrop to the singing."[19]

Nero not only created and directed blood tragedies in both the literal and literary sense, but he also acted in the tragedies of his tutor Seneca: "when *Seneca* . . . wrote tragedies, *Nero,* and the lords, might with lesse

[17]Thomas Heywood, *An Apology For Actors* [1612] (New York: Scholars Facsimiles and Reprints, 1941), Eiiiv.
[18]Edmund Bolton, *Nero Caesar, or Monarchie Depraved: An Historicall Worke* (London: Thomas Walkley, 1624), 64.
[19]*The Tragedy of Nero,* ed. Elliott Hill (New York: Garland Publishing Company, 1979), xxx.

reproofe bee actors. . . . *Oedipus, Hercules furious,* and *Thiestes,* are . . . among those in which *Nero* was an actor."[20] Thus, Nero acted in Senecan tragedies in which a prophecy of doom is fulfilled when a son kills his father and marries his mother; an insane father kills his children; and a vengeful brother kills his brother's children and serves them to their father at a banquet. Scholars have maintained that Nero's acting in such parts parallels the bloody roles he played as emperor.

When Piso and his conspirators decided to kill Nero in 64 A. D., they first chose to assassinate him while he was acting onstage. In *The Tragedy of Nero*, Scevinus explains the appropriateness of such an act:

> To make the generall liking to concurre
> With ours, were even to strike him in his shame,
> Or (as he thinks) his glory, on the Stage,
> And so too truely make't a Tragedy;
> When all the people cannot chuse but clap
> So sweet a close, and twill not *Caesar* be
> That shall be slaine, a Romane Prince;
> Twill be *Alcmaeon,* or blind *Oedipus.*   (2.3.118–25)

Subsequently, the conspirators scrapped this plan in favor of killing the emperor at the Neronian games in the Circus Maximus: "They decided to carry out their design on that day of the circus games, which is celebrated in honour of Ceres, as the emperor . . . used to go to the entertainments of the circus, and access to him was easier from his keen enjoyment of the spectacle."[21] However, Nero crushed the conspiracy before the assassination could be attempted, and, as a result, he sentenced the conspirators, who consisted mainly of actors and writers, to death. Tacitus quotes an ironic saying about Piso's plot which reveals the extent to which events in Nero's reign can be viewed within a dramatic context: "Even a saying of Flavus was popularly current, 'that it mattered not as to the disgrace if a harp-player were removed and a tragic actor succeeded him.' For as Nero used to sing to the harp, so did Piso in the dress of a tragedian."[22] Nero forced Seneca, Lucan (Seneca's nephew), and Petronius to commit suicide for their real or imagined roles in Piso's conspiracy.

---

[20] Bolton, *Nero,* 262.

[21] Tacitus, *The Annals,* in *The Complete Works of Tacitus,* tr. Alfred Church and William Broadrib, ed. Moses Hadas (New York: Random House, 1942), bk. 15, chap. 53, p. 385.

[22] Ibid., bk. 15, chap. 65, p. 393.

For these murders and other insane activities during his reign, Nero came to represent a type of the Antichrist, the embodiment of pagan Rome as persecutor of Christianity. As Emmerson explains: "The typological interpretation of Nero . . . is . . . the apocalyptic Antichrist. . . . Christians identified Nero with the 'mystery of iniquity,' the evil power presently at work of which Paul writes in 2 Thess. 2:7. . . . Since commentators accuse Nero of killing the apostles, persecuting the church, and doing the works of the devil—'his father'—his persecution is a figure of the . . . persecution to come under Antichrist."[23] Nero is often associated with the wounded and then healed head of the seven-headed sea beast described by St. John in Rev. 13:3: "And I sawe one of his heads as it *were* wounded to death, but his deadlie wounde was healed, and all the worlde wondred *and* followed the beast" (118v). The gloss explains that "This maie be understand of Nero, who moved the first persecution against the Churche, and after slewe him self, so . . . the familie of the Caesars ended in him."

In *The Spanish Tragedy*, Kyd applies the Neronian dramatic and Antichrist contexts to the Machiavellian villain Lorenzo, who devises and directs plots to kill his enemies and, in order to escape detection, his accomplices. After carrying out the murder of Horatio in the bower—the assailants enter disguised—Lorenzo sets up Serberine to be murdered by Pedringano, who is apprehended immediately by the Watch sent by Lorenzo to witness the crime. Lorenzo directs from the wings, so to speak, Pedringano's subsequent death scene on the gallows. Lorenzo has promised Pedringano his pardon, which is ostensibly contained in the empty box held by the mocking page. Pedringano indulges in last-minute and pathetic bravado on the scaffold—another name for a stage—before the audiences watching his demise. Yet after his role is over and he has been "turned off" by the hangman, Pedringano "returns" in the posthumous letter which undermines Lorenzo's direction of this scene.

In his effort to bring his son's murderers to justice, Hieronimo becomes detective, author, actor, and director, who seizes the right time to execute Lorenzo and Balthazar before their fathers in a playlet of his own devising. Nero had criminals put to death in his plays, and he acted in Senecan tragedies which he also carried out during his reign. Nero crushed Piso's conspiracy and caused the deaths of the writers Seneca, Lucan, and

---

[23]Emmerson, *Antichrist*, 28.

Petronius. Hieronimo, in a point-for-point reversal of Nero's activities, creates a Senecan blood revenge playlet in which he kills the condemned—unknown to them—villains, who are the representatives of Spain and Portugal, Babylon, Rome, Nero, the Pope, and Antichrist. In the playlet, Lorenzo and Balthazar speak in Latin and Italian, respectively, the languages associated with the Antichrist: ". . . Latin . . . noteth the Pope or Antichrist who useth in all things the Latin tonge. . . . [B]ecause Italie in olde time was called Latinum, the Italians are called Latini, so that thereby he noteth of what countrey chiefly he shulde come" (Rev. 13:18, 119 r, n). By killing Lorenzo and Castile, Hieronimo makes the king of Spain, like Nero, the last of his line: "I am the next, the nearest, last of all" (4.4.208).

The second allusion to a historical plot which Hieronimo will reverse in his revenge playlet occurs when he cites the "Italian tragedians" as precedent for the performance of a *tragedia cothurnata* at the wedding celebration. In chapter 4 this reference was placed within the apocalyptic context of the destruction of Babylon in one hour, but Hieronimo also alludes to the famous Pazzi plot in 1478 to kill Lorenzo de' Medici during High Mass at the cathedral when the sanctus bell was rung. However, the conspirators only wounded Lorenzo, who hunted down, tortured, and brutally executed those connected with the assassination attempt. In *The Spanish Tragedy* Hieronimo reverses this outcome by killing Lorenzo, whose name, Catholicity, and Machiavellian activities link him with Lorenzo de' Medici, duke of Florence.

During the Renaissance, the Medici were considered by Protestants to be the image of Italian Catholic perfidy. Because they were rich, ambitious, powerful, and had gained control of Florence through astute political maneuvers, the Medici—Lorenzo the Magnificent in particular—came to represent the essence of Machiavellianism. Gentillet explains that "he [Machiavelli] dedicates . . . [*The Prince*] to Lawrence de Medicis, to teach him the reasons and means to invade and obtaine a principalitie. . . . [T]hey [the Medici] (since that time) occupied the principalities of Florence, and changed that Aristocraticall free . . . citie into . . . a manifest tyrannie."[24] Henri Estienne argues that since the Medici are Italian, they

---

[24]Innocent Gentillet, *A Discourse Upon The Meanes of Wel Governing and Maintaining In Good Peace, a Kingdome. . . . Against Nicholas Machiavell the Florentine*, tr. Simon Patericke (London: Adam Islip, 1602), A2v.

naturally "tryumphe in treason: in murdering men in theyr bedds: and slaying men comming behinde them, or takynge all advantage possible. . . ." But Lorenzo surpassed his countrymen in the achievement of evil, because he was "a man consumed . . . in . . . villanies, whore-domes, and incestes, . . . blynded with ambition, . . . who wanted . . . power to commit most grevous evills."[25]

Because of their power, the Medici made important enemies in Florence and in the hierarchy of the Catholic Church. Pope Sixtus IV, his nephew Gerolamo Riario, Archbishop Salviati, and members of the Pazzi family—wealthy Florentine rivals to the Medici—concocted the plot to assassinate Lorenzo and his brother Giuliano while they were at Mass. A precedent for this act had been established on December 26, 1476, when Galeazzo Sforza was stabbed to death in the church of Santo Stefano in Milan by three assassins directed by Cola Montano, who had extolled the glories of tyrannicide. Harold Acton describes the repercussions of this assassination: "Murder in churches became fashionable. There was less risk in stabbing the victim in a holy place of worship; and since the assassins could claim classical precedents they found magniloquent apologists."[26]

In forming their plot, the Pazzi "thought that both brothers (Lorenzo and Giuliano) might be slain, either at a marriage, or at a play, or in a church."[27] They finally decided to execute their plot on Sunday April 26, 1478, at High Mass in the cathedral when the priest received the Host: "Having now decided upon the time, they resolved that the signal for the attack should be the moment when the priest who celebrated high mass should partake of the sacrament, and that, in the meantime, . . . Arch-bishop de' Salviati . . . should take possession of the palace."[28] During the attack, Guiliano was killed but Lorenzo escaped to revenge himself upon the Pazzi in bloody reprisals. After the capture of some of the conspirators at the church, a band of Salviati's followers was trapped in a locked room at the Signory and slaughtered: "He [Salviati] entered with only a few of

[25]Henri Estienne, *A Mervaylous discourse upon the lyfe, deides, and behaviours of Katherine de Medicis, Queene mother . . . .* (Heydelberg, 1575), 132, 8.

[26]Harold Acton, *The Pazzi Conspiracy: The Plot against the Medici* (London: Thames and Hudson, 1979), 52.

[27]Niccolo Machiavelli, *History of Florence and of the Affairs of Italy: From the Earliest Times to the Death of Lorenzo the Magnificent* (New York: M. Walter Dunne, 1901), bk. 8, chap. 1, p. 360.

[28]Ibid., 362–63.

his followers, the greater part of them being shut up in the chancelleria into which they had gone, whose doors were so contrived, that upon closing they could not be opened from either side, without the key."[29] The revenge was swift and terrible; people attacked and killed the helpless conspirators, whose bodies were carried on spears or dragged through the streets. However, in the midst of the carnage, eyewitnesses were impressed with the silent dignity of Francesco Pazzi, "who could not be induced, by any injurious words or deeds . . . to utter a syllable,"[30] but showed "onely the Signs of a most disdainful and lofty fierceness."[31]

Instead of destroying Medicean power, the Pazzi conspiracy resulted in the resurgence of Lorenzo's authority in Florence; to mark his phoenix-like rebirth, Lorenzo arranged for a number of civic spectacles and pageants designed to promote and memorialize the glory of his family. Such displays became an integral part of Medicean rule from the end of the fifteenth and throughout the sixteenth century.[32] The Medici also encouraged the creation of intermezzi, mythological interludes performed during the courtly plays and fetes celebrating dynastic marriages. In 1539, a series of seven intermezzi were staged at Cosimo's wedding to Eleanor of Toledo. In 1586, intermezzi performed at the marriage of Virginia de' Medici to Cesare d'Este contained the theme of the revival of the golden age and the punishment of evil in Hades. The 1589 intermezzi marking the marriage of Ferdinand de' Medici and Christina, Catherine de' Medici's granddaughter, presented scenes involving the return of Astraea, the operation of Necessity as depicted in the Myth of Er, and the final *naumachia* in the courtyard of the Pitti Palace depicting the struggle between Christians and Turks.[33]

The history of the Medici dynasty, including the Pazzi conspiracy against Lorenzo and the use by the Medici of spectacle and pageantry to promote their power, serves as the subtext to Hieronimo's terse reference to the "Italian tragedians." Hieronimo alludes to the Medici as Nero-like promoters of festivals and intermezzi designed to celebrate dynastic unions and to memorialize family history. Thus, on the one hand, the

[29]Ibid., 364–65.
[30]Ibid., 366.
[31]Antoine Varillas, . . . *The Secret History of the House of Medicis,* tr. Ferrand Spence (London, 1686), 127.
[32]Roy Strong, *Splendor at Court: Renaissance Spectacle and the Theater of Power* (Boston: Houghton Mifflin Co., 1973), 169–70.
[33]Ibid., 170–96.

Medici are Italian tragedians who use intrigue and the arts to create real political tragedies necessary for the maintenance and promotion of their tyranny. But, on the other hand, Hieronimo, in two closely related ways, serves as the Italian tragedian "so sharp of wit, / That in one hour's meditation / . . . would perform anything in action." The Machiavellian Lorenzo has arranged a dynastic wedding between his sister and his "prisoner," Prince Balthazar of Portugal, but, foolishly, Lorenzo allows Hieronimo to create a tragedy for the joyous occasion. Hieronimo turns the weapon of the Medici against their dramatic representative as he devises a murderous intermezzo which destroys Lorenzo's dynastic play.

In the second way, Hieronimo parallels, but surpasses, the Pazzi conspirators who, as "Italian tragedians," failed in their attempt to kill Lorenzo during the High Mass—the "one hour's meditation." Hieronimo successfully carries out his plot to kill Lorenzo and Balthazar onstage at the wedding celebration. And just as the fleeing assassins were trapped and slaughtered in the locked room at the Signory by the Medici forces, so too Hieronimo locks his victims onstage with the key given him by Castile, who, along with the assembled royalty, can enter only when the murders have been completed. After being apprehended, Hieronimo, like Francesco Pazzi, does not "utter a syllable," but, unlike Francesco, who was executed by his captors, he bites out his tongue and kills Castile and himself with the knife intended to mend his pen. Thus, Hieronimo has reversed the final element in the historical parallel in which Lorenzo de' Medici exacted a horrific revenge against his assailants and emerged from the plot against his life with more power than before. In *The Spanish Tragedy* Hieronimo has taken a brutal revenge against his son's killers with his creation and enactment of the Italian tragedy. The next chapter will concern Hieronimo's reversal of the third and most extensive of the historical analogies—the St. Bartholomew's day massacre enacted by the French tragedians under the direction of Catherine de' Medici.

6

The Paris Massacre: The Revenging of Saint Bartholomew's Day, August 24, 1572

THE THIRD ALLUSION TO a historical plot which Hieronimo will reverse in the revenge playlet occurs immediately after his reference to the "Italian tragedians." Lorenzo exclaims ". . . I have seen the like / In Paris, 'mongst the French tragedians," and Hieronimo retorts "In Paris? mass, and well remembered!" (167–69) The use of the expression "French tragedians" links this passage to the previous one and sets up another parallel between the historical allusion and the revenge playlet involving real tragedies. The words *Paris* and *mass* in conjunction with the "French tragedians" allude to the infamous Paris massacre of Huguenots on St. Bartholomew's day in 1572. The occasion for the massacre was the marriage between Margaret, daughter of the queen mother Catherine de' Medici, and the Protestant Henry of Navarre on August 18, 1572. This union was intended as a reconciliation between Catholics and Protestants which would put an end to the internecine French religious wars that had raged for a decade; but at the instigation of the French royal family and the duke of Guise the conciliatory wedding ceremony was transformed into a "blood wedding" that became a rallying cry for Protestant forces in the ensuing years. As a representative of Protestant England, Hieronimo, the divinely sanctioned revenger, will create a playlet through which he will turn the dynastic union of Bel-imperia, sister of the Machiavellian Lorenzo, and Balthazar into a blood wedding.

The three historical allusions preceding the revenge playlet are related to each other in a number of ways. First, they follow a chronological progression from the Piso conspiracy in 65 A.D., through the Pazzi plot in 1478, and, finally, to the Paris massacre of 1572. Secondly, the situations are dominated by the respective tyrannical figures, Nero, Lorenzo de' Medici, and Catherine de' Medici, celebrated for their use of art as state propaganda. Further, the three plots are connected with state or religious functions, the first with the Neronian games, the second with High Mass, and the third with the wedding of Margaret and Henry. The last two events are linked even more closely by the similarities in the Mass's being the occasion for the attacks, in the signals given for the beginning of the vio-lence—the sanctus bell and church bells, respectively—and in the Machia-vellian policies of Lorenzo and Catherine de' Medici, who are classified as the Italian and French tragedians, respectively. Gentillet links Catherine with her forebears when he declares that "our Machiavelistes of Fraunce . . . were authors and enterprisers of the Massacre of S. *Bartholomew*."[1]

This analysis of Hieronimo's allusion to the Paris massacre, which provides the largest subtext of the three preparatory historical parallels, will cover these areas: (1) the relationship between the city of Paris and the word *mass*, which is a dual pun on the St. Bartholomew's day massacre and the Nuptial Mass celebrating the Protestant–Catholic union, which was seized upon by Protestant commentators as the symbolic cause of the massacre; (2) the bloody events of the Paris massacre, primarily the murder of the Protestant hero Admiral Gaspard de Coligny; (3) the role of Catherine de' Medici as mastermind of the violence and as promoter of civic and religious fetes whose contents, Protestant observers claimed, foreshadowed and mirrored the Paris massacre; (4) The influence of d'Aubigné's *Les Tragiques* and accounts of the massacre and fetes on the plot, characters, and staging of *The Spanish Tragedy*.

When Hieronimo exclaims "In Paris? mass, and well remembered!" he clearly joins two words *Paris* and *mass* which would have evoked for English audiences, at least the "initiated" members of those audiences, the

[1]Gentillet, *Discourse*, 348.

infamous Paris massacre of French Huguenots in 1572. The association of Paris and massacre became almost proverbial in the years following this political and religious tragedy as Marlowe's *The Massacre At Paris* (1593?) indicates. In a significant conflation of literary and real tragic contexts, Guise exuberantly assigns roles and accessories to be worn during the initial attack:

> They that shall be actors in this massacre
> Shall wear white crosses on their burgonets
> And tie white linen scarfs about their arms.[2]

After he has been wounded, Coligny blames the assault on "the Guisians, / That seek to massacre our guiltless lives" (4.58–59). When Guise decides to murder Coligny and expand the violence to include more Huguenots, he declares that Coligny "[s]hall in the entrance of his massacre / Be murdered in his bed" (5.13–14), and urges his assassins "forward to the massacre" (6.57). Finally, George Whetstone epitomizes English Protestant outrage at the Paris massacre:

> For where was there a more savage crueltie ever committed, then the massacre at Paris, where by the traine of amitie, and the celebration of a marriage, betweene the king of Navarre, and the kinges sister: which in outward appearance, promised much peace and honour to the long afflicted realme: . . .[however] the good Admirall was slaine, and . . . many . . . thousand innocent . . . Protestants in Paris and other cities of Fraunce were cruelly murthered, which monstrous massacre . . . is remembred with the blame and exclamation of the cruellest Pagans in the worlde.[3]

The exclamation "In Paris? mass, and well remembered!" also contains an allusion to the role of the Mass as the symbolic cause of the Paris massacre. *Mass* is the shortened form of the oath "by the mass," but Hieronimo gives the simple oath a meaningful twist by placing it next to Paris. The marriage between Margaret of Valois and Henry of Navarre took place outside of Notre Dame Cathedral on Monday August 18, 1572, and after the ceremony a Mass was held inside the church. This two-part wed-

---

[2]Christopher Marlowe, *The Massacre At Paris*, in *The Complete Plays of Christopher Marlowe*, ed. Irving Ribner (New York: Odyssey Press, 1963), 4.29–31.

[3]Whetstone, *English Myrror*, 96.

ding arrangement was intended, as François Hotman put it, to "be the most streight bond of civill concorde,"[4] but it proved to be the prologue to the French tragedy:

> That dismall daie is come, the marriage must begin,
> Where were assembled solemnlie the chiefe of
>   everie kinne.
> And for because the Masse their minds might grieve
>   no more,
> The mariage was solemnised before the great
>   Church dore
> Of Paris. . . .
> Which done, into the church the Bride in solemne
>   maner went
> To heare a Popish Masse.[5]

Marlowe depicts Catherine's plan to transform the Mass into a blood wedding. Her son King Charles IX announces:

> And now . . . the marriage rites performed,
> We think it good to go and consummate
> The rest with hearing of a holy mass. . . .
> Come, mother,
> Let us go to honor this solemnitie.

Catherine replies:

> Which I'll dissolve with blood and cruelty.
>   (1.18–20,24–26)

The signal for the slaughter to begin was the ringing of three silver bells of St. Germain l'Auxerrois, the parish church of the Louvre.[6] N. M. Sutherland has identified three phases of the ensuing violence in what is known collectively as the St. Bartholomew's day massacre: (1) the abortive attack on Admiral Coligny's life on August 22; (2) the murder of Coligny

---

[4]François Hotman, *A true and plaine report of the Furious outrages of Fraunce, and the horrible and shameful slaughter of Chatillon, the Admirall* . . . (Edinburgh: Striveling, 1573), xxviii.

[5]Anne Dowriche, *The French Historie: That is, A lamentable Discourse of three of the chiefe, and most famous bloodie broiles that have happened in France for the Gospell of Jesus Christ* (London: Thomas Man, 1589), 21r.

[6]Hugh Williamson, *Catherine de' Medici* (London: Michael Joseph, 1973), 224.

and his retinue on August 23 and 24, the feast days of St. Bartholomew; (3) the subsequent spread of the massacre throughout Paris and France.[7] Coligny, the Protestant leader and hero, was noted for his bravery and piety, and contemporary accounts of his behavior after his being shot depict him as "the very prototype of the Protestant saint" who "spoke . . . in saintly terms, providing political advice for the king, a confession of faith for his followers, and forgiveness for his would-be assassin."[8] The murder of Coligny in his bed and the subsequent defiling of his body served as the focal point for Protestant outrage at the murderous frenzy of the French Catholics.

After Coligny was only wounded, the duke of Guise and Catherine de' Medici decided to kill him in his bed. Hotman depicts Catherine as a merciless Machiavel, determined "that within the space of one houre all the enimies may be slayne, and the whole name and race of those wicked men be utterly rooted out."[9] In order to set the plan in motion, a treacherous guard was set up outside the admiral's room. He was to admit the assassins at the right moment: "the Kings brother commaunded Cossin captaine of the Kings guarde, to place a certaine band of souldiers to ward before the Admirals gate. There could hardly a man be found more hatefull against the Admirals parte . . . than this Cossin, which the successe plainly proved."[10] The net was drawn tighter around Coligny's forces through the royal suggestion that they lodge with their wounded leader to make certain, as Hotman explains, that they could be killed in one swoop.

After the intruders stabbed Coligny to death, they threw the corpse out the window to their confederates below. Marlowe captures the grisly qualities of the horrible execution by having the dukes of Guise and Anjou exult over the corpse:

> Guise: Ah, base Chatillon and degenerate, . . .
> Thus, in despite of thy religion,
> The Duke of Guise stamps on thy lifeless bulk.

---

[7]N. M. Sutherland, "The Massacre of St. Bartholomew and the Problem of Spain," *The Massacre of St. Bartholomew: Reappraisals and Documents*, ed. Alfred Soman (Hague: Martinus Nijhoff, 1974), 15.

[8]Donald Kelly, "Martyrdom, Myths, and the Massacre: The Background of St. Bartholomew," *The Massacre of St. Bartholomew: Reappraisals and Documents* (Hague: Martinus Nijhoff, 1974), 196, 197.

[9]Hotman, *Report*, L.

[10]Ibid., xlvii–xlviii.

Anjou: . . . . Cut off his head and hands,
And send them for a present to the Pope.
And when this just revenge is finished,
Unto Mount Faucon will we drag his corpse;
And he that living hated so the cross
Shall . . . be hanged thereon in chains. (4.39–48)

The hanged corpse served as a symbol for Protestants of the homicidal madness of the Parisian Catholics and the royal family:

There it remayned certeine dayes as a banner of the people of *Parisis* victorie, and as a monument of their madnesse and crueltie, which they executed uppon him both quicke and dead: which deede will not only never be forgotten, but also bee the destruction of *Paris*. . . . When tidings of the slaughter at Paris was caried into *Ingland, Scotland,* and *Germanie* . . . it is incredible too tell how greate hatred it procured too the king and the Queene mother, specially forasmuch as in those feawe dayes, almost ten thousand Protestants . . . fled in too those countries . . . who making report that the Admirall was a noble gentleman, a great and wise capteine, and the glorie of their countrie, blazed the authors of that wickednesse for ranke murtherers.[11]

Protestants were convinced that the slaughter of St. Bartholomew's day was directed by Catherine de' Medici who was depicted by Dowriche as the exponent of "that divel of Florence, Machiavel, of whom she learned manie bad lessons."[12] Estienne indicted her tainted lineage, which has resulted in the "most terrible matters at her handes,"[13] and John Stubbs denounced her Italianate infiltration of French politics whereby she has "depose[d] natural magistrates and help[ed] her countrymen to the richest offices, promote[d] an Italian to be High Chancellor . . . , and

[11]François Hotman, *The Lyfe of the Most Godly, Valeant and Noble Capteine and maintener of the trew Christian Religion in Fraunce, Jasper Colignie Shatillion* . . . , tr. Arthur Golding (London: Thomas Vautrollier, 1576), H3r–v.

[12]Dowriche, *Historie*, 23 v, n.

[13]Estienne, *Discourse*, 19.

. . . [made] half Italians to be marshals of France."[14] In sum, her Medicean lineage, her continued prominence in French politics from the death of her son Francis II in 1560 when she became regent for her son Charles IX, her influence over her reigning sons Charles and Henry III, her alliance with the duke of Guise and the Holy League, her prominent efforts to create religious harmony in a war-torn France through her opulent fetes, and her putative role as mastermind of the St. Bartholomew's day massacre made Catherine the target of Protestant hatred. As N. M. Sutherland explains, Catherine was "depicted . . . as cold, cruel, calculating, treacherous, and evil. She was a monster of selfish ambition, who sacrificed her children, her adopted country, her principles. . . for power. . . . Catherine became . . . the wicked author of the massacre . . . and symbol of all that was degraded in the *mores* of the time."[15]

Protestant writers describe the Paris massacre as a French tragedy written and directed by the evil playwright Catherine de' Medici. Dowriche presents Catherine plotting the massacre after the wedding ceremony: "the Prologue endes, and heere begins the plaie. . . . The Mother Queene appears . . . upon the stage . . . planting . . . a bloodie plot. . . . 'So shall we quicklie on the rest performe our whole intent. Pluck up . . . your sprites, and play your manlie parts.'"[16] Treating the massacre as a blood tragedy, Gentillet declares that "our Machiavelists of Fraunce . . . were authors . . . of the massacre of S. *Bartholomew*. . . . [T]he great effusion of blood, which they have made, hath incontinent cried for vengeance to God, who . . . hath heard the voice of that blood."[17] Finally, Stubbs sums up Catherine's roles as author, actor, director, and stage manager of the French tragedy:

> In this tragedy she played her part naturally and showed she governs all France. Her daughter Margaret was the stale to lure and allure them that otherwise . . . could not be gotten. . . . [T]he mother as setter-forth of this earnest game, stood holding the book (as it were) upon the stage and told her children

[14]John Stubbs, *The Discoverie Of A Gaping Gulf Whereinto England Is Like To Be Swallowed by an other French marriage . . .* , ed. Lloyd E. Berry (Charlottesville: University Press of Virginia, 1968), 89.

[15]N. M. Sutherland, "Catherine de' Medici: The Legend of the Wicked Italian Queen," *Sixteenth Century Journal* 9 (1978): 45.

[16]Dowriche, *Historie*, 23r–v.

[17]Gentillet, *Discourse*, 348–49.

and every other player what he should say; the last act was very
lamentable . . . the marriage of a king's sister imbrued with
blood; . . . little ones christened before to Christ were now
dipped again to Antichrist.[18]

The St. Bartholomew's day massacre also was interpreted by Protestant writers as the predictable outcome of Catherine's Machiavellian policies which she promoted through the grand fetes staged to celebrate
national and dynastic events. Catherine was a polished practitioner of the
Medicean art of lavish festivals designed to impress foreigners with the
power and wealth of the French court, to promote national pride, and,
most significantly, to reconcile warring religious factions by having them
participate in peaceful masquerades and stately dances. However, as
Frances Yates has pointed out, Catherine's fetes were often marred by
political and religious acrimony and threats of violence, which came to a
horrible fruition in the festivities marking the marriage of Margaret and
Henry.[19] As a result of the massacre, Catherine's preceding series of conciliatory fetes became tainted, being perceived as the Machiavellian preparation for the slaughter of the Huguenots in 1572. It is important to trace the
history of these fetes, because with Hieronimo's allusion to the French tragedians and the Paris massacre and his subsequent murder of his son's killers within a deadly wedding playlet, Kyd's drama is pointing to the ways
in which Hieronimo reverses Catherine's pageants to produce a Protestant
victory over Babylon/Spain.

Catherine staged the first of her "politique magnificences" in March
of 1563 at Chenonceaux to celebrate the establishment of peace after the
first religious civil war. In 1564 at Fontainebleau she created her next conciliatory fete after rejecting Catholic demands for harsher action against
Protestantism. As Roy Strong explains, the celebration at Fontainebleau
established the pattern for future pageants, with fetes occurring over a
number of days, and different people responsible for the specific presentations.[20] King Charles and his brother Anjou appeared as "deux grands
Princes" who vanquished a giant and released enchanted ladies. Symbolically, this plot reflected the hope for the end of religious strife and the cre-

---

[18]Stubbs, *Discoverie*, 26–27.

[19]Frances Yates, *The Valois Tapestries* (London: The Warburg Institute, 1959), 51–52,
60–65.

[20]Strong, *Splendor*, 132.

ation of an ordered and tolerant country under Charles and his mother, Catherine.[21]

In 1565 a very important fete was held at Bayonne on the Spanish frontier from June 15 to July 2. Philip II sent his wife, Isabella, Catherine de' Medici's daughter, to demand that France eliminate heresy, banish Huguenot ministers, exclude Huguenots from political office, and effect the orders of the Council of Trent. However, Catherine refused to comply with Philip's demands; thus, in effect, the Bayonne fetes were designed to celebrate a nonexistent French–Spanish accord. In the dance on the final day, the audience was invited to participate in the peaceful virtues expounded by the court fete.[22] Despite the apparent irenic nature of the presentations, Protestant observers later assigned darker motivations to Bayonne, seeing it as a preparation for the St. Bartholomew's day massacre:

> these fetes represented . . . hope . . . of a Franco–English alliance through a marriage between one of Catherine's children (Charles IX) and Elizabeth. . . . [T]he Huguenots afterwards maintained that the Massacre of St. Bartholomew was deliberately planned at Bayonne. . . . The rumour shows how contemporaries associated the tragedies . . . of Catherine's religious policy with the splendid fetes that marked its phases.[23]

The "magnificence" staged on the Wednesday following the marriage between Henry and Margaret involved the irenic nature of the union between Catholic and Protestant, Valois and Navarre. An allegorical combat *Paradis d'Amour* was staged in the Salle de Bourbon of the Louvre, depicting the attempted assault on Paradise by errant knights, Henry of Navarre and the Huguenots—the Protestant forces—who were defeated and cast into hell by King Charles and his two brothers—the Catholic forces. However, upon the intercession of the nymphs who had been saved from abduction, the royal brothers released their captives, thus testifying to the conciliatory power of love as found in the Navarre–Valois wedding.[24] But

[21]Margaret McGowan, "Introduction," *Le Balet Comique, by Balthazar de Beaujoyeulx: A Facsimile* [1581] (Binghamton, New York: Medieval and Renaissance Texts and Studies, 1982), 36.
[22]Strong, *Splendor*, 133–37.
[23]Frances Yates, *The French Academies of the Sixteenth Century* (1947; rpt. Nedeln, Liechtenstein: Kraus Reprint, 1968), 254.

on the second day of the entertainment, a more ominous presentation took place, a tilting match between the Valois brothers, costumed as Amazons, and the Huguenots, dressed as Turks, indicating perhaps their status as unbelievers. On the next day, Coligny was wounded, and the violence escalated into the massacre during the weekend of August 23 and 24.

After the massacre occurred, Protestant writers retrospectively concluded that the treachery had been planned from the outset and that the fete involving the Huguenots dressed as Turks attacked by the royal family symbolically mirrored and introduced the ensuing carnage. Simon Goulart, author of *Memoires de L'Estat de France sous Charles Neuviesme . . .* (1578), believed that the plans for the massacre had been drawn up at Bayonne and that they initially involved the actual murder of the Huguenot leaders during one of the dramatic presentations:

> he [Goulart] regards the *Paradis d'Amour* as a very menacing performance. . . , a prophecy of the massacre. . . . [T]he charging of court entertainment with the dynamics of contemporary theology and politics . . . reached a terrific intensity. A romantic tourney of knights before ladies. . . . The knights are Huguenots and Catholics fighting for heaven.[25]

Ironically, the marriage intended to terminate religious conflict produced an event which haunted Protestants for decades and became a rallying cry for their resistance to the Counter-Reformation.

Even after the horror and infamy of the St. Bartholomew's day massacre, Catherine did not give up her "magnificences." The final festival took place in 1581 to celebrate the wedding of Henry III's favorite, Anne, duke of Joyeuse, and Marguerite, sister of Henry III's wife, Queen Louise of Lorraine, on September 24. However, this entertainment differed from the preceding ones because it was not directed primarily toward conciliation between antagonistic religious factions, but was intended to ally the French crown with the ultra-Catholic Guise faction. Nevertheless, the subject matter of the spectacles involved the traditional themes of the healing power of love and the calming of man's passions through music and dance. The climax of the series was, appropriately, *Le Balet Comique de la Reyne*, which epitomized Catherine's past irenic aims and pointed to the

---

[24]Strong, *Splendor*, 149–50.
[25]Yates, *French Academies*, 256.

unfounded hope that civil war would be eliminated. In *Le Balet Comique* Henry III defeats Circe, the enslaver of men, and serves as an embodiment of the cardinal virtues who symbolically vanquishes the dragon of civil war that has attacked France for decades.[26]

In addition to allying the Valois line with the ultra-Catholic faction, another purpose of the Joyeuse fetes was the attempt to arrange a union between France and England through the marriage of Queen Elizabeth and Duke Francis of Anjou (Alençon). In England, Anjou participated in the "barriers" festival, which demonstrated how love and destiny had brought the prince to Elizabeth. However, the contemplated marriage between Alençon and Elizabeth aroused the staunch opposition of English Protestants, who remembered the tragedies resulting from the dynastic marriages between Catherine de' Medici and Henry II, Philip II and Queen Mary, and Margaret and Henry. Denouncing the proposed union of Elizabeth and the "frog prince," John Stubbs compared the horrible repercussions of the marriage of Alençon's parents, Catherine and Henry, to the evils which descended upon Judah after the wedding of King Jehoram and the wicked Athaliah, daughter of Jezebel and Ahab:

> whoso matcheth with any wicked race do make themselves . . . partakers of the sins of that race. . . . And the match of France with the Italian Athaliah and her furies in that land, especially those at the marriage of her daughter Margaret, will . . . prove the sin and punishment of such wicked . . . matches between Christian true Jews and Popish bastard Israelites.[27]

Similarly, Sidney warned Elizabeth not to marry Alençon because "common people will know . . . that he is the sonne of that Jezabel of our age: that his brothers made oblacion of their owne sisters mariadge the easier to make massacres of all sexes."[28]

Elizabeth's persistence in pursuing the Alençon match served to strengthen Protestant memories of the Catholic persecution under Queen Mary and Philip II and the bloodshed resulting from the Catholic–Protestant marriage in Paris in 1572. As A. G. Dickens explains, the two past wed-

[26]Strong, *Splendor*, 155, 159–64.
[27]Stubbs, *Discoverie*, 14.
[28]Sir Philip Sidney, *A Discourse of Syr. Ph. S. to the Queenes Majesty*, in *The Prose Works of Sir Philip Sidney*, 3 vols., ed. Albert Feuillerat (London: Cambridge University Press, 1912), 3:52.

dings and the proposed one were joined in the English popular mind as a threat to national identity and independence.[29] Stubbs reflects these fears when he denounces Alençon's family as cruel Roman emperors and representatives of Babylon:

> This man [Alençon] is a son of Henry the Second, whose family, ever since he married with Catherine of Italy is fatal . . . to resist the gospel, and have been . . . one after another, as a Domitian after Nero, . . . a Trajan . . . , and . . . Julianus . . . , whose manifest cruelties . . . against God's church have been severally sealed with his visible marks of vengeance, written not upon the wall, but successively on their carcasses with a heavenly finger . . . insomuch as Belshazzar [Henry II], the father, had his *Mene* graven in the apple of his eye. . . . His first son [Francis] had his *Tekel* told in his ear, which had rotted him while he was yet alive. And his next son [Charles IX] had his *Peres* marked in every vent of his body.[30]

Thus, Stubbs places the "crimes and punishment" of the Valois line within a Danielic context, just as Kyd has depicted Hieronimo's act of vengeance against the "French tragedians" as the divinely sanctioned stroke against France and Babylon/Spain.

Kyd's dramatic action, staging, and characterization are influenced by the contemporary accounts of the St. Bartholomew's massacre and the Valois program of civil and religious fetes. In the bower murder scene, the lovers are betrayed by Bel-imperia's servant Pedringano, whom she describes "as trusty as my second self" (2.4.9). With the connivance of Pedringano, the assailants enter the bower and create the "murd'rous spectacle" (2.5.9), the "bloody corpse dishonour'd here" (21).

Pedringano's betrayal and the subsequent murderous spectacle of the hanged corpse parallel the descriptions of the betrayal of Coligny and the defiling of his corpse as contained in the accounts of Dowriche, Estienne, Golding, Hotman, and Marlowe. Assigned to protect the wounded Coligny

---

[29]A. G. Dickens, "The Elizabethans and St. Bartholomew," *The Massacre of St. Bartholomew: Reappraisals and Documents* (Hague: Martinus Nijhoff, 1974), ed. Soman, 68.

[30]Stubbs, *Discoverie*, 22–23.

after the first attempt on his life, the treacherous Marshal Cossin instead allowed the attackers to enter Coligny's room:

> Cossin when he sawe the noblemen drawe neere, knocked at the gate, which . . . he was commaunded . . . to kepe. Whereupon many applyed the olde proverbe, A goodly guarde to make the woolfe keeper of the sheepe. When he . . . entered without . . . any difficultie, he carried in with him a great companie of armed men.[31]

After stabbing Coligny to death, his assassins threw his body out the window to the courtyard below and the duke of Guise stamped on it exultantly. Later, the mutilated body was placed on the Montfaucon gallows—Marlowe calls it "this tree" (10.11)—where it became a spectacle for mocking onlookers, including the royal family:

> what a beautifull spectacle this was, for so noble princes to behould. . . . I can not conceave to what extent she [Catherine] dyed it, onlesse it were to embolden them in all kinds of bloudy cruelty, and so to frame them to her own nature, which is such, that no kinde of tyrannous sight, can so far quaile hir cruel kind, as therein to diminish her pleasure . . . , or to cause her to absent her self, from the presence of the same.[32]

The final playlet scene also parallels some of the motifs contained in the accounts of Catherine de' Medici's role in the massacre and in the creation of the fetes. The union between Spain and Portugal as represented by the marriage of Bel-imperia and Balthazar is the analogue to the disastrous weddings in contemporary history which haunted the English consciousness: the union of Philip II and Queen Mary, that of Henry of Navarre and Margaret of Valois, as well as the contemplated union of the duke of Alençon and Queen Elizabeth. Hieronimo reverses the effects of these weddings, which resulted in Catholic persecution of Protestants, by killing the representatives of Catholic Spain–Portugal, Italy, and France during and after the wedding playlet.

---

[31]Hotman, *Report*, liv.
[32]Estienne, *Discourse*, 102–3.

Hieronimo alludes to the Paris marriage of Henry and Margaret and the Elizabeth–Alençon affair by having Bel-imperia speak in courtly French during the playlet—"because . . . / Bel-imperia hath practised the French / In courtly French shall all her phrases be" (4.1.177–78). Unlike the Valois–Navarre marriage and the Alençon–Elizabeth situation, Bel-imperia and Balthazar share the same religion, but Bel-imperia turns against Balthazar by helping Hieronimo to cause the fall of Babylon/ Spain–Portugal. In this way, she becomes an analogue of Queen Elizabeth, the image of "beautiful power," "Phoebe, Flora, or the Huntress" (4.1.148), and, in the final judgment scene, the virgin goddess of justice Astraea rewarded with an Elysian apotheosis—"I'll lead my Bel-imperia to those joys / That vestal virgins and fair queens possess" (4.5.21–22). [33]

The motif of the real deaths, being effected within a dramatic production celebrating a dynastic marriage, fits the context of the reversal, by Hieronimo, of the Valois fetes promoted by Catherine. The allegations that the Bayonne fete of 1565 was the origin of a plot to actually kill Protestants, and that the symbolic war between Protestants and Catholics in the "Paradis d'Amour" fete in 1572 was a planned introduction to the Paris massacre underlie the motif that Hieronimo employs in the "Soliman and Perseda" playlet. This motif stresses the difficulty of distinguishing between the play and reality. In the historical context of the 1572 massacre, the distinction between drama and reality was erased as the fetes, ostensibly intended to promote harmony between the warring religions, led directly to the brutal slaughter of Huguenots. Similarly, Hieronimo presents a playlet in which his enemies will serve as actors who do not know that they are participating in a real tragedy, with their actual deaths as its purpose. Although Hieronimo's ostensible roles in the play and playlet are that of the Spanish lord marshal and the Turkish bashaw respectively, he is in fact the representative of Protestant England, who joins with the "beautiful power" of Elizabeth to defeat Babylon/Spain within a dramatic context that he has created and controlled, with the exception of Bel-imperia's decision to commit suicide.

For these reasons, Hieronimo emerges as the foil to Catherine de' Medici in her role as author, director, and stage manager of the Paris massacre. As Stubbs commented: "the mother, as setter-forth of this earnest game, stood holding the book (as it were) upon the stage and told her chil-

dren and every other player what he should say." Hieronimo sets forth the
earnest plot of turning the playlet celebrating the marriage of the Spanish
king's niece into a lamentable last act—from the Iberian perspective—by
controlling the book and assigning all the parts. Catherine had the
wounded Coligny and his supporters lodge in the same building as ostensible protection against further attacks, but her real reason, according to
Hotman, was "that within the space of one houre all the enimies may be
slayne, and the whole name and race of those wicked men be utterly
rooted out." In the playlet, Hieronimo is so sharp of wit that "in one
hour's meditation" (4.1.165) he performs anything in action, destroying
the lines of accession to the Iberian thrones and causing the Spanish king
to lament "I am the next, the nearest, last of all" (4.208). Similarly, as
Stubbs pointed out, Catherine, after the deaths of her husband and four
sons, was the last of her line.

In the aftermath of the St. Bartholomew's day massacre, Catholics
and Protestants produced works defending the necessity for the action or
decrying its perfidy. French Catholics hailed the event as a providential triumph, a preventive strike against Protestant forces intending to attack
Paris during the wedding of Henry and Margaret. On the other hand, Protestants placed the event within an apocalyptic context which contained
the promise that God would revenge the martyred Huguenots in the
unfolding of time. Jacob Brocardo, who divided history into apocalyptic
periods or seasons, asserts that the St. Bartholomew's massacre marks the
end of the fifth and the onset of the sixth and final season, and he identifies "the universal murders [begun] in *Fraunce* in . . . 1572 the 24 of
August" as the second of the three woes described in Revelation 8 and 9.[34]
Dowriche has Coligny on his deathbed apocalyptically denounce the
treachery of the Catholics:

> Though yet you do not feele the sentence that is due
> . . . yet know that you shall rue
> Your breach of . . . faith . . . ;
> There is a God . . . that will revenge our smart.[35]

[34]Jacob Brocardo, *The Revelation of S. Jhon Reveled*, tr. James Sanford (London, 1582),
95v.

[35]Dowriche, *Historie*, 26v.

Similarly, in *The Massacre At Paris*, Navarre uses the same reference (Rev. 6:9–10) as Hieronimo does (4.1.33–34) to promise that God "will revenge the blood of innocents" (1.44). Predictably, when Charles IX died at the age of twenty-four, two years after the massacre, Dowriche declared that ". . . Charles . . . from Gods revenging hand / By bloodie death, repaies the blood he shed within his land."[36]

Kyd drew upon these sources for the historical subtext of his allusion to the Paris massacre and for the action and staging in some key scenes, as I have shown. However, the work which provides the most significant philosophical and metadramatic parallels to Kyd's use of the massacre is Theodore Agrippa d'Aubigné's epic poem *Les Tragiques*, which was written between 1574 and 1600, but not published until 1616. D'Aubigné, poet-prophet, scholar, and politician, traces the history of the Huguenots during the civil wars, denouncing the Valois princes, the chambers of justice, and the Catholic martyrdom of the Huguenots. Kyd may have known *Les Tragiques* in manuscript or by reputation; d'Aubigné's apocalyptic Protestantism closely resembles Spenser's nationalism and anti-Catholicism in *The Faerie Queene*, and Kyd may have imbibed this influence from his former Merchant Taylors schoolmate. Whatever the source of the influence, it is certain that d'Aubigné, Spenser, and Kyd share the highly charged Protestant apocalyptic fervor of the time and use similar themes and methods to convey their convictions.

Les Tragiques consists of seven books, 9,302 lines, and it represents d'Aubigné's efforts to console his fellow Huguenots by recording their unmerited suffering and bravery.[37] Like Calvin, d'Aubigné believes that God works in mysterious ways, but that in the course of time the good will be rewarded and the evil punished. The epic poem receives unity from its apocalyptic structure, style, and content, all of which point to the justification of God's chosen people: "*Les Tragiques* is a poetic vision in which the sense of history, past, present, and future becomes manifest and through which the destiny of the Huguenots as the modern chosen people is made known. . . . In the Revelation of St. John d'Aubigné found a correspondence between the situation of the early Christians in Rome and that of the Huguenots in France."[38] D'Aubigné uses apocalyptic imagery to

---

[36]Ibid., 36v.

[37]Keith Cameron, *Agrippa d'Aubigné* (Boston: G. K. Hall, 1977), 39.

[38]Richard Regosin, *The Poetry of Inspiration: Agrippa d'Aubigné's "Les Tragiques"* (Chapel Hill: University of North Carolina Press, 1970), 14–15.

connect his villains with the Antichrist; Catherine, the Pope, and Philip II are related to the emperor Nero, and all of them are contrasted with the just Protestant ruler Queen Elizabeth.

Throughout the poem, d'Aubigné creates a sense that justice will be accomplished in the Last Judgment rendered by a vengeful God. Like Kyd, d'Aubigné uses the apocalyptic image of the faithful waiting for the divine vengeance which must come.[39] At the end of the fifth book, which contains the gruesome account of the Paris massacre, d'Aubigné presents God as the unsleeping revenger:

> Vous saurez que toujours son ire ne sommeille,
> Vous le verrez debout pour rendre la pareille,
> Châtier de verveine ou punir par le fer
> Et la race du ciel et celle de l'enfer.   (5.1,561–64)

In sum, the poem represents God's revelation of the destiny of the Protestant people to the divinely inspired author who will show that providence will lead to the fall of Babylon:

> Venge ta patience en l'aigreur de ta peine:
> Frappe du ciel Babel: les cornes de son front
> Défigurent la terre et lui ôtent son rond.
>   (1.1,378–80)

Although the work is an epic poem, it also qualifies as a *tragedia cothurnata* dedicated by d'Aubigné to Melpomene (1.79). Each of the books serves as an act in a play, offering a series of tableaux of the present, the past, and the future, on earth and in heaven. D'Aubigné pictures the world as a stage—"ce triste échafaud" (1.76)—on which the tragic history of the French civil wars takes place with God and the angels as both spectators and actors and the Huguenots as protagonists. The angels create tableaux of the French civil wars which are viewed by Admiral Coligny and the Huguenot martyrs who have ascended to heaven and now watch the events which led to their deaths and apotheosis.[40] In this way, the entire work becomes a play-within-the-play which is watched by various audiences with different perspectives.

---

[39] Agrippa d'Aubigné, *Les Tragiques* (Lausanne: Editions Rencontre, 1968), 4.53.
[40] Imbrie Buffum, *Agrippa d'Aubigné's Les Tragiques* (New Haven: Yale University Press, 1951), 54.

The first perspective is that of the otherworldly audience consisting of God and his angels, who are the authors and unseen actors in the play, and Admiral Coligny and his fellow martyrs who constitute the elect reviewing the course of historical events which they experienced on earth. Now they are in heaven able to see the events retrospectively and to discern the destiny leading to the triumph of the good and the punishment of the evil. Further, d'Aubigné declares in "Aux Lecteurs" that he has included in *Les Tragiques* certain "apopheties" (385), prophecies of events that already have occurred, to enhance his role as prophet-poet.

Admiral Coligny serves as the focal member of the elect audience. He is presented as the Protestant hero, the analogue to the Roman hero Scipio the Younger who, in Cicero's *De Republica,* ascends to heaven in a dream and foresees the future success he will have (2.1,428–36). D'Aubigné parallels Coligny to Scipio as the Protestant martyr who is killed and ascends to heaven where he obtains a superior perspective on the earthly action which he now sees as a comedy for the Huguenots and a tragedy for their antagonists.

The next perspective is that of the French Catholics and royal family who look upon the autos-da-fé which they create and attend as comedies, not tragedies (3.613–24). This audience is blind to the sufferings of the Protestants and to the final outcome of these sacrifices—the tragedy which will be theirs when God punishes them in the Last Judgment. They are participants in a play, but not as the superior audience they see themselves as; there is a celestial audience watching and evaluating their actions:

> From this vantage point [the otherworldly perspective], the Catholic bankers and judges, and the zealots present at the *autos-da-fé* are only spectators to a play within a play. They are the audience to a spectacle which is at the same time a microcosmic reflection of the larger universal drama and a small scene in it. . . . From the celestial vantage point, the Admiral is a spectator to a dramatic comedy: the characters are of lower station than the Elect. . . . [T]he essential action progresses from misery on earth to eternal happiness in Heaven.[41]

The fifth book, *Les Fers,* contains the gruesome description of the Paris massacre. As in the Book of Job, Satan asks God to allow him to

[41]Regosin, *Inspiration*, 47.

tempt people on earth, and, granted permission, he enters the body of Catherine de' Medici, who sets in motion the slaughter of the Huguenots. As he approaches his depiction of this event, d'Aubigné sees his pen as the future apocalyptic sword of vengeance: "Dieu met en cette main la plume pour écrire / Ou un jour il mettra les glaives de son ire" (5.307-8). D'Aubigné places the massacre within a dramatic context as dawn draws back the curtains and the deadly spectacle is enacted before the heavenly audience. The evil Charles IX and his decadent mistresses stand at the windows of the Louvre overseeing the tragedy unfolding below them. They laugh at the victims, and d'Aubigné compares their sadistic delight to the cruel pleasures of Neronian Rome when the slaughter of people was turned into a cruel spectacle for the enjoyment of debauched audiences:

> Cependant que Néron amusait les Romains
> Au théâtre et au cirque à des spectacles vains,
> Tels que ceux de Bayonne . . . .   (5.963-65)

After the horrors of the massacre have occurred, book 6, *Les Vengeances*, presents the punishments visited upon biblical, Roman, and contemporary Catholic tyrants who have persecuted God's people. In the process of drawing the analogy between past and present tyranny, d'Aubigné links Nebuchadnezzar, Nero, Charles IX, and Philip II as evil rulers punished by God. Opposed to their perfidy is Queen Elizabeth, the epitome of the beneficent and powerful ruler under the protection of God, who has enabled her to defeat the Spanish Armada:

> Les mers avec les vents, l'air haut, moyen et bas,
> Et le ciel, partisans liés à tes combats,
> Les foudres et les feux choquent pour ta victoire,
> Quand les tonnerres sont trompettes de ta gloire.
>   (3.982-85)

In the final book, *Jugement*, God gives d'Aubigné, who has been narrator, historian, and writer of the poem, the right to administer the Last Judgment. In this way, the poet, through his tragic and epic poem *Les Tragiques*, becomes the instrument of divine justice (7.7-10). The poet possesses the "pacquet à malheurs ou de parfaicte joye" (22), which enables him to separate the elect from the damned. After depicting the horrors to be endured for all eternity by the wicked Catholics and the joys to be experienced by the triumphant Protestants, d'Aubigné undergoes the apotheosis foreshadowed by Coligny's ascent and the reference to the

Dream of Scipio. The present and the future have been joined to create a timeless eternity consisting of the Protestant comedy and the Catholic tragedy. D'Aubigné has created an apocalyptic tragicomedy which has revealed, through the agency of divine inspiration, the providential course of history in strife-torn Renaissance France.

Kyd's debt to d'Aubigné primarily involves religio-political, generic, and metadramatic concerns. Like Kyd, d'Aubigné, using the Apocalypse as the source of much of his imagery, structure, and analogues, writes a Book of Revelation which shows the Protestants the process of destiny leading to the accomplishment of God's justice and the fall of Babylon. Under the rubric of the hated Whore of Babylon, Kyd and d'Aubigné gather the same enemies: Nero, Catherine de' Medici, Philip of Spain, and the Pope. Both authors invite their audiences to share the superior perspective of their otherworldly audiences in order to see how past events have led inevitably to the Protestant comedy and the Catholic tragedy. Of course, d'Aubigné is the more obviously committed Protestant writer than Kyd who places his play within the mystery context and adopts the pose, through his author-figure Hieronimo, of the hierophant initiating the elect audience into the secrets of providential design. D'Aubigné borrows the techniques of the English martyrologist John Foxe, presenting in book 4 a series of grisly descriptions of the torture and murder of Huguenots;[42] by contrast, Kyd's Protestant apocalypticism belongs to his covert subtext, which can be discovered by deciphering the political mystery.

Les Tragiques and *The Spanish Tragedy* also share generic qualities of high tragic import. D'Aubigné dedicates his poetic epic to Melpomene and calls it a *tragedia cothurnata*. Similarly, Kyd identifies *The Spanish Tragedy* by analogy with the "Soliman and Perseda" playlet as a

> stately-written tragedy,
> *Tragedia cothurnata*, fitting kings,
> Containing matter, and not common things.
>
> (4.1.159–61)

Ultimately, when viewed from the perspective of their Last Judgment scenes, the two works are tragicomedies, as the seeming victims of Catholic tyranny become the elect, and the forces of Antichrist who have held sway are changed into the victims of God's apocalyptic wrath.

[42]Tresley, "Commentaries," 102–3.

Further, both works are essentially plays-within-the-play which contain otherworldly perspectives on the dramatic action. Although Andrea, unlike Scipio and Coligny, undergoes a descent to the underworld followed by a return to earth, he too sees in a dream and a play a destiny which leads to the justification of his friends, the damnation of his enemies, and his own apotheosis. At the end of the play, Andrea is given the right to assign the rewards and punishments, just as d'Aubigné, who is an actor in his own work, is given the right to judge the elect and the damned.

The limited perspectives of the villainous audiences in the various plays-within-the-play of both works are similar. In *Les Tragiques* when the debauched Catholic audiences watch the autos-da-fé, they imagine they are seeing comedies without actual deaths, but they are surprised later when they experience the tragedy imposed on them for their callous treatment of the Huguenots. Similarly, in *The Spanish Tragedy* when the onstage audience of Iberian royalty attends the "Soliman and Perseda" playlet they think they are watching a playlet with no real consequences, but they are in fact witnessing the deaths of Lorenzo, Balthazar, and Belimperia. Both audiences see only playacting instead of the tragic reality thrust upon them.

By means of terse and covert allusions to past precedents, Kyd creates an historical context for Hieronimo's act of vengeance. In the Pisonian, Pazzi, and Paris conspiracies, the forces of Antichrist defeated their antagonists: Nero and Lorenzo de' Medici avenged their attempted murders with savage cruelty, and the Catholic rulers of France slaughtered their Protestant enemies during an ostensibly irenic marital and dynastic union. Hieronimo reverses these past events by killing the contemporary representatives of Babylon at the court of Spain. In the final two chapters, I will trace the manner in which Kyd creates the subtext for the allusion to the climactic plot which Hieronimo will defeat—the attempt by Philip II to conquer England in 1588.

7

The *"Annus Mirabilis"* of 1588: Apocalypse and Armada

$\mathcal{T}$HE SECOND HALF OF the sixteenth century was marked by a sense of apocalyptic gloom caused by dire geological and astrological portents and pessimistic numerological, philosophical, eschatological, and historical arguments. Many observers believed that the world was in an irreversible process of decay as evinced by "a supposed decline in the fruitfulness of the soil and the vigor of vegetation, in the corruption of the air, in a decline in man's physical strength, length of life, stature and moral inclinations, in the alterations of the natural course of the heavens."[1] The "alterations of the natural course of the heavens" included the appearance of the nova of 1572, the comet of 1577, the earthquake of 1580, and the ominous conjunction of planets in 1583, 1588, and 1593. Moreover, as Douglas Bush has argued, the scientific improvements in tracking the heavens and the proliferation of conflicting philosophies concerning the nature of the world exacerbated the Renaissance strain of pessimism about man's earthly tenure.[2]

The eschatological arguments for the approaching doom were linked inextricably with the practice of numerological prophecy. The books of Daniel and Revelation contain puzzling references to symbolic periods of time such as 1,260, 1,290, 1,335, and 2,300 days, seventy weeks, and five and forty-two months which allude to the advent, reign, and fall of Antichrist followed by the establishment of Christ's monarchy. With the success of the Protestant Reformation and the concomitant decline in papal

---

[1]Bauckham, *Tudor Apocalypse*, 152.
[2]Douglas Bush, *English Literature in the Earlier Seventeenth Century* (New York: Oxford University Press, 1945), 278.

power, many Protestants believed that Babylon/Rome would mount a counterattack culminating in a decisive battle equivalent to the Armageddon predicted in Rev. 16:16. Hence, there was an increased interest in the calculation of the date of the imminent conflict.

The years 1583, 1588, and 1593 were singled out as the fateful dates for the fulfillment of the apocalyptic prophecies, but it was 1588 that received the most attention because of the currency of a verse predicting that it would be the *annus mirabilis*. Misattributed to Regiomontanus, the famous mathematician and astrologer who had died in 1475, the prophetic verse was written by Kaspar Brusch, the German humanist, historian, and poet, who expanded four lines of German doggerel into eight lines of elegant Latin in 1553 which declared "Octogesimus octavus mirabilis annus."[3] In 1564, Cyprian Leowitz used Brusch's Latin verses as proof that the world was ending in his *De conjunctionibus magnis*, which was reprinted throughout Europe and became the direct means of the popularization of the prophecy, first translated into English in 1569 by John Securis in *A Newe Almanacke and Prognostication*. In his translation of Sheltco à Geveren's *Of the End of this Worlde, and second comming of Christ . . .* , which was published in 1577, 1578, 1582, and 1589, Thomas Rogers reproduced the prediction:

> When after Christs birth there be expirde
> Of hundreds, fifteene yeeres, eightie and eight,
> Then comes the time of dangers to be feard,
> And all mankind with dolors it shall freight:
> For if the world in that yeere do not fall,
> If Sea and Land then perish, ne decaie,
> Yet Empires all, and kingdomes alter shall,
> And man to ease himselfe shall have no way.[4]

The prediction for 1588 was analyzed in important treatises on numerological and astrological prognostications. In *An Astrological Discourse . . .* , Richard Harvey declares that the fateful year 1588 "is now so rife in every mannes mouth and was so resolutely defended as a publique disputation in the laste Commencement. . . . Astrologers . . . have . . . prognosticated . . . a marvellous feareful and possible alteration of Em-

---

[3]Qtd. in Walter Stone, "Shakespeare and the Sad Augurs," *JEGP* 52 (1953): 460.
[4]Geveren, *End of World* (1589), 18v.

pyres, Kyngdomes, . . . togither with other wonderful . . . Accidents."[5] In *A Discoursive Probleme concerning Prophecies*, Richard's brother John emphasizes the fame and ominousness of the prophecy, which "is universally more feared . . . than all . . . togither, as being more credibly, or probably grounded upon some surer foundation of lawfull Art."[6]

Some Protestant writers place their predictions for 1588 within an optimistic apocalyptic context, changing the projected doom to the inevitable triumph of Christ over the Antichrist. Helisaeus Reslyn describes the propitious significance of the conjunction of Saturn and Jupiter in 1588: "Wherefore seeing the 7 conjunction is now imminent, . . . it is surely to be judged that seaventh and last time of the Apocalypse to be at hand, wherein Christ with the two edged sword, and spirit of his mouth, being to destroy the beast with the pseudo-prophet, shall deliver his church."[7] In his addendum to Richard's treatise, John Harvey declares that in 1588 "some . . . cruell Antichrist, some . . . irreligious Mahomet . . . shall arise . . . who wil furiously assault the holy citie of Jerusalem. . . . But he that keepeth Israel, shal . . . [not] sleepe: . . . Adonay . . . wil confound this helhound . . . to his . . . overthrow and confusion."[8]

Other Protestant commentators divide history into a series of apocalyptic cycles of multiples of seven and ten, with the climactic year of 1588 marking the fall of Babylon. In 1576 James Sandford predicted that the final cycle of seventy years, the length of the Babylonian Captivity, would be completed in 1588 by the release of Protestantism from captivity: "the Captivitie of Babylon endured 70 yeares, whiche may be thought to prefigure the Captivitie of the Gospel in these later dayes: for from the yeare of Our Lorde 1518 in the which Martine Luther began truely to preache Gods word . . . to 1588 are just 70 yeares, in the which . . . some greater thing shall bee done."[9] Geveren cites the numerological parallels between the cycles beginning with Christ's life and the final one culminating in 1588 as proof of God's "wonderfull mysterie,"[10] which will mark the advent of

[5]Richard Harvey, *An Astrological Discourse upon the great and notable Conjunction of the two Superiour Planets, Saturne and Jupiter* . . . (London, 1583), 44.

[6]John Harvey, *A Discoursive Probleme concerning Prophecies* (London, 1588), 88.

[7]Helisaeus Reslyn, *Theoria nova coelestium meteorum* (1578), qtd. in ibid., 105.

[8]John Harvey, *An Astrological addition, or Supplement to be Annexed to the Late Discourse* (London, 1583), C4r–v.

[9]Lodovico Guicciardini, *Houres of Recreation* . . . , tr. James Sandford (London, 1576), A5r–v.

[10]Geveren, *End of World* (1589), 20r.

the golden age when he will establish his perfect justice: "With everie 500 and . . . fiftie yeere there doe commonly happen some singular alterations in the Church and commonweales . . . the eightie eight yere now at hand, which is the yere of the world, 5550 shal bee fullie perfect. . . . And therefore . . . do seeme to presage . . . a golden worlde . . . everlasting . . . , in which the justice of God shal be fulfilled."[11]

Inevitably, Spain, according to English Catholic and Protestant apologists, interpreted the fateful year of 1588 as the time for its destined victory over England. In *An Admonition to . . . England . . .*, Cardinal William Allen denounces English Protestants for making Elizabeth "a verie nationall idol . . . and [for] blaspheminge the other [King Philip], . . . as a . . . devill or Antechriste."[12] Citing a series of glorious Catholic triumphs as precedents, Allen declares that

> for the greatnes of power given him by the almighty, . . . for the infinite injuries . . . done to his majestie and people by *Elizabethe*, and . . . for his speciall pietie and zeale towardes Gods house and the See Apostolike . . . , his majestie wold take upon him in the name of God almightie, this sacred and glorious enterprise.[13]

Protestant apologist James Lea argues in *A True . . . description of a straunge Monstar borne in . . . Rome . . .* that Philip's invasion plans were encouraged by the militant Holy League, so that "in the saide yeare of 88 there should be but one king, one pastor and one flocke, the interpretation whereof they apply, the King, to be Phillip of Spayn, the pastor to be the Pope, and the flocke to be al people and nations of . . . Europe."[14] Francis Marquino summarizes the delusory and doomed apocalyptic desires of Spain when it sent the Armada against England with the grandiose motto "Exurge, domine, et vindica causam tuam":[15]

[11]Ibid., 34r–v.

[12]William Allen, *An Admonition to the Nobility and People of England . . . Concerninge the Present Warres made for the execution of his Holines' Sentence, by the highe and mightie Kinge . . . of Spaine* (Antwerp, 1588), vi.

[13]Ibid., xlix.

[14]James Lea, *A True . . . description of a straunge Monstar borne in . . . Rome . . .* (London, 1590), A3r.

[15]Garrett Mattingly, *The Armada* (Boston: Houghton Mifflin, 1959), 215.

the Spanish nation, is at hir highest degree, and shalt therefore no more ascende but descend: Because she goeth about not only to take and invade hir neighbours countries, but she dare say, she will have the fift Monarchie, that onely appertaineth to Jesus Christ, who will give it to whom it pleaseth him, and will not give it unto them: but . . . he will give it unto Englishmen, which have received him.[16]

The victory over the Spanish Armada in 1588 gave England assurance that it was the divinely favored nation in the struggle with Babylon/Spain and the Antichrist. English biblical commentators considered the Armada defeat as the fulfillment of the predictions concerning 1588 and the numerological and eschatological prophecies contained in Daniel and Revelation. In the expanded introduction to the 1589 edition of Geveren's *Of the End of this worlde . . .* , Thomas Rogers explains that Geveren's calculations have been confirmed because

> A yeere admired is eightie eight, by fall of Popish
>   crue:
> And happie deemd by good successe.[17]

In his own work, *An Historical Dialogue Touching Antichrist and Popery . . .* , Rogers asserts that *"He that seeth not a speciall regard of God towardes us, . . .* and an angrie countenance on th'other side . . . as upon the whore of Babilon described by S. John is verie blind."[18]

Protestant apologists conflate the destruction of Babylon and the Tower of Babel to describe the defeat of the Armada. Daniel Archdeacon compares Philip II to Nimrod, the builder of the ill-fated Tower of Babylon, "who hath by hys ships, made like Babel towers, vaunted himselfe to make us afraid."[19] James Lea repeats the word *confounded* to signal the fall of Babylon/Rome:

> We knowledge thee [the Pope] to bee confounded.
> Al the earth judgeth thee to be the father of confusion. . . .

[16]Francis Marquino, *A Politike Discourse most excellent for this time present . . .* (London, 1589), A1v.

[17]Geveren, *End of World* (1589), A2v.

[18]Thomas Rogers, *An Historical Dialogue Touching Antichrist and Poperie . . .* (London, 1589), 90.

[19]Daniel Archdeacon, *A True Discourse of the Armie which the King of Spaine caused to bee assembled . . . in . . . 1588, against England* (London: John Wolfe, 1588), 8.

> Confounded, confounded, confounded: Lord of
> Babaloth.[20]

Rogers also declares that universal confusion has been brought upon Babylon/Spain by its defeat: "the God of Gods had them in derision, and brought . . . in the publique view of th'universall world most horrible confusion upon them all."[21]

Certain aspects of the battle against the Spanish Armada were interpreted as reenactments and fulfillments of the visions depicted in the Apocalypse. John Napier parallels the destruction in one hour of Babylon's great ships (Rev. 18:7) to the overthrow of the Spanish "marriners with their great Galliasses . . . of that Antichristian flote who . . . in 1588 . . . have been so redie . . . to have overwhelmed us."[22] Jean Baptiste Morel argues that the defeat of the Armada was predicted in Rev. 15:2 (the sea of glass mingled with fire), and the blood in which the robe of Christ is dipped (Rev. 19:13) is the blood shed by the Spanish slain by the English.[23] Finally, Edward Hellwis equates Queen Elizabeth in her role as victorious monarch with the "woman clothed with the sunne, and the moone . . . under her feete, and upon her head a crowne of twelve starres" (Rev. 12:1, 118v): "Time, revealer of hidden secrets, delivereth demonstration that God . . . hath erected the woman . . . in the twelfth chapter of the revelation . . . , that nowe . . . by Gods great favour . . . [is] placed . . . in strange enterprises by Sea to bee atchieved and . . . happily finished."[24] Hellwis says that this woman, whose name he can not divulge—but whose identity, paradoxically, is obvious to the reader—"hath revealed the holie misteries . . . of God . . . and unto . . . [her] the Lord . . . hath given power" to overthrow "this foresaid Dragon and his Antichrist."[25]

---

[20]James Lea, *An Answer to the Untruthes Published and Printed in Spaine in Glorie of their Supposed Victorie . . . against our English Navie* (London, 1589; rpt. New York: Da Capo Press, 1969), 30.

[21]Rogers, *Historical Dialogue*, 74.

[22]Napier, *Discovery*, 223n.

[23]Jean Morel, *De Ecclesia ab Antichristo liberanda; eaque ex Dei promissionibus reparanda* (London, 1594), A4v–6r.

[24]Edward Hellwis, *A Marvell Deciphered, An Exposition of the 12th Chapter of Revelation* (London, 1589), B1v–B2r.

[25]Ibid., 2, 7.

In addition to the exegetical celebration of the apocalyptic significance of the English victory over Spain, the importance of the Armada
defeat was marked by public ceremonies, iconographic commemorations,
and historical and literary accounts of the battle and its heroes. There were
many English celebrations of the victory, but perhaps the most significant
one was held at St. Paul's Cathedral on November 24, 1588, when "the
Queen's Majestie . . . was carried . . . in a tryumphant chariot . . . unto the
Cathedrall Church of St. *Paul*, out of the which the ensignes and colours
of the vanquished Spaniards hung displayed. . . . Her Majestie . . . together
with her Clergie and Nobles gave thanks unto God."[26] The Armada victory
was hailed also by the coining of money commemorating the sea battle.
Meteren remarks that "upon the one side . . . was represented a ship fleeing, and a ship sincking: on the other side foure men making prayers . . .
unto God . . . with this sentence: *Man purposeth; God disposeth*, 1588."[27]
Similarly, William Camden describes new coins stamped "with a Fleet
flying with full Sails, and this inscription, *Veni, vidit, fugit* . . . ; others in
Honour of the Queen, with Fire-ships and a Fleet all in Confusion,
inscribed, *Dux foemina facti*, that is, A Woman was Conductour in the
Exploit."[28]

The victorious Lord Admiral Charles Howard supervised the making
of diagrams, charts, maps, and drawings reconstructing the various sea
battles between the Armada and the English fleet. He also commissioned
two Dutch artists, the designer Hendrick Vroom of Haarlem and the
weaver François Spierincx of Delft, to create from Augustine Ryther's
engravings ten spectacular tapestries, measuring from nineteen to
twenty-nine feet in width and fifteen feet in length. These sumptuous
wall hangings reconstruct the specific engagements with such detail that
the viewer can follow the battles from beginning to end. In the borders of

---

[26]Emanuel van Meteren, *The miraculous victory atchieved by the English Fleete . . . Upon
the Spanish huge Armada*, tr. Richard Hakluyt, *Elizabethan Backgrounds: Historical Documents
of the Age of Elizabeth I . . .* , ed. Arthur Kinney (Hamden, Conn.: Archon Books, 1975), 273–
74.

[27]Ibid., 273.

[28]William Camden, *The History of the Most renowned and Victorious Princess Elizabeth
Late Queen of England Selected Chapters*, ed. Wallace MacCaffrey (Chicago: University of Chicago Press, 1970), 327.

each tapestry appear portraits of the leading commanders, with Howard occupying the central position along the top edge.[29]

In the highly nationalistic period following the victory of 1588, more pamphlets were produced about the battle and its significance than on any other event in Elizabeth's reign.[30] The most popular account is *The Copie of a Letter Sent Out of England to Don Bernardino Mendoza* (1588), which received three English editions and was translated into French and Italian. Supposedly written by an anonymous English Catholic to the former Spanish ambassador concerning the actual state of England after the defeat of the Armada, this pamphlet was a highly propagandistic encomium to English power and stability written by William Cecil. The anonymous pamphlet *A Relation of Proceedings* (1588), a detailed account of the various sea battles and the roles of the English leaders and the names of their ships, was translated into Italian by the Florentine Petrucchio Ubaldino and then retranslated into English as *A Discourse Concerning the Spanish Fleet Invading England in the year 1588* (London, 1590). Daniel Archdeacon's *A True Discourse of the Armie which the King of Spaine caused to bee assembled . . . in 1588* contains authoritative lists of Spanish leaders and their squadrons.

The most detailed and objective account of the Armada defeat is provided by Emanuel van Meteren's Latin treatise *The miraculous victory atchieved by the English Fleete . . . Upon the Spanish huge Armada*, which was translated by Richard Hakluyt in his 1598 edition of *The Principal Navigations, Voyages, . . . and Discoveries of the English Nation*. The chronicle histories of Elizabeth's reign by William Camden, John Speed, and John Stow also provide graphic reconstructions of the Armada defeat, including analyses of the strengths of the Spanish and English leaders and their ships.

Aware of the apocalyptic and historical significance of the 1588 victory and supplied with the details of the struggle from the numerous accounts and the letters from the English commanders preserved in the state papers, Protestant writers created literary works which combine classic myth, contemporary history, and native and maritime legend.[31]

---

[29]Bryce Walker, *The Armada* (Alexandria, Virginia: Time–Life Books, 1981), 132; Robert Kenny, *Elizabeth's Admiral: The Political Career of Charles Howard Earl of Nottingham 1536-1624* (Baltimore: The Johns Hopkins Press, 1970), 160.

[30]Meteren, *Elizabethan Backgrounds*, 239.

[31]Elkin C. Wilson, *England's Eliza* (1930; rpt. New York: Octagon Books, 1966), 287.

Learned poems in many languages were written to honor Elizabeth as Gloriana, Queen of the Seas, favored by God in her struggle against Catholic Spain.[32] Armada poems published in England also emphasize the divine championing of England against the superior Spanish forces. In his long poem entitled *The Blessedness of Brytaine, or A Celebration of the Queenes Holyday . . . Newly set foorth with a New Addition Containing the Late Accidents and Occurrents of this yeare 88 . . .* (1588), Maurice Kyffin declares that Spain mistakenly believed that God was on its side, but Catholic corruption caused God to favor England. Immediately after the defeat of the Armada, Thomas Deloney issued three broadside ballads describing the capture of the Spanish commander Don Pedro de Valdes, Elizabeth's inspiring visit to the camp at Tilbury, and the inhuman tortures prepared by the Spanish sailors for the English in the event the Armada won. Deloney maintains that the English victory was achieved through "the mighty power and providence of GOD . . . to the great encouragement of all those that willingly fight in the defence of His Gospel and our good Queen of England."[33]

In 1588, James Aske wrote *Elizabetha triumphans . . .* in which he describes Elizabeth's stirring speech to the army at Tilbury and the naval battle with Spain, whose "bigge-made Barkes with huge and mightie Mastes, / Like Churches . . . with steeples very high,"[34] were defeated by little England aided by the winds of God. Three additional volumes of Armada poetry were issued in 1589. The first of these, published in Oxford and London, was the anonymous *Skeltonicall Salutation*, an amusing satire on Spanish military and religious arrogance. The second one was Christopher Ockland's *Elizabetheis. . . . In quo, praeter caetera, Hispanicae classis profligatio, Papisticarumque molitionum et consiliorum hostilium mira subversio, bona fide explicantur.* The Cheltenham schoolmaster Ockland glorified the Tudors so successfully in his three-volume Latin history (1580, 1582), of which the *Elizabetheis* is the third volume, that his works were prescribed by the Privy Council as required reading in the schools.[35] The

[32]Leicester Bradner, "Poems on the Defeat of the Armada," *JEGP* 43 (1944):447–48.

[33]Thomas Deloney, "A joyful new Ballad declaring the . . . obtaining of the great Galleazzo, wherein Don *Pedro de Valdes* was the chief," *An English Garner: Tudor Tracts 1532–1588*, ed. Edward Arber and rev. Thomas Seccombe (1877–90; rpt. New York: Cooper Square Publishers, 1964), 485.

[34]James Aske, *Elizabetha triumphans* (London, 1588), 28.

[35]Leicester Bradner, *Musae Anglicanae: A History of Anglo-Latin Poetry 1500–1925* (New York: Modern Language Association of America, 1940), 37.

third book published in Geneva, a collection of Greek and Latin poems entitled *Triumphalia de victoriis Elisabethae . . . contra classem instructissimam Philippi Hispaniarum . . .* , contains a poem by the pseudonymous N. Eleutherius, who declares that the prophecy for 1588 has been fulfilled by "vastis / Vasta cadat Babylon ruinis."[36]

Two Latin poems by Thomas Watson and Thomas Campion place their treatments of the Armada conflict within an infernal context. In the sixth eclogue of *Amintae Gaudia* (1592), Pluto and Jupiter engage in an epic struggle described as a chess game. Pluto objects to Jupiter's announcement of the birth of Elizabeth as Astraea and the return of the golden age to England, because these events will deprive him of evil souls. Ultimately Pluto, who, as Bradner says, represents Satan and Philip II, is defeated.[37] Like Watson, Thomas Campion, in his long Latin poem *Ad Thamesin* (1595), depicts Spain as the representative of the devil in its attack against Protestant England. The epic work gets its title from the poet's congratulations to the Thames upon its deliverance from the Spanish threat. Most of the poem describes the devil's attempts to incite Spain into attacking England. Before the Armada sails, the Spanish are feted at a hellish banquet during which they vow to conquer England. However, the Armada is defeated and Elizabeth's glory celebrated.[38] In both of these works, the Armada is connected with underworld machinations and infernal conclaves, whereas in *The Spanish Tragedy*, the spirit of Revenge arises from the underworld to prophesy mystically the English victory over Spain-Portugal.

Other English Armada poems include William Warner's *Albion's England*, and William Wodwall's *The Acts of Queen Elizabeth*. Written from 1586 to 1606, Warner's recital of English history and legend declares that Spain was defeated because "God did patronize our Ile."[39] Wodwall's long poem presents the conflict between Spain and England under Elizabeth in the form of an allegory pitting the World, the Flesh, and the Devil against Conscience, whom they are trying to dispossess from Castle Coeur (England). The opposition between these characters is depicted in six

[36]Qtd. in Stone, "Sad Augurs," 476.
[37]Bradner, *Musae Anglicanae*, 48–49.
[38]Ibid., 53.
[39]William Warner, *Albion's England: A Continued Historie of the same Kingdome, from the . . . first Inhabitants . . . unto and in, the happie Raigne of . . . Queene Elizabeth* (London, 1596), bk.9, chap. 48, p. 226.

assaults, each of which forms a separate canto. The climactic sixth canto concerns the victory over the Armada, which results from the providence of God.[40]

The most important poem influenced by the Armada is Edmund Spenser's *The Faerie Queene,* the allegorical epic dedicated "To the Most Mightie and Magnificent Empresse Elizabeth, by the Grace of God Queene of England, France, and Ireland Defender of the Faith."[41] There is evidence, as critics have pointed out, that Spenser revised *The Faerie Queene* near the end of the 1580s to reflect the Armada victory.[42] The overthrow of the Souldan by the power of the magic shield has been interpreted as the defeat of the Armada at sea through divine providence (5.8.28–45). René Graziani has associated the Souldan's Phaeton-like loss of control over his horses with Philip II's *imprese* depicting Apollo driving his chariot across the heavens.[43] Spenser turns Philip's own image against him by undermining its claim to imperial power. Graziani also relates the Souldan's chariot "With yron wheeles and hookes arm'd dreadfully" (28) to the ships of the Armada and the lightning flash from Arthur's shield (37–38), which causes the Souldan's horses to bolt, with the fire ships that the English sent against the Spanish Armada. Similarly, Angus Fletcher maintains that "[t]he Souldan's chariot horses stampede, out of control, like the galleons of Medina Sidonia blown by the 'protestant wind.'"[44] Other episodes involving the struggles against the three Spanish giants Geryoneo, Grantorto, and Orgoglio have been interpreted as representing "the victory of . . . Protestantism over . . . Catholicism."[45]

The war against the Spanish Armada was viewed by some writers as a drama enacted upon the stage of history before the world. The attempted invasion of England contained all of the ingredients for a heroic drama: the powerful Catholic country, Spain, assembling a huge fleet to subdue

[40]Wilson, *England's Eliza,* 326.

[41]Edmund Spenser, "Dedication to *The Faerie Queene*" (1590), *The Complete Poetical Works of Spenser,* ed. R. E. Neil Dodge (Boston: Houghton Mifflin Company, 1980), 130.

[42]Tresley, "Commentaries," 19n.

[43]René Graziani, "Philip II's *Impresa* and Spenser's Souldan," *JWCI* 27 (1964): 322–24.

[44]Fletcher, *Prophetic Moment,* 210.

[45]S. K. Heninger, "The Orgoglio Episode in *The Faerie Queene*," *Essential Articles for the Study of Edmund Spenser,* ed. A. C. Hamilton (Hamden, Connecticut: Archon Books, 1972), 133.

little England, which nevertheless defeats the Spanish Whore of Babylon and Antichrist with the help of divine providence and excellent military leadership. John Harvey had anticipated the dramatic context for this war when he predicted that "there want not some probable . . . significations . . . of a Tragedy insuing in this world, . . . as hath not often been . . . upon this mortall stage and fraile Theater."[46] In his long poetic encomium *Englands Eliza . . .* (1610), Richard Niccols depicts God as author and director of the Spanish tragedy:

> Great *Joves* command, perform'd upon the foes,
> Th'*Eolian* King call'd home his windes againe;
> Then ceast the storme; then did the seas disclose
> The armes, the painted robes, and spoiles of
>   Spaine, . . .
> Where *Jove* did act their fleets black tragedie.[47]

And at the end of *The History of Great Britaine . . .* (1611), John Speed calls the Spanish defeat and English victory in 1588 a "*Tragico-Comedy.*"[48]

Elizabethan writers also saw the Armada defeat as a revenge tragedy in which God punished the Spanish for their overweening pride and greed. In *A True. . . description of a straunge Monster. . . ,* James Lea depicts God as the unsleeping revenger who causes the fall of Babylon/Spain: "he that keepeth Israel doeth neyther slumber nor sleepe. Babell is falling. . . . [T]he righteous God hath revenged our wronges on the proudest of our foes."[49] Thomas Nun extols God as the revenger who sends the destructive winds and actually participates in the battle: "Mightie was thine armie as was *Baracke*, but Jehovah would have the glorie as then hee had, his windes revenged thy quarel. . . . Jehovah . . . thou wast our man of warre on that day."[50] John Speed describes how God punished the arrogance of the "Invincible Armada": "The *Invincible Navie*, and terrour of *Europe*, as the Papals both tearmed and tooke it to bee, . . . loosed Anchor from *Lisbon* . . . and made unto the Groine in *Gallicia* . . . but suddenly the heavens hating such hostile actions, powred doune revenge, by a . . . tempest."[51]

[46]John Harvey, *A Discoursive Probleme*, 130.

[47]Richard Niccols, *Englands Eliza: or The Victorious And Triumphant Reigne of That Virgin Empresse of Sacred memorie . . .* (London: Felix Kyngston, 1610), 838.

[48]John Speed, *The History of Great Britaine . . .* (London, 1611), bk.9, ch.24, p. 863.

[49]Lea, *True description*, 15.

[50]Thomas Nun, *A Comfort Against the Spaniard* (Oxford: John Windet, 1596), C2r.

[51]Speed, *History*, 9, 24, 859.

The nationalism inspired by the rivalry with Spain grew even more fervid after 1588, and it led to an increased interest in the dramatic representation of past and contemporary historical events. As Felix Schelling has argued: "the popularity of the Chronicle Play . . . [had] its origin in the . . . sense of national unity which reached its climax in . . . 1588."[52] Gabriel Harvey reflects the demand for such dramas when he declares in *Pierces Supererogation . . .* (1595) that the heroic exploits of English naval leaders should be presented on the stage:

> The date of idle vanityes is expired: awaye with these scribling paltryes: there is . . . no wanton leasure for the Comedyes of Athens. . . . [T]he winde is chaunged, and there is a busier pageant upon the stage. . . . [R]ead the report of the . . . hoatt welcome of the terrible Spanishe Armada to the coast of Inglande that came in glory, and went in dishonour. . . . [T]he report of the resolute encounter about the Iles Azores, betwixt the Revenge of Ingland, and an Armada of Spaine; in which encounter brave, Sir Richard Grinvile most vigorously and impetuously attempted the extreamest possibilities of valour and fury.[53]

As a result of the upsurge in nationalism and the emphasis on the Armada battle as a revenge tragedy, Elizabethan writers became interested in "dramatizing the repulse of the Spanish Armada."[54] These works contain patriotic allusion, historical parallels, allegorical and symbolical representation, and historical reenactment of the defeat of Spain. The first type of reference is intended as a nationalistic gesture and often concerns the power of England to repel foreign invasions. For example, in Robert Greene's *The Historie of Orlando Furioso* (ca. 1591), King Brandemart praises the power of the Isles to fend off invaders:

---

[52]Felix Schelling, *The English Chronicle Play: A Study In The Popular Historical Literature Environing Shakespeare* (New York: MacMillan, 1902), 39.

[53]Gabriel Harvey, *Pierces Supererogation Or A New Prayse of The Old Asse*, in *The Works of Gabriel Harvey*, 3 vols., ed. Alexander Grosart (1884; rpt. New York: AMS Press, 1966), 2:95–97.

[54]Felix Schelling, *Elizabethan Drama 1558-1642: A History of the Drama*, in *England from the Accession of Queen Elizabeth to the Closing of the Theaters*, 2 vols. (1908; rpt. New York: Russell and Russell, 1959), l:xxxix.

> And what I dare, let say the Portingale,
> And Spaniard tell, who, mand with mightie fleetes,
> Came to subdue my Ilands to their King,
> Filling our seas with stately Argosies,
> . . . hulkes of burden great;
> Which Brandyemart rebated from his coast,
> And sent them home ballast with little wealth.[55]

Brandemart summarizes the defeat of the Armada, destroyed in the attempt to invade the divinely protected British Isles.

In works that lack overt references to the Armada defeat, there may be historical parallels established by the plots and characters. In the anonymous play *Locrine* (1595) Humber has invaded Britain and is victorious until he is conquered by Locrine. Ribner maintains that Humber's lament over his defeat (3.6.1,300–30) contains parallels to the destruction of the Armada.[56] Similarly, E. A. J. Honigman has argued that the plot, characters, and language of Shakespeare's *King John* can be related to the events and characters involved in the attempted invasion of England by the Spanish Armada:

> the pope . . . invites . . . [a] king to invade England (III.i.181), . . . a foreign invasion is attempted (IV.ii.110). . . . [T]heir navy is providentially wrecked off the English coast (V.v.12), English unity being . . . achieved through the failure of the invasion (V.vii.115)—frequent 'Armada idiom' hammering home the topicality of the play.[57]

The third and fourth types of Armada plays are allegorical, symbolical, and historical representations of the Spanish war and the English victory. These include: Robert Greene's *The Spanish Masquerado* (1589); Robert Wilson's *The Three Lords and Three Ladies of London* (1589) and *The Cobler's Prophecy* (1594); Lyly's *Midas* (1591); *England's Joy* (1603); Thomas Dekker's *The Whore of Babylon* (1606); and Thomas Heywood's *If you know not me, You Know No Body, Or The Troubles of Queen Elizabeth* (1606, 1632).

[55]Robert Greene, *The Historie of Orlando Furioso, One of the Twelve Peeres of France*, *The Life and Complete Works of Robert Greene in Prose and Verse*, 15 vols., ed. Alexander Grosart (1881–86; rpt. New York: Russell and Russell, 1964), 13:89–96.

[56]Ribner, *History Play*, 240.

[57]William Shakespeare, *King John*, ed. E. A. J. Honigman (London: Methuen, 1959), xxix.

They form a subgenre within the larger genre of chronicle or history plays, and they are meant to celebrate onstage the magnificent victory over the Spanish Armada, which was defeated by its own pride and divine providence.

Greene's *Spanish Masquerado* is a highly symbolic treatment of the destruction of the Spanish Armada, replete with anti-Catholic and apocalyptic imagery.[58] Although *The Spanish Masquerado* is not a play, its title reveals its masquelike characteristics as Greene presents twelve emblematic scenes with Latin mottos which are followed by extensive glosses. The twelve "devises" concern the defeat and lamentations of the Pope (characterized as the Beast of the Apocalypse), Philip II (the Pope's tool), Roman Catholic cardinals, clergy of Spain and Rome, Spanish nobility and military leaders, Don Martines de Ricaldo (duke of Medina), and Don Pedro de Valdes. The second scene presents Philip II who, persuaded by the papal Antichrist, "provideth a great Armado, his Shippes huge and monstrous, his men the chosen Cavaliers of *Spaine, Portugal, Italie,* and other Provinces. . . . God hearing their great braves against him and his people . . . scattered them as dust before the wind."[59] God encouraged the forces of Antichrist to attack England "to shew them [the Spanish] that he favoreth his people, and useth revenge against the despisers of his Gospell" (257).

Greene refers to the conflict between Spain and England in terms of heraldic designs and portents, which seemed to point to a Spanish victory, until the English leaders under God's direction defeated the Armada:

[the Spanish] Hierogliphicall Simbols, Emblems, impresses, and devises, did prognosticate (as they supposed) their triumphant victorie, and our . . . miserable overthrowe, . . . [They] no sooner came alongst our Coaste, and were encountred with our Fleete, filled with Noblemen of invincible courage, . . . our Lord Admirall, the Lord *Charles Howard.* . . . Next . . . , the terrour of *Spaine,* . . . Sir Francis Drake.   (271–72)

In sum, Greene presents the Armada defeat as a divine revenge play with God effecting vengeance against Babylon/Spain: " God who holdeth revenge in his hand, let loose the windes and threw a storme into the sea,

[58]Robert Esler, "Robert Greene and the Spanish Armada," *ELH* 32 (1965):331.
[59]Greene, *Works,* 5:255.

that any of their shippes which escaped our handes, perished on the
Rockes: using the Sea for revenge, as he did against Pharao . . ." (275).

Robert Wilson wrote the allegorical Armada play *The Three Lords and
Ladies of London*, a sequel to his *The Three Ladies of London* (ca. 1587), for
the queen's company in 1589. The three ladies, Love, Conscience, and
Lucre, are joined by three lords, Policy, Pomp, and Pleasure, in a patriotic
play showing the defeat of the Armada as symbolized by the three Spanish
lords, Pride, Ambition, and Tyranny. Much of the play involves preparation for the coming of the Armada and the allegorical description of the
virtues and vices representing the Spanish and English forces. The Spanish
march onstage and Pride has a peacock as his "impress . . . the word *Non-
pareil*; his Page, SHAME, . . . having a pendant gilt with this word on it, *Sur
le Ciel*. AMBITION, his impress a black horse saliant, with one hinderfoot
upon the globe of the earth, . . . his word *Non sufficit orbis*."[60]

Tyranny and his page Terror are accompanied by the herald Shealty
whose "coat must have the arms of Spain before, and a burning ship
behind" (462). When the English virtue Policy asks Shealty the significance of the burning ship on his shield, he replies: "To signify the burning
of your fleet / By us Castilians" (470). After the defeat of the Castilians, the
play concludes with the marriage of the three lords and ladies, and a prayer
is said for the queen who receives all blessings and bestows them upon
England.

Wilson's *The Cobler's Prophecy* (1594) is, as David Bevington has
explained,[61] an Armada play which concentrates on the domestic factions
within England at the time of the Armada attack. The details of the victory
are related summarily near the end of the play by the Messenger with no
attempt to reconstruct the battle as Wilson had done in *The Three Lords
and Three Ladies of London*. Boetia defeats its unnamed enemy because it
is favored by the gods, who finally rouse the country to martial fervor
after a protracted period of unrest.

In its emphasis on the role of the gods in the destined Boetian victory, *The Cobler's Prophecy* parallels *The Spanish Tragedy*, but, unlike Kyd's
play, the gods are actors in as well as observers of the dramatic action. The
play begins with a heavenly council convened by Mercury, who is dis-

---

[60]Robert Wilson, *The Three Lords and Three Ladies of London*, in *A Select Collection of
Old English Plays* (1744), ed. W. C. Hazlitt (London: Reeves and Turner, 1874), 6:461.

[61]David Bevington, *Tudor Drama and Politics: A Critical Approach to Topical Meaning*
(Cambridge: Harvard University Press, 1968), 192-94.

turbed by Venus' deceiving of Mars, whose languor and indifference to Boetian affairs have produced turmoil in that country. To resolve the situation, Mercury makes the humble cobbler Raph a prophet and his wife Zelota a madwoman who commits the divinely sanctioned murder of Ennius, a disloyal lord who attempts to kill the duke. In a doggerel prophecy, Raph predicts that Ruin, the illegitimate offspring of the lustful union between Venus and the vice Contempt, will dominate the country until Mars regains his traditional fierceness. When this occurs, Boetia, led by the veteran soldier Sateros, defeats the attempted invasion.

In its simple depiction of the enactment of the will of the gods, *The Cobler's Prophecy* parallels Pickering's *Horestes* in which Horestes' revenge is approved by the country's leaders as an act of beneficial nemesis restoring the nation to order. In *The Cobler's Prophecy*, Raph is raised to the role of national prophet and his wife, driven mad, is given the right to commit murder through "the secret judgement of the Gods."[62] Similarly, Hieronimo becomes the representative of England in his revenge playlet, and his murder of his son's killers, which has been seen as an act of homicidal madness, is the divinely sanctioned defeat of England's enemy, Spain.

John Lyly's play *Midas* (1589) also concerns the role of prophecy in the struggle with Spain. *Midas* is an allegorical depiction of Philip II's desire to control the world through the amassing of wealth and power. Midas, King of Phrygia, wishes to turn everything that he touches to gold because he believes that money corrupts everyone and that it will help him conquer all the countries he wants to dominate, especially the island of Lesbos, or England under Elizabeth. However, once given the golden touch, Midas discovers that he still cannot conquer the brave and incorruptible people of Lesbos, who are "protected by the Gods, by Nature, by . . . vertue ."[63]

After receiving asses' ears for choosing Pan over Apollo in a music context, Midas consults the Delphic oracle to find out how to rid himself of the ears. Apollo responds plainly, "because thou art dul" (5.3.79), that Midas must stop trying to conquer Lesbos. Midas, paradoxically, sees this plain prophecy of Apollo as a "darke answere [which] is to mee the glistering of a bright sunne. I perceive . . . that Lesbos will not be touched by gold, by force it cannot: that the Gods have pitched it out of the world, as

[62]Robert Wilson, *The Cobler's Prophecy* (London: Malone Society Reprints, 1914), 1647.
[63]John Lyly, *Midas, The Complete Works of John Lyly*, 3 vols., ed. R. Warwick Bond (1902; rpt. London: Oxford University Press, 1967), 3:3.1.54.

not to bee controlde by any in the world" (99–103). Thus, Midas learns to read a mysterious yet plain riddle which tells him not to conquer Lesbos/ England. Unlike his historical counterpart Philip II, who used prophecy as a spur to his doomed invasion of England, Midas avoids defeat by heeding Apollo's prophetic warning.

The next work, an allegorical treatment of England's glorious victories under Elizabeth, may never have been performed. C. W. Hodges explains that the only evidence we have of this play is the description of *The Plot of the Play called England's Joy* contained in a playbill. In 1602, Richard Venner promised to put on the play described in the playbill at the Swan, but he vanished with the gate receipts without providing the production. However, Hodges argues that even this "dud prospectus" reveals a great deal about the nature of such symbolic representations of history.[64] The sixth scene "whereupon is set forth the battle at Sea in '88, with Englands victory" could have been performed in the ground yard.[65] Hodges concludes that the symbolic scenes resemble *tableaux vivants* and the entertainments at Kenilworth and Elvetham, and in keeping with such pageants, the final scene involves an apotheosis of the queen, who is crowned in heaven as she sits on the Throne of Honour, while "beneath . . . the stage . . . divers black and damned souls, [are] wonderfully described in their several torments."[66]

Thomas Heywood's *If You Know Not Me, You Know Nobody . . .* is a straightforward account in two parts of various aspects of Elizabeth's reign, including the various plots against her, the establishment of Gresham's Royal Exchange, and the defeat of the Armada. In the second part, subtitled *With the Building of the Royall Exchange: and the famous Victories of Queene Elizabeth in the Yeare 1588*, the Spanish invasion of the "fateful year" is described:

> The proud Spaniard . . . sends forth a fleet,
> Three whole yeares in preparing, to subvert,
> Ruine, and quite depopulate this land.
> Imagine you now see them under sail,

---

[64]C. Walter Hodges, *The Globe Restored: A Study of the Elizabethan Theatre* (London: Ernest Benn Ltd. 1953), 48–49.

[65]Ibid., 49, 185.

[66]Ibid., 162.

Swell'd up with many a proud, vainglorious boast,
And newly enter'd in our *English* coast.[67]

The Spanish leaders, Don Medina Sidonia, Pedro de Valdes, John Martinus Ricaldus, and others, enter to brag about the ease with which they will invade small and powerless England. Medina calls upon Ricaldus to relate the "potency of . . . our great Armado, / Christend, by th'Pope, the Navy Invincible" (335). Elizabeth assembles her troops at Tilbury and asks Lord Hunsdon to assess the Spanish fleet: "there's a power above both them and us, / That can their proud and haughty menaces / Convert to their owne ruins" (338). After the three posts dutifully recite the progress of England's victory over Spain, Sir Francis Drake issues the roll call of victorious English ships, including his own flag ship the *Revenge* (343). Queen Elizabeth attributes the victory to God:

And to the audience in our name declare
Our thanks to Heaven, in universal prayer,
For though our enemies be overthrown,
'Tis by the hand of Heaven, and not our own. (343)

The history of Elizabeth's reign culminates in the defeat of the Armada.

The last and most complex of the Armada plays in this group is Thomas Dekker's *The Whore of Babylon*, which combines apocalyptic, allegorical, symbolic, and historical elements "to set forth (in Tropicall and shadowed collours) the . . . Heroicall vertues of our late Queene . . . and . . . the inveterate malice . . and . . . bloody strategems of that Purple whore of Roome."[68] The play begins with a dumb show which presents the death of the Catholic Queen Mary and the accession ceremony of Elizabeth during which she receives the Bible, and Truth, the daughter of Time, is restored. Indebted to the Antichrist plays of Bale and Foxe and *The Faerie Queene*, *The Whore of Babylon* recounts the various plots against the faerie queen, Titania (Elizabeth), by the Empress of Babylon, who finally sends the Armada against England:

---

[67]Thomas Heywood, *If You Know Not Me, You Know Nobody* . . . in *The Dramatic Works of Thomas Heywood*, 6 vols., ed. R. H. Shepherd (1874; rpt. New York: Russell and Russell, 1964), 1:333.

[68]Thomas Dekker, *The Whore of Babylon*, in *The Dramatic Works of Thomas Dekker*, 4 vols., ed. Fredson Bowers (1953; rpt. London: Cambridge University Press, 1962), 2:1–6.

> vast *Argozies,*
> Huge Galeasses and such wooden Castles,
> As by enchantment on the waters move:
> . . . a brave *Armado,* such a Fleete,
> That may breake *Neptunes* backe to carry it.
>   (3.1.251–56)

As England prepares to withstand the attack, Time promises to take revenge against Babylon:

> I'll flie hence to the fleete of *Babylon.*
> And from their tacklings and their mainemost tops,
> *Time* shal shoote vengeance through his bow of
>   steele. . . .
> Ile cut their Princes downe as blades of grasse,
> As this glasse, so the Babilonian power,
> The higher shall runne out to fill the lower.
>   (5.3.56–58, 60–62)

During the battle, the Spanish leaders behave cowardly and soon are defeated. The vanquished empress chastises her leaders and declares that "Never was day to me thus *Tragical,* / Great *Babylon* thus lowe did never fall" (5.6.137–38).

Judith Spikes has cogently argued that these history plays, along with *Henry VIII, Sir John Oldcastle* (ca. 1600), and *Thomas Lord Cromwell* (1602), belong to an emerging national myth of England as God's elect nation which would defeat the Antichrist and cause the fall of Babylon.[69] Based on the apocalyptic structure of history as delineated in John Foxe's *Acts and Monuments* and Bale's commentary on Revelation and his Protestant morality and history plays, they are characterized

> by a philosophy which viewed world history as the temporal
> manifestation of the cosmic warfare, of God's Elect . . .
> against . . . Antichrist. . . . [T]he action . . . ends when the good
> character or his cause triumphs, not a victim of fate but its
> instrument, in an action not tragic but tragicomic, as is the
> action of the Christian drama itself. . . . [T]hey . . . find their

---

[69]Judith D. Spikes, "The Jacobean History Play and the Myth of the Elect Nation," *Renaissance Drama* 8 (1977): 119.

context and their meaning—as did the mystery and miracle plays . . . they resemble—as late-Reformation versions of the religious drama.[70]

In the Armada plays, the defeat of Spain in 1588 becomes the culmination of the apocalyptic course of history leading to England's apotheosis as the elect nation.

Similarly, *The Spanish Tragedy* is an apocalyptic history play which culminates in Hieronimo's defeat of Babylon/Spain within the fateful revenge playlet. As the representative of Kyd and England, Hieronimo fulfills the prophecy with which Revenge began the play and toward which the action has inevitably led. In the last chapter, I will detail the specific ways in which Kyd draws upon contemporary interpretations of the *"annus mirabilis"* to symbolically represent the defeat of the Spanish Armada in 1588, with Hieronimo serving as the analogue to Lord Admiral Charles Howard, who, along with Sir Francis Drake, captain of the *Revenge*, led England to victory.

[70]Ibid., 118–19.

8

The Spanish Tragedy as Armada Play: The Triumph of English Revenge

THE SPANISH TRAGEDY IS DOMINATED by the sense of destiny achieved in the unfolding of time. Prophecies are made, and then we watch them being fulfilled through a series of events which are revealed to be inextricably connected and inexorably directed toward the accomplishment of destiny. The characters in the earthly play-within-the-play are unaware of the unfolding providential design, but Revenge, who represents Kyd, and Proserpine as the embodiment of destined revenge, show Andrea and the theater audience how to interpret the play as the revelation of the mystery of divine providence. Revenge issues the prophecy that Balthazar will be killed by Bel-imperia, and at the end of each of the first three acts, Revenge promises to lead Andrea's enemies to their punishment, which is imposed on them at the conclusion of the fourth act when they are sentenced to their "endless tragedy."

Connected with the motif of the fulfillment of prophecies is the topos of *Veritas filia temporis*. When Hieronimo and Isabella discover their son's corpse in the bower, Isabella expresses her faith that "[t]ime is the author both of truth and right, / And time will bring this treachery to light" (2.5.58–59). However, they are not aware that truth is coming to light as we learn in a series of judgment scenes that appear on one level to be entirely fortuitous but ultimately are seen to be fated.[1] Alexandro is condemned to death because, according to Villuppo, he has killed Balthazar. But the Portuguese ambassador arrives with the letters from Spain

---

[1]Ardolino, *"Veritas Filia Temporis,"* 57–60; Ronald Broude, "Time, Truth, and Right in *The Spanish Tragedy,"* SP 68 (1971): 130–45.

proving that Balthazar is still alive and that Alexandro has been falsely accused. As a result of the truth about the past revealed in the letters, the viceroy releases Alexandro and condemns Villuppo.

Similarly, when Hieronimo searches for the identities of his son's murderers, Bel-imperia's letter, written in her blood, drops almost miraculously from above, telling him the truth about Horatio's murder. But he cannot give credence to its revelations until he has further proof, which is furnished by the incriminatory letter found on Pedringano's body by the hangman. Having learned the truth about the past, Hieronimo now revises his lost student play into a version of the immediate past and fulfills destiny through his writing. The onstage Iberian audience remains confused about the reasons for Hieronimo's revenge, but the theater audience understands that it has witnessed the process by which destiny is fulfilled on earth.

The scheme of truth coming to light in the play is related to the political theme of the Elizabethan accession as the onset of truth in England after the persecution and confusion of her Catholic sister's reign. In the processional pageant occurring on the day before her coronation on January 14, 1558, Elizabeth was associated with "Truth, the daughter of Time." Truth was led from a cave by old Father Time, and she gave Elizabeth a copy of the English Bible, which had been banned during Mary's reign. In this way, Elizabeth's succession was depicted as the coming to light of truth in the course of time.[2] Kyd uses this temporal scheme in connection with writing as the instrument of its accomplishment. The letters from Portugal, Pedringano's posthumous letter, and Bel-imperia's bloody letter all serve as the means of revealing the truth. Finally, Hieronimo's playlet, translated into English and endowed with apocalyptic significance, becomes the means of achieving the vengeance which fulfills the nationalistic ethos of the play.

In creating the temporal scheme of the past being repeated in the present and both leading to an inevitable future, Kyd is presenting a future which has already been accomplished. This technique is found in Tudor history plays which announce the future as if it had not happened already and then have it accomplished during the play. The Elizabethan theater audiences realize that they are being shown a version of their past

---

[2]Soji Iwasaki, "*Veritas Filia Temporis* and Shakespeare," *ELR* 3 (1973):251–52.

presented as a future to be fulfilled. Marjorie Garber has explained the nature of this temporal paradox:

> The history play seems to say to the audience: "this is your past." In the experience of the playgoer, however, the past becomes a future: when the audience enters the theater, the historical events are yet to come. The history as such is thus lodged in the paradoxical temporality of what the French call the *future anterieur,* the prior future.[3]

Kyd sets *The Spanish Tragedy* in the recent past, the Iberian rivalry of the 1580s and has the play culminate in the symbolic reenactment of the already accomplished English victory over the Armada in 1588, the *annus mirabilis.* Elizabethan audiences are expected to penetrate the veil of mystery and recognize how and why the events of their shared past have led inevitably to this triumph. In this way, the temporal structure of the play parallels the historical and apocalyptic interpretation of the prophecies concerning 1588. The predictions remained ambiguous about the nature of the events which would take place in the fateful year, but when defeat came to the Armada, England retrospectively interpreted the victory as the fulfillment of its apocalyptic destiny. Everything which had happened prior to 1588 had led inevitably to this end; history had been planned by God as the accomplishment of the apocalyptic defeat of Babylon/Spain. Similarly, the earthly play begins with the prophecy of Balthazar's death, but the ramifications of this prediction, the reasons for it and its connections with the other characters and events to come, are not perceived at that time. However, by the end of the play when the prophecy has been satisfied, we see its full significance; we go back retrospectively and then forward to perceive how everything has led to its accomplishment. As Stillman says of Spenser's use of the defeat of the Armada in the Souldan episode of book 5: "[Spenser] uses the 1588 conflict . . . to adjust our perception of earlier incidents in the struggle against Spanish . . . injustice. The . . . victory reveals itself as a type and a prophecy of the final victory of the English, once one penetrates to the veil that conceals the apocalyptic import . . . and . . . significance of the destruction of the Spanish fleet."[4]

---

[3]Marjorie Garber, "'What's Past Is Prologue': Temporality and Prophecy in Shakespeare's History Plays," *Renaissance Genres: Essays on Theory, History, and Interpretation,* ed. Barbara Lewalski (Cambridge: Harvard University Press, 1986), 306.

[4]Stillman, "Elect England," 222.

Kyd builds an intricate network of analogies between the revenge playlet and contemporary historical accounts and literary depictions of the defeat of the Spanish Armada in 1588. Kyd symbolically reenacts the momentous victory with a series of covert allusions to important people, ships, and events involved in the Spanish war. It is this historical context which makes *The Spanish Tragedy* an integral part of the tradition of Armada works which present the glorious English victory over the Spanish Antichrist.

As with the terse and covert allusions to the Piso, Pazzi, and Paris conspiracies, the Armada subtext fits the mystery rubric, being introduced by the repetition of the signal word *revenge* four times within four lines. Directly before the enactment of the Spanish–Portuguese tragedy in the playlet, Hieronimo recalls the murder of his son and the suicide of Isabella:

> Behoves thee then, Hieronimo, to be reveng'd:
> The plot is laid of dire revenge:
> On then, Hieronimo, pursue revenge,
> For nothing wants but acting of revenge. (4.3.27–30)

Of course, the word *revenge* is repeated four times to signal the onset of the fatal playlet and the accomplishment of revenge. But along with the obvious function of the repetition, there is an incantatory quality, an urging into action of revenge as if it were an embodiment of the forces that Hieronimo represents. Hieronimo's exhortation parallels Andrea's four demands at the end of act 3 that the sleeping Revenge awaken and punish Lorenzo and Balthazar. To silence Andrea, Revenge produced the Hymen dumb show which predicted the death of Andrea and Hieronimo's enemies. Now Hieronimo will fulfill that prophecy by means of his revenge playlet.

The Spanish Tragedy is dominated by revenge: by repetitions of the word *revenge* and its variants, by the ethos of revenge, by the character Revenge who presents the revenge play to Andrea and to us, and by interlocking acts of revenge. With Hieronimo's invocation before the enactment of his playlet, another dimension of revenge is introduced—the role of Sir Francis Drake's flagship *Revenge* in the defeat of the Armada. Ronald Broude has described the connection between the Protestant ethos of revenge, the Armada defeat, and the revenge play:

The Reformation . . . led Englishmen to an intense interest in
the various manifestations of divine retribution and to the
conviction that theirs was an age in which God's vengeance
was . . . turned loose on a degenerate world. . . . [I]n 1588 the
flagship of . . . Drake . . . was named the *Revenge*, suggesting
that she would be one of the instruments through which God
would punish Spain. The revenge play . . . was a most effective
form for the expression of this grim world view.[5]

A naval context analogous to Hieronimo's invocation of revenge
occurs in the masque at Elvetham staged in September 1591 on the estate
of the earl of Hertford. There was a mock battle between the sea gods and
the wood gods, which was precipitated when Sylvanus was pitched into
the water; whereupon Sylvanus emerged and rallied his land troops with
cries of "Revenge, Revenge."[6] After the battle, Neaera asked Elizabeth to
bless her boat, and the queen did so, naming it, after herself, the *Elizabeth
Bonaventure*.

As Bergeron explains, Queen Elizabeth serves as the central presence
in the Elvetham pageant, which uses the mock-battle as the means of
praising her and English military power.[7] In addition, the pageant is
intended, as Boyle and Valentino have argued, to celebrate the victory
over Spain in 1588 and to justify the subsequent naval policies of Lord
Admiral Charles Howard.[8] Boyle links Howard with Nereus, who serves as
the masque presenter and controller and represents naval power as
opposed to the land power of Sylvanus, identified as Jack Norris. Sylvanus'
cry for "revenge" alludes to the loss of the *Revenge* in the battle against the
Spanish Armada in the Azores one month before the Elvetham pageant
was held. Elizabeth's christening of her ship signalled the replacement of
the lost *Revenge* with the *Elizabeth Bonaventure*. The use of revenge as the

[5]Broude, "Three Forerunners," 501–2.
[6]*The Honorable Entertainment given to the Queen's Majestie in Progresse, at
Elvetham . . .* , *Entertainments for Elizabeth I*, ed. Jean Wilson (Totowa, New Jersey: Rowman
and Littlefield, 1980), 110.
[7]David Bergeron, *English Civic Pageantry 1558–1642* (Columbia: University of South
Carolina Press, 1971), 63–64.
[8]Harry Boyle, "Elizabeth's Entertainment at Elvetham: War Policy in Pageantry," *SP* 68
(1971): 146–66; Lucille Valentino, "Playing for Power: The Meanings of Elizabethan Entertainment" (Ph.D. diss., Wayne State University, 1983), 86–96. See also Curt Breight, "Realpolitik
and Elizabethan Ceremony: The Earl of Hertford's Entertainment of Elizabeth at Elvetham,
1591," *RQ* 45.1 (1992): 20–48.

motivation for an allegorical naval battle, the invocation of real ships which were employed in the struggle against Spain, the exaltation of the queen as Astraea and Diana, and the use of Howard in the role of prophetic poet, masque presenter, and victorious leader of English sea power—all these characteristics link the Elvetham pageant with Hieronimo's revenge playlet during which Babylon/Spain–Portugal will be destroyed in a symbolic reenactment of the Armada sea battle with Bel-imperia and Hieronimo serving, respectively, as analogues to Queen Elizabeth and Lord Charles Howard, as will be argued shortly.

Hieronimo's allusion to Drake's flagship prepares the initiated audience to understand the Armada subtext of the revenge playlet. The role of the *Revenge* as a fighting ship was well publicized in Elizabethan accounts of the wars with Spain. The *Revenge* was a specialized fighting ship, weighing five hundred tons, carrying a crew of 250 men, and containing thirty to forty guns of different sizes.[9] The ship was launched from Deptford in 1577, but in the ensuing decade experienced a number of mishaps which gave it a checkered reputation. In 1582, upon returning from Ireland, the ship struck a sandbar and narrowly escaped sinking. In 1586 embarking from Portsmouth harbor it ran aground and was unable to proceed on the journey. And in 1589 while lying in the harbor at Chatam, the *Revenge* was overturned by a sudden storm. But during the wars with the Armada in 1588 and 1591, it performed heroically and became the subject of stirring accounts of the battles.[10] Kyd draws upon these contemporary accounts for his symbolic use of the *Revenge* in *The Spanish Tragedy*.

During the struggle with Spain in 1588, the *Revenge* served as the chief ship of a squadron commanded by Sir Francis Drake, who, along with his ship, achieved renown for daring attacks against the Spanish Armada. Meteren explains that even though the Spanish discharged a "great store of ordinance . . . they [the English] lost not . . . one shippe or person of account . . . albeit Sir *Francis Drake's* shippe was pierced with shot above forty times, and his very cabben was twise shot thorow."[11] In *The Spanish Masquerado*, Greene says that Drake "valiently standing in the

[9]Alexander McKee, *From Merciless Invaders: An Eyewitness Account of the Spanish Armada* (London: Souvenir Press, 1963), 85; Julian S. Corbett, *Drake and the Tudor Navy*, 2 vols. (London: Longmans, Green, and Co., 1898), 1:372n.

[10]Edward Arber, "Introduction," *English Reprints* 8.29 (1871; rpt. New York: AMS Press, 1966), 8.

[11]Meteren, *Miraculous Victory*, 267.

fore roome [of the *Revenge*], delivered with Cannon his Ambassage to the Enemie" (272–73). Heywood describes Drake's brave drawing of Spanish artillery in careful detail

> At his poor single vessel. . . .
> He now finding
> Most of their present fury spent at him
> Fires a whole tyre at once, . . . having emptied
> a full broadside. . . .
> He takes advantage both of winde and tide, . . .
> Scouring along, as if he would besiege them
> With a new wall of fire, . . .
> Insomuch, that blood . . . was seene
> To pour out of their portholes.[12]

In the 1588 pamphlet *A Packe of Spanish Lyes . . .* , the anonymous author is moved by certain rumors about Drake's supposed capture to state categorically that "*Drake* is returned with honour: his shippe called the *Revenge* is in harborow, ready for a revenge by a newe service."[13]

Although the *Revenge* achieved renown in 1588 under Drake, it received even more glory under Sir Richard Grenville for its ill-fated final battle against the great *St. Philip*, "Prince of the twelve Sea Apostles," and the rest of the Spanish Armada in the Azores in 1591. The three contemporary accounts by Raleigh, Markham, and Linschoten emphasize the bravery of the doomed vice-admiral and his ship against the superior forces of the Spanish Armada, which nevertheless suffered great losses. Analyzing the struggle, Francis Bacon explains that even though Grenville died and the *Revenge* was captured and then destroyed, it was, in effect, a victory for the undermanned English:

> In the yeare 1591, was that Memorable Fight, of an *English Ship* called the *Revenge*, under the Command of Sir *Richard Green-vill*; Memorable . . . to the Height of some Heroicall Fable. And though it were a Defeat, yet it exceeded a Victory; Being like the Act of *Sampson*, that killed more Men at his Death, than he

---

[12]Heywood, *If You Know Not Me*, Pt. 2, 339–40.
[13]*A Packe Of Spanish Lyes, Sent Abroad In The World . . . Now . . . , by just examination condemned, as conteyning false, corrupt, and detestable wares . . .* (London: Christopher Barker, 1588), 4.

had done in the time of . . . his Life. . . . This brave ship the
Revenge, being manned only with 200 . . . , after a Fight main-
tained . . . of 15 hours [had] . . . two Ships of the Enemy sunke
by her side; Besides many more torne and battered. . . ; The
Enemies themselves having in admiration the Vertue of the
Commander, and the whole Tragedy of that ship.[14]

Bacon uses the analogy with Samson to describe the *Revenge's* triumphing
in death over its antagonists, just as Kyd has Hieronimo parallel Samson in
his suicide and the destruction of his enemies within a revenge playlet.

In some accounts, the death of Grenville, the destruction of the
Revenge, and the great losses suffered by the Spanish are depicted as a
blood revenge tragedy with God punishing the evil Spanish for their
attack on the English. After the capture of the *Revenge*, the battered ship
was towed by the Spanish until a storm arose and sent it to the bottom of
the ocean along with some of the accompanying Spanish ships. Camden
says, "So . . . the *Revenge* . . . perished not unrevenged, and by this one . . .
victory cost the Spaniards much blood."[15] Richard Niccols writes that
"Englands blacke Revenge, alone at length / Did work him [Don Alonso
Bacan, Captain of the Spanish Fleet] shame with all his navale strength."[16]
In *The Fight and Cyclone at the Azores* (1598), Jan Huygen van Linschoten
has Grenville's body, which had been buried at sea by the Spanish, going
down to hell to raise up the devils in revenge against Spain:

whereby may bee considered what great losse and hinderance
they received at that time . . . [which] was esteemed to be
much more then was left by their . . . Armado . . . that came for
England, and . . . it was no other than a just plague purposely
sent by god upon the *Spaniards*, and that it might . . . bee said,
the taking of the *Revenge* was justlie revenged uppon them . . .
by the power of God, as some of them openly said . . . : saying
further yat so soone as they had throwne the dead bodie of the
Viceadmirall Sir *Richard Greenfield* overborde, . . . hee presently sunke . . . into Hell, where he raysed up all the devilles to

[14]Francis Bacon, *Considerations touching a Warre with Spaine, Certaine Miscellany Works*, ed. Dr. Rawley (1629), 52–53, qtd. in Arber, *English Reprints* 8.29, 8.

[15]William Camden, *Annales: The True and Royal History of the Famous Empresse Eliza-beth . . .* , tr. Richard Norton (London: Benjamin Fisher, 1630), 4:32.

[16]Niccols, *England's Eliza*, 849.

the revenge of his death: and that they brought so great stormes . . . upon the Spaniards.[17]

The accounts of the exploits of Drake and Grenville on the *Revenge* and the allegorical use of its name within revenge drama and naval contexts indicate that Kyd's elect audience would have been attuned to Hieronimo's invocation of this ship within a similar framework. Moreover, as part of this historical subtext, many characters in *The Spanish Tragedy*, excluding Horatio among the major figures, have names related to English and Spanish ships, squadrons, and leaders. The presence of such names tells Kyd's audience that the revenge playlet symbolically reenacts the war with Spain in 1588.

The Elizabethan interpretation of the names of ships as having political significance is illustrated by two accounts of sea battles in which the defeat of the Spanish *St. Philip* is seen as the defeat of Catholic Spain under Philip II. In "a breefe relation of the notable service performed by Sir Francis Drake upon the Spanish Fleete . . . in . . . Cadiz . . . in . . . 1587," Hakluyt explains the importance of the name of the Spanish carack *St. Philip* captured by Drake on his flagship the *Elizabeth Bonaventure*: "this was the first Carak that ever was taken comming forth of the East Indies; which the Portugals tooke for an evil signe, because the ship bare the Kings owne name."[18] Similarly, in *The Most Honorable Tragedie of Sir Richard Grinvile, Knight* (1595), Gervase Markham depicts the *Revenge* as "the scourge which doth controule, / The recreants that *Errors* right applaud," whose victory over "[t]he great *San-phillip*, which all *Spayne* did call / Th'unvanquisht ship, *Iberias* soule and faith," will "her selfe, by name and fame enroule . . . / Within eternall Bookes of happie deeds."[19]

The names of the English and Spanish ships engaged in the wars of 1588 were published in Camden, Speed, Heywood, Greene, and in *A True Discourse of the Armie which the King of Spaine caused to bee assembled in . . . Portugall, in . . . 1588, against England*, and thus would have been familiar to English audiences.[20] The Spanish ships primarily were named

[17]Jan Huygen van Linschoten, *The Fight and the Cyclone at the Azores*, in *English Reprints*, 8.29, 95.

[18]Richard Hakluyt, *The Principal Navigations, Voyages, Traffiques and Discoveries of the English Nation* . . . (New York: E. P. Dutton, 1907), 284–85.

[19]Gervase Markham, *The Most Honorable Tragedie of Sir Richard Grinvile, Knight*, in *English Reprints* 8.29, 63, 66.

[20]For the lists of the English and Spanish ships, I am indebted to John Knox Laughton's collection of the *State Papers Relating to The Defeat of The Spanish Armada* . . . *1588*, 2 vols. (1894; rpt. New York: Burt Franklin, 1971), 2:323–41, 376–87.

after saints, while English ships received allegorical names like *Victory*, *Defiance*, and *Revenge*; biblical names like *Daniel*, *Samson*, and *Solomon*; the names of prominent figures like *Dudley*, *Drake*, and *Leicester*; spiritual names like *Virgin God save her*, *the Gift of God*, and *the Grace of God*; and names derived from the queen like *Elizabeth Jonas* and *Elizabeth Bonaventure*.[21] Andrea's name is found in three Spanish ships, one listed under the "Armada of hulks, whereof Juan Gomes de Medina hath charge" and the others under "Patasses and zabras, whereof Don Antonio Hurtado de Mendoza hath charge." Isabella's name is present as *la Isabela* in the "Armada of Biscay, whereof Juan Martinez de Recalde is Captain-general." The *San Jeronimo* is listed under "Patasses and zabras, whereof Don Antonio Hurtado de Mendoza hath charge," and the *Capitana San Lorenzo*, which will be discussed in greater detail later, appears in the "Galleasses of Naples under the charge of D. Hugo de Moncada." As namesakes for Don Pedro, the brother to the Portuguese viceroy, there are three Spanish ships, the galleon *San Pedro* in the squadron of "Castille, whereof Diego Flores de Valdes is Generall," and the paired hulks *San Pedro Major* and *San Pedro Minor*. The duke of Castile, Don Pedro's counterpart as brother to the Spanish viceroy, is connected with the hulk *Castillo Negro* and with the Castilian squadron of the Armada, consisting of sixteen ships and 4,177 men under the command of General Diego Flores de Valdes.[22]

Although Bel-imperia has no exact nominal naval counterpart, it is possible to relate her to ships named for the queen like the *Elizabeth Jonas* and *Elizabeth Bonaventure*. As Laughton explains, it was the custom to name English ships after the reigning sovereign, and the *Elizabeth Jonas* "was so named by her Grace in remembrance of her own deliverance from the fury of her enemies, from which . . . she was no less miraculously preserved than . . . Jonas from the belly of the whale.'"[23] Just as the naming of the *Elizabeth Jonas* indicated gratitude for the past, so too the christening in 1561 of the *Elizabeth Bonaventure*, which was reenacted in the Elvetham pageant, expressed confidence in Queen Elizabeth's future. Rebuilt in 1581, the *Bonaventure* achieved a long and meritorious service as Drake's flagship and in the wars against Spain in 1588 and 1591.

Bel-imperia, which means "beautiful power," is an analogue to Queen Elizabeth, who serves as Hieronimo's accomplice in the revenge

[21]Marcus, *Puzzling Shakespeare*, 87.
[22]Laughton, *State Papers*, 2:379–81, 397.
[23]Egerton MS. 2642, f.150, qtd. in ibid., 2:334.

playlet in which the fall of Babylon/Spain is accomplished. When assigning her the role of Perseda, Hieronimo tells her to dress "[l]ike Phoebe, Flora, or the Huntress" (4.1.148), mythological figures often associated with Queen Elizabeth. The reference to Diana, the Huntress, may be related to the role of the ship *Diana* against the Armada in 1588.[24]

Although Balthazar, like Bel-imperia, does not have a nautical namesake, there are a number of possible Armada analogies to his name, character, and role in the play. The existence of the English coaster *Daniel*[25] suggests the Danielic context of Balthazar's role as the doomed ruler of Babylon. Secondly, a Spanish adventurer Balthazar de Zuñiga served on the Capitana *General San Martin*, the huge flagship of the commander of the Armada, Duke Medina-Sidonia.[26] When Medina-Sidonia wanted his *Relation* delivered to Philip II, he sent Balthazar de Zuñiga to deliver the letter and to say "[w]hat our armada did thereupon."[27]

The appearance of the all-but-silent Don Pedro, who arrives in Spain for the wedding of Bel-imperia and Balthazar, may also be related to Balthazar as an Armada figure. Don Pedro is mentioned early in the play by the Spanish general who describes how

> Don Pedro, their chief horsemen's colonel,
> Did with his cornet bravely make attempt
> To break the order of our battle ranks.   (1.2.40–42)

Near the end of the play, after witnessing the death of his son Balthazar, the Portuguese viceroy tells his brother Don Pedro to "[t]ake up our hapless son untimely slain" (4.4.210).

The most important Armada figure named Don Pedro was Don Pedro de Valdes, the captain-general of the Andalusian squadron, who was considered by Sir Francis Drake to be "a man of greatest estimation with the King of spain, and thought next in his army to the Duke of Sidonia."[28] Valdes was captured by Drake when his galleon, the *Nuestra Señora del Rosario*, "became foul of another ship which spoiled and bare overboard his foremast and bowsprit, whereby he could not keep company with their fleet, but being with great dishonour left behind by the Duke [Medina-

---

[24]Ibid., 2:327.
[25]Ibid., 2:330.
[26]Archdeacon, *True Discourse*, 36.
[27]Laughton, *State Papers*, 2:369.
[28]Ibid., 1:364.

Sidonia], fell into our hands."[29] In *The Spanish Masquerado*, Greene depicts Valdes as the "surpassing great hope amongst the Spaniardes" (276), whose "Banners and Ensignes which he hoped to have displaied in *England* to our great reprooch, were to his deepe dishonour hanged to the joy of all true English heartes, about the Battlementes and crosse of *Paules*, and on *London* bridge . . ." (279).

Controversy surrounded Don Pedro's capture and imprisonment in England. When his flagship *Nuestra Señora del Rosario* became disabled, Duke Medina-Sidonia attempted to tow it, but as a result of the advice of Diego Flores de Valdes, Pedro's hated cousin, the duke sailed back to the rest of the Armada leaving the *Rosario* a prey to Drake. Don Pedro blamed the duke for deserting him, but when a hearing was conducted in Spain after the Armada returned home, the duke was exonerated and Diego Flores was imprisoned for fifteen months. Pedro's behavior in this affair was also suspect because he made no attempt to repair the damaged ship, and then when Drake attacked he did not return fire and surrendered meekly.[30]

Despite his capture of the rich prize of Valdes' flagship, Drake received criticism for leaving the English fleet to plunder the helpless ship.[31] Martin Frobisher became particularly incensed at Drake concerning the division of the spoils of the *Rosario*, to which he felt he had a legitimate claim because of the help he gave Drake in the battle against the *Rosario* and the accompanying ships:

> Further, saith he [Drake], he hath . . . took Don Pedro. For after he had seen her [*Rosario*] in the evening, that she had spent her masts, then, like a coward, he kept by her all night, because he would have the spoil. He thinketh to cozen us of our shares of fifteen thousand ducats; but we will have our shares, or I will make him spend the best blood of his belly.[32]

The booty from the *Rosario* was about thirty thousand ducats, of which Howard and Drake took three thousand each, with the rest being spent in the service of the queen. Don Pedro and his fellow prisoners were

[29]Ibid., 1:8.
[30]Ibid., 2:133–36, 357–58; David Howarth, *The Voyage of the Armada: The Spanish Story* (New York: Penguin Books, 1982), 127–31.
[31]Howarth, *Voyage*, 129.
[32]Laughton, *State Papers*, 2:102.

put into the custody of Sir Francis Drake, who turned them over to his rel-
ative Richard Drake for housing until the ransoms could be arranged.
However, Pedro remained a prisoner for three years before he was ran-
somed for three thousand pounds, the sum which Drake originally
claimed from the booty.[33] Although Valdes chafed throughout his imprisonment at his inability to negotiate his ransom, he nevertheless enjoyed a
privileged status, receiving, as he put it, "the best usage and entertainment
that may be."[34] Don Pedro was given the freedom to participate in English
court life as a guest rather than an enemy:

> Don Pedro de Valdes abideth five miles from London as hith-
> erto; for although they imputed to him a desire to escape and
> imprisoned him for the same, Francis Drake, to whom always
> he hath recourse, hath arranged everything, so as he goeth a-
> hunting and to other pleasure parties as in the time when he
> was not in prison.[35]

The capture of Pedro Valdes, the dispute over the booty, the problem
of Valdes' ransom, and his paradoxical status as "friendly prisoner" form
the background of Balthazar's presence at the Spanish court. When Balthazar was captured by Horatio after killing Andrea in battle, a dispute
arose over who was responsible for his capture. Both Lorenzo and Horatio
presented their claims to the Spanish king, who decided that Horatio
should receive Balthazar's armor and ransom money, and Lorenzo should
be given the horse, weapons, and custody of the prince:

> Nephew, thou took'st his weapon and his horse,
> His weapons and his horse are thy reward.
> Horatio, thou didst force him first to yield,
> His ransom therefore is thy valour's fee: . . .
> But nephew, thou shalt have the prince in guard.
> (1.2.180–85)

After making this judgment, the king promises to "feast our prisoner as
our friendly guest" (197).

---

[33]John Knox Laughton, "Sir Francis Drake," *Dictionary of National Biography*, ed. Leslie
Stephen and Sidney Lee (London: Oxford University Press, 1921–22), 5:1,343.
    [34]Laughton, *State Papers*, 2:136.
    [35]Ibid., 2:374–75.

However, while Balthazar is being treated as Spain's "friendly pris-oner," in Portugal the viceroy believes his son has been killed by Alexan-dro, whom the treacherous Villuppo has accused of murder. But Alexandro is exonerated and Villuppo condemned when the ambassador returns with news of Balthazar at the Spanish court. Through the dynastic plan of the king and Lorenzo to solidify the union between the two coun-tries, Balthazar is promoted as Bel-imperia's husband, whose "son . . . shall enjoy the kingdom after us" (2.3.21). Lorenzo and Balthazar kill Ho-ratio to further these plans, which culminate in the wedding celebration. Ironically, when Hieronimo assigns the roles for his fatal playlet, he reveals that Horatio's ransom money is financing the performance:

> with the ransom that the viceroy sent
> So furnish and perform this tragedy,
> As all the world shall say Hieronimo
> Was liberal in gracing of it so.   (4.1.151–54)

The money that was supposed to ransom Balthazar is now being used to stage a death playlet during which the viceroy, who earlier had thought his son had been murdered, will see his son killed and the dead son of Hieron-imo revealed as the reason for the revenge death.

By paralleling the names of his characters with English and Spanish ships and saints, Kyd not only endows the revenge playlet with the histor-ical relevance of Armada battles but at the same time subverts Spanish political and religious symbols of power. Important insights into Kyd's method of subversion can be gained by an analysis of "An Address to the Captains and Men on the Armada," which was issued immediately before its departure. Christ is depicted as the captain of the Armada and the Spanish saints as his sailors. When they reach England, they will be joined by the Catholic victims of Protestant persecution, who are compared to the apocalyptic saints crying out from under the altar for divine ven-geance:

> . . . God, in whose sacred cause we go, will lead us. With such a
> Captain we need not fear. The saints . . . will go in our com-
> pany, and particularly the holy patrons of Spain; and those of
> England . . . cry aloud to God for vengeance. . . . There we
> shall find awaiting us the aid of . . . John Fisher, . . . Thomas
> More, . . . and of . . . holy Carthusians, Franciscans, . . . who
> call to God to avenge them. . . . [W]e [shall] have the help of

Edmund Campion, . . . and many . . . priests . . . whom Elizabeth has torn to pieces with . . . cruelty. . . . With us, too, will
be the blessed and innocent Mary queen of Scotland, . . . who
bears . . . witness to the cruelty . . . of Elizabeth, and directs
her shafts against her.[36]

The address ends with a presentation of the horrors exacted by Elizabeth upon her Catholic victims, which parallels the impassioned
accounts of the slaughter of the Protestants during the Paris massacre:
"There also will await us the groans of . . . imprisoned Catholics, the tears
of widows who lost their husbands for the faith, the sobs of maidens . . .
forced to sacrifice their lives rather than . . . their souls." Kyd opposes the
Spanish ethos expressed in this address by reversing the power of the
saints Lorenzo and Jerome and by invoking the power of the martyred
Huguenots, especially Coligny, as the vindication of Hieronimo's vengeance.

Lorenzo's name is, as has been argued in chapter 5, related to
Hieronimo's reversal of the Pazzi conspiracy in which Lorenzo de' Medici
was almost killed. Further, when Hieronimo kills Lorenzo within the
revenge playlet, which has as its major historical subtext the Spanish war
of 1588, Kyd alludes to a significant event of that struggle, which took
place on August 9, 1588: the *San Lorenzo*, the *Capitana* galleass of Don
Hugo de Moncada, son of the viceroy of Valencia, ran aground near Calais
and was captured by Lord Admiral Charles Howard in the *Ark Royal*. In
order to understand the significance of this victory, as Kyd alludes to it, it
is necessary to investigate the role of St. Lorenzo in sixteenth-century
Spain.

When Spain defeated France at St. Quentin on the feast day of St.
Lorenzo, August 10, 1557, Philip II gave thanks to the third-century
martyr and promised to build the greatest church in Spain for him. The
church would serve as royal palace, mausoleum, and Hieronymite monastery. After choosing Madrid as the site for San Lorenzo de Escorial, Philip
explained to the Hapsburg empire his reasons for building the magnificent architectural monument, which was completed in 1586.

[36]*Calendar of Letters and State Papers Relating to English Affairs . . . , 1587-1603*, ed.
Martin Hume (1899; rpt. Germany: Kraus Reprint, 1971), 295.

[W]e found and erect the Monastery San Lorenzo el Real, near
the town of El Escorial, . . . the which we dedicate in the name
of the Blessed St. Lawrence, on account of the special devotion
which . . . we pray to this glorious saint, and in memory of the
favor and victories which on his day we received from God.
Moreover, we found it for the order of St. Jerome, on account
of our special affection . . . for this order, and that which was
also bestowed upon it by the emperor and king, my father.[37]

The Escorial was built in the shape of the gridiron upon which St. Lorenzo
was burned to death, and the monastery came to symbolize for Catholics
"the zeal of the Counter-Reformation . . . [and] Spain at its imperial apo-
gee";[38] but for the English Protestants the Escorial was

> the vain bubble of *Iberian* pride
> That over-croweth all the world beside.
> Which rear'd to raise the crazy Monarch's fame.
> Strives for a court and . . . Colledge name.[39]

The defeat of the powerful galleass *San Lorenzo* on the eve of the feast
day of St. Lorenzo in 1588 reverses the Spanish association of good fortune with the revered saint. The narrative of Howard's capture and plun-
dering of the *San Lorenzo*, "so princely a vessel, the very glory and stay of
the Spanish army,"[40] became a set piece of Armada accounts. Camden
reports that after the fire ships scattered the Armada, the ". . . *Admirals
Galleasse* had her Rudder broken, and went almost adrift, and the day
following, . . . after a doubtfull fight . . . was taken, *Hugh Moncada*, the
Captaine, being slaine, . . . they [Howard's men] found and carried away a
great quantity of gold."[41] In a letter to the queen, Lord Henry Seymour
explained that "it fell out that the galleass distressed [*San Lorenzo*] altered
my Lord's [Charles Howard] former determination, as I suppose, by pros-
ecuting the destruction of her, which was done within one hour after,"[42]
just as Hieronimo performed his action in "one hour's meditation"

[37]Qtd. in Mary Cable, et al., *El Escorial* (New York: Newsweek, 1971), 30–31.
[38]Ibid., 11.
[39]Joseph Hall, *Virgidemiarum, The Collected Poems of Joseph Hall, Bishop of Exeter and Norwich*, ed. A. Davenport (Liverpool: Liverpool University Press, 1949), 5.2.37–40.
[40]Laughton, *State Papers*, 1:348.
[41]Camden, *Annales*, 3.262 [misnumbered 280].
[42]Laughton, *State Papers*, 2:2.

(4.1.165). The ship named after the patron saint of Philip II—who had recently added Lorenzo's shoulder bone to the treasures of the Escorial[43]—was defeated, and the remainder of the Armada scattered in the ensuing three days. History had been reversed: Spain defeated France at St. Quentin on August 10, 1557, and the St. Bartholomew's day massacre occurred in August 1572, but England destroyed the Spanish Armada in August 1588. August, the month associated with the virgin goddess of Justice Astraea and the virgin huntress Diana,[44] appropriately is the time of England's greatest victory under the Virgin Queen Elizabeth, whose dramatic analogue, Bel-imperia, is apotheosized as the Elysian virgin.

Another hagiographic irony may be seen in the parallel between Hieronimo and St. Hieronymus or Jerome, the patron saint of the powerful Hieronymite Order which flourished in Renaissance Spain, Portugal, Italy, and France.[45] As Philip II explained in his plans for the Escorial, St. Jerome enjoyed a special relationship with the Hapsburg monarchy, but again Kyd reverses the beneficent Spanish association by having St. Jerome's namesake cause the fall of Babylon/Spain. Throughout the play, Kyd uses its own symbols of power against Babylon/Spain, the Antichrist enemy of Protestant England.

Hieronimo, the ostensible Spanish lord marshal, becomes the instrument of Protestant revenge against the Spanish Antichrist in his creation of the revenge playlet. As the lord marshal, who creates the revenge playlet, exhorts the action of revenge as ethos and English flagship, and murders Lorenzo and Castile, Hieronimo functions as an analogue to Lord Admiral Charles Howard, who defeated Spain in 1588 and avenged the Catholic massacre of Protestants in August 1572. In order to understand how Kyd uses the Howard analogy in *The Spanish Tragedy*, it is necessary to investigate the history of the illustrious, but also troubled, Howard family, which included a number of lord admirals, marshals, and chamberlains.

The Howard family is very important in English history, containing in its genealogy "the blood of Plantagenet, . . . Capet, . . . Mowbray,

[43]James A. Froude, *The Spanish Armada* (1895; rpt. Lawrence, K1ansas: Coronado Press, 1972), 62.

[44]Paul McLane, *Spenser's Shepheardes Calender: A Study in Elizabethan Allegory* (Notre Dame: Notre Dame University Press, 1961), 343-44.

[45]Eugene Rice, *Saint Jerome in the Renaissance* (Baltimore: The Johns Hopkins University Press, 1985), 168, 170.

Bigod, Warrenne, Fitz-Alan, Percy, and the flower of the English baron-age."[46] The most relevant part of the Howard participation in English history begins in the second half of the fifteenth century with the second duke of Norfolk, Thomas Howard (1443–1524), who became a Knight of the Garter, a member of the privy council, and in 1510, earl marshal.[47] His first wife Elizabeth Tilney bore ten daughters, one of whom married Thomas Boleyn and gave birth to Anne Boleyn, Queen Elizabeth's mother.

The eldest son of the second duke of Norfolk, Thomas Howard (1473–1554), became lord admiral and achieved military fame as the leader of the English army at Flodden in 1513, was appointed president of the privy council in 1529, and in 1533 became earl marshal. However, after a power struggle with Edward Seymour, earl of Hertford, Norfolk and his son Henry Howard, earl of Surrey, were condemned to death in 1546. Surrey was executed, but his father narrowly escaped death. Surrey's son, Thomas Howard (1536–72), succeeded his grandfather as earl marshal in 1554, but was executed in 1572 for involvement in the Ridolfi plot.[48]

The second son of the second duke of Norfolk was Lord William Howard (?1510–1573), who served as lord high admiral from 1554 to 1557 and as lord chamberlain from 1558 to 1572. His eldest son was Charles Howard (1536–1624), who was made lord chamberlain in 1584, and in the following year became the fifth member of his family to be appointed lord admiral.[49] He was also a member of the three-man commission serving as joint earl marshal in 1590.[50]

As lord chamberlain, Charles Howard served as the officer in the royal household concerned with the queen's wardrobe, travel, reception of ambassadors, and courtly entertainment. The chamberlain was the immediate superior of the master of the revels, who was responsible for the arrangement, supervision, and financing of dramas performed at court. Edmund Tilney, a relation of Charles Howard, filled this office from 1579 to 1609.[51] Hieronimo parallels the duties of these officers when he

[46]Gerald Brenan and Edward Statham, The House of Howard, 2 vols. (London: Hutchinson and Co., 1907), 1:18.
[47]Ann Hoffmann, Lives of the Tudor Age 1485–1603 (New York: Harper and Row Publisher, 1977), 260–61.
[48]Ibid., 262–63.
[49]Ibid., 255, 265–66.
[50]Robert Kenny, Elizabeth's Admiral, 166.
[51]The Reader's Encyclopedia of Shakespeare, ed. Oscar Campbell and Edward Quinn (New York: Thomas Y. Crowell Co., 1966), 467, 506.

presents the historical pageant at the end of act 1 and when he stages the revenge playlet.

The knight marshal of England was "an officer of the English royal household, who had judicial cognizance of transgressions 'within the king's house and verge.'"[52] Hieronimo fulfills this function when he attends Pedringano's execution and, ironically, when he pursues justice in the murder of his son. Ultimately, the knight marshal's search for justice extends to the satisfaction of the apocalyptic ethos of revenge represented by Andrea and Revenge.

The lord high admiral was concerned with both military and legal matters as the principal administrator of the queen's navy, who also judged civil and criminal cases involving maritime activities.[53] As Elizabeth's lord high admiral during the war with Spain in 1588, Charles Howard led the royal navy into battle against the Armada. Howard's role in the defeat of the Armada was well documented by Elizabethan writers. William Cecil praises Howard as the lord admiral by noting his illustrious lineage: "the Queenes Navie . . . [is divided] into three companies: the greatest under . . . Charles L. Haward . . . , whose father, grandfather, uncles, and other of his house . . . had also bene high Admirals afore him, whereof both Fraunce and Scotland have had proofe."[54] In *The Spanish Masquerado*, Greene contrasts the cowardly Spanish leaders with brave Howard who "stood upon the upper decke, resolutely and valiantly encouraging his men to fight for the honour of their Countrie" (272).

Howard was praised as a biblical, classical, and knightly hero whose worth should be proclaimed to all the world. James Lea makes Howard the deliverer of Israel/England from Egypt/ Spain, declaring that "[i]f he [God] gave to the people of Israel for theyr bringing out of Egypt, a *Moyses*, an *Aaron*, . . . : To thee [England] he hath given . . . a Charles Howard, . . . whom the Lord had ordained . . . for the defense of his universall church and this . . . kingdome." Lea compares Howard to classical heroes and asserts that if the lord admiral had been the victorious leader of the Armada he would be venerated for his brave leadership:

> time shal make your name as fearefull to the Spaniards, as was that of high minded *Scipio* against the Numidians. . . . [I]f the

---

[52]*OED*, 6b.

[53]Ibid., 2.

[54]William Cecil, *The Copie of a Letter Sent Out of England to Don Bernardin Mendoza* . . . (London: Richard Field, 1588), 15.

Duke of *Medina* . . . had gotten the like glorious conquest [of] our English Navie . . . ; the chronicles of Spain had bin stuffed with his praises, the cleargie had soong him in, with *Te Deum*, thorow the streets of Toledo, . . . and in fine Deified . . . and registred him amidst their catalogue of Saints.[55]

In his dedicatory sonnet "[t]o the Right Honourable . . . Lord Ch. Howard, Lord High Admiral . . . , Knight of the . . . Garter, and One of Her Majesties Privie Counsel," Spenser announces that Howard is the equal "[o]f th' old heroes," because he has vanquished the haughty Spanish:

> With those huge castles of Castilian king,
> That vainly threatned kingdomes to displace,
> Like flying doves did before you chace,
> And that proud people, woxen insolent
> Through many victories, didst first deface.   (141)

Finally, Thomas Heywood depicts Howard as a figure of St. George defeating the Spanish dragon:

> Where Royal *Englands Admirall* attended
> With all the *Chivalry* of our brave nation
> The name of *Howard* through the earth extended
> By *Naval* triumph o're their proud
> Invasion where victory on the *Red-Crosse*
>   descended.[56]

The extent to which the victory over the Armada is associated with the Howard family is shown by the number of English captains related to Charles Howard.

Charles Howard was also the patron for the Admiral's Men, an acting company founded in 1576 which changed its name in 1585 when Howard was made lord admiral. In 1589, the great actor Edward Alleyn joined the Admiral's Men, and the following year the company combined with Lord Strange's Men at James Burbage's Theater.[57] However, after an argument with Burbage in 1591, the hybrid company moved to the Rose Theater

[55]Lea, *Answer to Untruths*, 24, A2r–v.

[56]Thomas Heywood, *Troia Britanica: Or Great Britaines Troy* (London: W. Jaggard, 1609), Canto 3, St. 6, p. 54–55.

[57]*Reader's Encyclopedia of Shakespeare*, 8.

where it presented the first recorded performances of *The Spanish Tragedy* in the early months of 1592.[58] Considering these facts, it is entirely appropriate for Kyd to celebrate Howard/Hieronimo's role as the patron, producer, director, author, actor, and stage manager of the revenge playlet in which he brings about the apocalyptic fall of Babylon/Spain. Charles Howard, lord high admiral, lord chamberlain, and joint lord marshal, who was tutored in his younger years by John Foxe,[59] whose dramatic and polemical works influenced Kyd, is the central historical analogue to Hieronimo, the sacred Protestant revenger.

Hieronimo accomplishes his revenge against the filial representatives of Spain and Portugal before an onstage audience composed of Iberian royalty and patriarchs. Kyd joins Spain and Portugal as victims of Hieronimo's vengeance because of the historical union between the Iberian countries created when Philip II annexed Portugal in 1580 after the battle of Alcantra and in 1582 appointed his nephew as viceroy. In May 1588, the "Invincible Armada" was launched from Lisbon with the "Armada of Portugal, under the charge of the Duke of Medina-Sidonia," serving as one of its major divisions.[60] Antonio Pérez links the two countries in the attack on England: "in the yeere 1588 the king of Castile in his Fleet and armie by sea, . . . sent two Regiments of Portugals, each of them consisting of 800 men. . . . These forces (notwithstanding . . . his usurpation of the countrey . . .) yet . . . promised to serve him faithfully . . . in the fight . . . against the Englishmen."[61]

Although Kyd changes the actual historical situation by having the Spanish king fight a war against the Portuguese viceroy, he nevertheless establishes the equation between the two countries at the outset of the historical masque, when the king declares that "Spain is Portugal, / And Portugal is Spain, we both are friends . . ." (1.4.132–33). The masque contains three scenes from the past in which England conquers both Portugal and Spain. These victories presage the destruction of Babylon/Spain–Portugal in the revenge playlet presented to celebrate the wedding of Belimperia and Balthazar, whose disruption symbolizes the Iberian unity and power destroyed by the defeat of the combined Armada.

[58]Edwards, *Spanish Tragedy*, lxvi.
[59]Hoffmann, 180.
[60]Laughton, *State Papers*, 2:376.
[61]Antonio Pérez, *A Treatise Paraeneticall, . . . Wherein is shewed . . . the right way . . . to resist the violence of the Castilian king . . .* (London: William Ponsonby, 1598), 27.

The onstage audience watching the fall of Babylon/Spain–Portugal is composed of equivalent figures of Iberian power. The Portuguese viceroy is the double of the Spanish king in the historical sense because Philip II ruled Spain and Portugal and appointed his nephew as viceroy. Both rulers are also linked by their witnessing the severance of their respective lines of succession in the playlet. Further, the viceroy is the counterpart of the duke of Castile since both are fathers who have lost their sons. Don Pedro, who arrives in Spain to attend the wedding of his nephew Balthazar, is also analogous to the duke of Castile as the brother of the monarch. Finally, Don Pedro, who may, as we have argued, represent Don Pedro de Valdes, may also stand for the historical ruler of Portugal and Castile known as Pedro I—both Pedro I, son of Alfonso IV, who reigned from 1357 to 1367 and Pedro I "The Cruel," who ruled the united kingdoms of Castile and Leon from 1350 to 1369.[62] In the preface to The History of the World Raleigh says that in comparison to Pedro "The Cruel" "all the tyrants of Sicily, our Richard the Third . . . were but petty ones; this Castilian, of all Christian and heathen kings, having been the most merciless."[63] John Loftis explains that in Lope de Vega's play Don Lope de Cardova the prince named Don Pedro "prides himself on his name and his cruelty, associating himself with the Castillian and Portuguese Pedros the Cruel."[64] Kyd uses the near-silent Don Pedro as the image of Iberian royal cruelty which is now defeated by Hieronimo—England.

Castile's death presents another synecdochic image of the destruction of Iberian power. Many critics have argued that the murder of the innocent Don Cyprian, duke of Castile, provides the final proof that Hieronimo has become a homicidal maniac. But Castile's demise is related to the defeat of the Armada in two ways. First, Castile was the name of one of the principal squadrons of the Armada consisting of sixteen galleons under the command of Diego Flores de Valdes.[65] Castile also is linked to the description of the Armada ships, which, because of their size and the presence on their decks of defensive towers known as castles, were described as looking like huge castles on the ocean. In Albion's England, William Warner describes the Armada as

[62]L. F. Wise and E. W. Egan, Kings, Rulers and Statesman (New York: Sterling Publishing Co., 1967), 324, 374.
[63]Raleigh, History, 2:xxiv.
[64]John Loftis, Renaissance Drama in England and Spain: Topical Allusion and History Plays (Princeton: Princeton University Press, 1987), 250.
[65]Laughton, State Papers, 2:377.

> Fleete of eightscore
> Ships and od, the *Ocean* never bore,
> So huge, so strong, and so compleate, . . .
> That seemed so many Castels their tops the cloudes
>   to tuch.[66]

In the arms of Spain, the symbol for Castile is a castle;[67] thus, the Armada ships can be seen as the nautical representatives of the power of Castile as synecdoche for Spain–Portugal. Spenser includes the pun on castle/Castile in the sonnet to Charles Howard when he describes the ships of the Armada as "those huge castles of Castilian king."

The final image of the defeated Armada is that of the doomed ship evoked by the grief-stricken viceroy. As he tells his brother to carry Balthazar away, he ironically echoes Hieronimo and Isabella's dirge for their dead son and parallels the Spanish king's lament for Castile:

> Take up our hapless son, untimely slain
> Set me with him, and he with woeful me,
> Upon the mainmast of a ship unmann'd
> And let the wind and tide haul me along
> To Scylla's barking and untamed gulf,
> Or to the loathsome pool of Acheron.   (4.4.210–15)

The image of the "unmann'd ship" signifies the annihilation of the royal lines of Iberian accession, and at the same time it represents the defeated Armada as a doomed ship, without its crew, sinking into the depths of the underworld, a destination which presages the otherworld punishment of Pedringano, who is "dragg'd through boiling Acheron, / . . . dying still in endless flames" (4.5.42–43). Joseph Schick says the viceroy's lines "recall, by their choice of simile—a mysterious ship setting out into the boundless sea—. . . the Viking-burial . . . in *Beowulf*, the Passing of Arthur in *Layamon* . . . [and] the greatest Englishman of the time of *The Spanish Tragedy*, the sea-king of terrible and glorious memory, Sir Francis Drake."[68]

It is ironic that Schick sees the death of Drake in these lines, because their context is the defeat of the Armada. A flaming ship symbolizes the

---

[66]Warner, *Albion's England*, 9, 49, 227.

[67]Ottfried Neubecker, *A Guide to Heraldry* (New York: McGraw-Hill, 1979), 140.

[68]Thomas Kyd, *The Spanish Tragedy*, ed. Joseph Schick (New York: J. M. Dent, 1898), 14n.

Armada in Wilson's *Three Lords and Three Ladies of London* when Policy explains that the burning ship on the shield of Shealty

> means your commonwealth's on fire
> About your ears, and you were best look home.
> A commonwealth's compared to a ship:
> If yours do flame, your country is hot.   (470)

Similarly, the coins celebrating the English victory showed "a ship fleeing and a ship sincking,"[69] and in *The Spanish Masquerado* Greene presents Juan Martinez de Recalde, admiral of the fleet and commander of the Biscay Squadron, who "standing in the Haven, and seeing his tattered Shippes, considering what goodlye Vessels were taken and drowned, and what store of men and munition they had lost, leaning his backe against a broken ancker, . . . saith thus. O Neptune, quantas epulas una coena devorasti?" (274) The sinking ship in the viceroy's lament epitomizes the loss of the Armada ships off the coast of England, the wrecks of the fleeing ships on the coast of Ireland, and the long mournful procession of the broken Armada back to Spain.

The date of *The Spanish Tragedy* has long been debated by scholars. The proposed dates of composition have ranged from 1582 to 1592, with 1587 being the most frequent choice. Arthur Freeman has argued that in a nationalistic play with a strong anti-Spanish sentiment, the absence of a celebratory reference to England's defeat of Spain in 1588 must make Kyd's play pre-Armada, most probably 1587.[70] As Freeman indicates, the problem of the dating is directly related to the problem of the play's historical context. Philip Edwards, who has argued that *The Spanish Tragedy* has little, if any, relation to past and contemporary Anglo–Iberian conflicts, concludes that it was written around 1590 because of its "style and manner."[71]

Despite the increase in scholarly awareness of the historical context of *The Spanish Tragedy* as explained in the work of Johnson, Broude, Hill, and Justice, no critic has argued as I have that the central political subtext

---

[69]Meteren, *Miraculous Victory*, 273.
[70]Edwards, *Spanish Tragedy*, xxvii.
[71]Freeman, *Kyd*, 77, 79.

involves the defeat of Spain in 1588. As a nationalistic ritual, *The Spanish Tragedy* has revealed to its "initiated" audiences the mystery of the process of destiny which led to the English victory over Spain. This subtext may account for the popularity of *The Spanish Tragedy*, which from 1592 to 1597 was the third most popular play.[72] Even if some Elizabethan audiences did not comprehend its full significance, many of Kyd's contemporaries must have at least sensed the nature of the play's religious and patriotic appeal. However, in the ensuing years, awareness of the religio-political subtext was lost and the revenge theme became the dominant focus of critical inquiry. It has been the purpose of this book to restore the apocalyptic and historical meanings to *The Spanish Tragedy*, which was written in the period after the defeat of the Armada and before its first performance in early 1592.

[72]D. F. Rowan, "The Staging of *The Spanish Tragedy*," *The Elizabethan Theater V*, ed. G. R. Hibbard (Hamden, Connecticut: Shoe String Press, 1975), 113.

Bibliography

Primary Sources

Allen, William. *An Admonition to the Nobility and People of England . . . Concerninge the Present Warres made for the execution of his Holines' Sentence by the highe and mightie Kinge . . . of Spaine.* Antwerp, 1588.

Archdeacon, Daniel. *A True Discourse of the Armie which the King of Spaine caused to bee assembled . . . in . . . 1588, against England.* London, 1588.

Aske, James. *Elizabetha triumphans . . . .* London, 1588.

Bale, John. *A Comedy concerning Three Laws of Nature, Moses, and Christ. The Dramatic Writings of John Bale Bishop of Ossory.* Edited by John S. Farmer (1907). Reprinted Guildford, England: Charles W. Traylen, 1966.

———. *The Image of Bothe Churches after the moste wonderfull and heavenly Revelacion of Sainct John . . . .* Antwerp? 1548.

———. *John Bale's King Johan.* Edited by Barry Adams. San Marino, California: Huntington Library, 1969.

Beaujoyeulx, Balthazar de. *Le Balet Comique . . . : A Facsimile* (1581). Binghamton, New York: Medieval and Renaissance Texts and Studies, 1982.

Bernard, Richard. *A Key of Knowledge for the Opening of the Secret Mysteries of St. Johns Mysticall Revelation.* London, 1617.

Bolton, Edmund. *Nero Caesar, or Monarchie Depraved . . . .* London: Thomas Walkley, 1624.

Brightman, Thomas. *A Most Comfortable Exposition . . . of Daniel . . . .* Amsterdam, 1635.

———. *A Revelation of the Revelation . . . of St. John opened clearely . . . .* Amsterdam, 1615.

Brocardo, Jacob. *The Revelation of S. John Reveled.* Translated by James Sanford. London, 1582.

Broughton, Hugh. *Daniel his Chaldie visions and his Ebrew . . . .* London: Richard Field, 1596.

Bullinger, Heinrich. *A Hundred Sermons Upon the Apocalypse of Jesu Christ.* Translated by John Day. London, 1573.

Calendar of Letters and State Papers Relating to English Affairs . . . , 1587–1603. Edited by Martin Hume (1899). Reprinted Germany: Kraus Reprint, 1971.

Calvin, John. *Commentaries of that divine John Calvine upon the Prophet Daniell.* Translated by Arthur Golding. London, 1570.

———. *Commentaries on the Book of the Prophet Daniel.* Translated by Thomas Myers, 2 vols. Edinburgh: Calvin Translation Society, 1852.

Camden, William. *Annales: The True and Royall History of . . . Elizabeth.* Translated by Richard Norton. London: Benjamin Fisher, 1630.

———. *The History of the Most Renowned and Victorious Princess Elizabeth Late Queen of England Selected Chapters.* Edited by Wallace MacCaffrey. Chicago: University of Chicago Press, 1970.

Cecil, William. *The Copy of a Letter Sent Out of England to Don Bernardin Mendoza. . . .* London: Richard Field, 1588.

D'Aubigné, Agrippa. *Les Tragiques.* Lausanne, Switzerland: Editions Rencontre, 1968.

Dekker, Thomas. *The Whore of Babylon. The Dramatic Works of Thomas Dekker.* Edited by Fredson Bowers. Vol. 2. London: Cambridge University Press, 1964.

DeLoney, Thomas. "A joyful new Ballad declaring the . . . obtaining of the great Galleazzo, wherein Don *Pedro de Valdez* was the chief." *An English Garner: Tudor Tracts 1532-1588.* Edited by Edward Arber and rev. Thomas Seccombe (1877-90). Reprinted New York: Cooper Square Publishers, 1964. 485-91.

Dent, Arthur. *The Ruine of Rome or An Exposition upon the whole Revelation . . . .* London, 1603.

Dowriche, Anne. *The French Historie . . . .* London: Thomas Man, 1589.

Estienne, Henri. *A Mervaylous discourse upon the lyfe, deides, and behaviours of Katherine de Medicis, Queene mother . . . .* Heidelberg, 1575.

Foxe, John. *Two Latin Comedies by John Foxe the Martyrologist: Titus et Gesippus [and] Christus Triumphans.* Edited and translated by John H. Smith. Ithaca: Cornell University Press, 1973.

Garter, Thomas. *The Commody Of the most vertuous and Godlye Susanna.* Oxford, England: Malone Society Reprints, 1936.

The Geneva Bible: A Facsimile of the 1560 Edition. Madison: University of Wisconsin Press, 1969.

Gentillet, Innocent. *A Discourse . . . Against Nicholas Machiavell the Florentine.* Translated by Simon Patericke. London: Adam Islip, 1602.

Geveren, Sheltco à. *Of the End of this Worlde, and second Comming of Christ . . . .* Translated by Thomas Rogers. London, 1577 and 1589.

Gifford, George. *Sermons Upon the Whole Book of Revelation.* London, 1596.

Greene, Robert. *The Historie of Orlando Furioso, One of the Twelve Peeres of France. The Life and Complete Works in Prose and Verse of Robert Greene.* Edited by Alexander Grosart (1881-86). Vol. 13. Reprinted New York: Russell and Russell, 1964.

———. *The Spanish Masquerado . . . . The Life and Complete Works . . . of Robert Greene.* Vol. 5.

Gualter, Rudolph. *Antichrist, That is to saye: A true reporte, that Antichriste is come . . . .* London, 1556.

Guicciardini, Lodovico. *Hours of Recreation . . . .* Translated by James Sandford. London, 1576.

Hakluyt, Richard. *The Principal Navigations, Voyages, Traffiques and Discoveries of the English Nation* (1598). New York: E. P. Dutton, 1907.

Hall, Joseph. *Virgidemiarum. The Collected Poems of Joseph Hall, Bishop of Exeter and Norwich.* Edited by A. Davenport. Liverpool: Liverpool University Press, 1949.

Harvey, Gabriel. *Pieces Supererogation or New Prayse of the Old Asse. The Works of Gabriel Harvey.* Edited by Alexander Grosart (1881). Vol. 2. Reprinted New York: AMS press, 1966.

Harvey, John. *An Astrological Addition, or Supplement to be Annexed to the Late Discourse.* London, 1583.

———. *A Discoursive Probleme concerning Prophecies.* London, 1588.

Harvey, Richard. *An Astrological Discourse upon the great and notable Conjunction of the two Superiour Planets, Saturne and Jupiter . . . .* London, 1583.

Hellwis, Edward. *A Marvell, Deciphered, An exposition of the 12th ch. of Revelation.* London, 1589.

Heywood, Thomas. *An Apology For Actors* (1612). New York: Scholars Facsimiles and Reprints, 1941.

———. *If You Know Not Me, You Know Nobody, or The Troubles of Queen Elizabeth. The Dramatic Works of Thomas Heywood.* Edited by R. H. Shepherd (1874). Vol. 1. Reprinted New York: Russell and Russell, 1964.

———. *Troia Britanica: Or Great Britaines Troy.* London: W. Jaggard, 1609.

The Honorable Entertainment given to the Queen's Majestie in Progresse, at Elvetham . . . . Entertainments for Elizabeth I. Edited by Jean Wilson. Totowa, New Jersey: Rowman and Littlefield, 1980.

Hotman, François. *The Lyfe of . . . Jasper Colignie . . . .* Translated by Arthur Golding. London: Thomas Vautrollier, 1576.

———. *A True and Plaine report of the Furious outrages of Fraunce . . . .* Edinburgh, Scotland: Striveling, 1573.

Hughes, Thomas. *The Misfortunes of Arthur. Early English Classical Tragedies.* Edited by John Cunliffe. Oxford: Clarendon Press, 1912.

Jerome, Saint. *Jerome's Commentary on Daniel.* Translated by Gleason L. Archer. Grand Rapids: Baker Book House, 1958.

Joye, George. *The exposicion of Daniel the Prophete.* Geneva, 1545.

Kyd, Thomas. *The Spanish Tragedy.* Edited by Philip Edwards. London: Methuen, 1959.

———. *The Spanish Tragedy.* Edited by Joseph Schick. London: J. M. Dent, 1898.

Lea, James. *An Answer to the Untruthes Published and Printed in Spaine in Glorie of their Supposed Victorie . . . against our English Navie.* London, 1589. Reprinted New York: Da Capo Press, 1969.

———. *A True . . . description of a straunge Monster borne in . . . Rome . . . .* London: John Wolfe, 1590.

Linschoten, Jan Huygen van. *The Fight and the Cyclone at the Azores. English Reprints* (1871) 8.29. Edited by Edward Arber. Reprinted New York: AMS Press, 1966. 90–96.

Ludovico Ariosto's Orlando Furioso. Translated by John Harington and edited by Robert McNulty. London: Oxford University Press, 1972.

Lyly, John. *Midas. The Complete Works of John Lyly.* Edited by R. Warwick Bond. Vol. 3. London: Oxford University Press, 1967.

Machiavelli, Niccolo. *History of Florence And of the Affairs of Italy* . . . . New York: M. Walter Dunne, 1901.

Markham, Gervase. *The Most Honorable Tragedie of Sir Richard Grinvile, Knight. English Reprints* (1871) 8.29. Edited by Edward Arber. Reprinted New York: AMS Press, 1966. 35–87.

Marlorat, Austin. *A Catholic Exposition Upon the Revelation of St. John.* Translated by Arthur Golding. London, 1574.

Marlowe, Christopher. *The Massacre At Paris. The Complete Plays of Christopher Marlowe.* Edited by Irving Ribner. New York: Odyssey Press, 1963.

Marquino, Francis. *A Politike Discourse most excellent for this time present* . . . . London, 1589.

Mede, Joseph. *The Key of the Revelation* . . . . London, 1643.

Meteren, Emanuel van. *The Miraculous Victory Atchieved by the English Fleete . . . Upon the . . . Spanish huge Armada* (1590). Translated by Richard Hakluyt. *Elizabethan Backgrounds: Historical Documents of the Age of Elizabeth I* . . . . Edited by Arthur Kinney. Hamden, Connecticut: Archon Books, 1975. 245–75.

Mirk, John. *Festial.* Westminister, 1483.

More, Henry. *A Plain and Continued Exposition of . . . Daniel.* London, 1681.

Morel, Jean. *De Ecclesia ab Antichristo liberanda, eaque ex Dei promissionibus reparanda.* London, 1594.

Napier, John. *A Plaine Discovery of the whole Revelation of Saint John* . . . . Edinburgh, 1593.

Newton, Isaac. *Sir Isaac Newton's Daniel and the Apocalypse* . . . . Edited by William Whitla. London: John Murray, 1922.

Niccols, Richard. *Englands Eliza: or The Victorious and Triumphant Reigne of that Virgin Empresse of Sacred Memorie* . . . . London: Felix Kyngston, 1610.

Norton, Thomas, and Thomas Sackville. *Gorboduc, or Ferrex and Porrex. Early English Classical Tragedies.* Edited by John Cunliffe. Oxford: Clarendon Press, 1912.

Nun, Thomas. *A Comfort Against The Spaniard.* Oxford: John Windet, 1596.

A Packe Of Spanish Lyes, Sent Abroad In The World . . . Now . . . , by just examination condemned . . . . London: Christopher Baker, 1588.

Pareus, David. *A Commentary upon the Divine Revelation of the Apostle and Evangelist John.* Translated by Elias Arnold. Amsterdam, 1644.

Patten, William. *The Calendar of Scripture.* London, 1575.

Peele, George. *The Battle of Alcazar. The Dramatic Works of George Peele.* Edited by John Yolkavich. Vol. 2. New Haven: Yale University Press, 1961.

Pérez, Antonio. *A Treatise Paraeneticall, . . . Wherein is shewed . . . the right way . . . to resist the violence of the Castilian king* . . . . London: William Ponsonby, 1598.

Raleigh, Sir Walter. *The History of the World. The Works of Sir Walter Raleigh.* 6 vols. Oxford, 1829. Reprinted New York: Burt Franklin, 1964.

Respublica. English Morality Plays and Moral Interludes. Edited by Edgar T. Schell and J. D. Schuchter. New York: Holt, Rinehart and Winston, 1969.

Rogers, Thomas. *An Historical Dialogue Touching Antichrist and Poperie* . . . . London, 1589.

Shakespeare, William. *King John.* Edited by E. A. J. Honigman. London: Methuen & Co., 1959.

Sidney, Sir Philip. *A Discourse of Syr. Ph. S. to the Queenes Majesty. The Prose Works of Sir Philip Sidney.* Edited by Albert Feuillerat. Vol. 3. London: Cambridge University Press, 1912.

Speed, John. *The History of Great Britaine* . . . . London, 1611.

Spenser, Edmund. *The Complete Poetical works.* Edited by R. E. Neil Dodge. Boston, 1908.

State Papers Relating to the Defeat of The Spanish Armada Anno 1588 (1894). Edited by John Knox Laughton. 2 vols. Reprinted New York: Burt Franklin, 1971.

Stubbs, John. *The Discoverie Of A Gaping Gulf Whereinto England Is Like To Be Swallowed by an other French marriage* . . . . Edited by Lloyd Berry. Charlottesville: University Press of Virginia, 1968.

Tacitus. *The Annals. The Complete Works of Tacitus.* Translated by Alfred Church and William Broadrib and edited by Moses Hadas. New York: Random House, 1942.

The Tragedy of Locrine. Edited by Ronald B. McKerrow. London: Malone Society Reprints, 1908.

The Tragedy of Nero. Edited by Elliott Hill. New York: Garland Publishing Company, 1979.

Traheron, Bartholomew. *An Exposition of the 4. Chapter of S. Johns Revelation.* Wesel, Germany, 1557.

Varillas, Antoine. . . . *The Secret History of the House of Medicis.* Translated by Ferrand Spence. London, 1686.

Warner, William. *Albion's England* . . . . London, 1596.

Whetstone, George. *The English Myrror* . . . . London: G. Seton, 1586.

Wilson, Robert. *The Cobler's Prophecy.* London: Malone Society Reprints, 1914.

——. *Three Lords and Three Ladies of London. A Select Collection of Old English Plays.* Vol. 6. Edited by W. C. Hazlitt (1744). Reprinted London: Reeves and Turner, 1874.

Secondary Sources

Acton, Harold. *The Pazzi Conspiracy: The Plot Against the Medici.* London: Thames and Hudson, 1979.

Adams, Barry. "The Audiences of *The Spanish Tragedy.*" *JEGP* 68 (1969): 221–36.

Aggeler, Geoffrey, "The Eschatological Crux in *The Spanish Tragedy.*" *JEGP* 86 (1987): 319–31.

Arber, Edward. "Introduction." *English Reprints* (1871) 8.29. Reprinted New York: AMS Press, 1966. 3–9.

Ardolino, Frank. "The Bearing of Deadly Letters: Uriah's Letter in Marlowe, Kyd, and Shakespeare." *Journal of Evolutionary Psychology* 6 (1985): 292–300.

——. "Corrida of Blood in *The Spanish Tragedy:* Kyd's Use of Revenge as National Destiny." *Medieval and Renaissance Drama in England* 1 (1983): 37–49.

———. "The Hangman's Noose and the Empty Box: Kyd's Use of Dramatic and Mythological Sources in *The Spanish Tragedy* (III.iv.viii)." *Renaissance Quarterly* 30 (1977):334-40.

———. "The Hangman, the Villain, and the Playwright: Kyd's Ironic Use of Morality and *Commedia* Traditions in *The Spanish Tragedy*." *Allegorica* 13 (1992):53-63.

———. "Hieronimo as St. Jerome in *The Spanish Tragedy*." *Études Anglaises* 36 (1983):435-37.

———. "'In Paris? Mass, and Well Remembered': Kyd's *The Spanish Tragedy* and the English Reaction to the St. Bartholomew's Day Massacre." *Sixteenth Century Journal* 21.3 (1990):401-9.

———. "'Now Shall I See the Fall of Babylon': *The Spanish Tragedy* as Protestant Apocalypse." *Shakespeare Yearbook* 1 (1990):93-115.

———. "'Now Shall I See the Fall of Babylon': *The Spanish Tragedy* as a Reformation Play of Daniel." *Renaissance and Reformation* 14 (1990):49-55.

———. *Thomas Kyd's Mystery Play: Myth and Ritual in The Spanish Tragedy.* New York: Peter Lang, 1985.

———. "*Veritas Filia Temporis*: Time, Perspective, and Justice in *The Spanish Tragedy*." *Studies in Iconography* 3 (1977):57-69.

Baines, Barbara. "Kyd's Silenus Box and the Limits of Perception." *Journal of Medieval and Renaissance Studies* 10 (1980):41-51.

Barish, Jonas. "*The Spanish Tragedy*, or The Pleasures and Perils of Rhetoric." In *Elizabethan Theatre (Stratford-Upon-Avon-Studies 9).* Edited by J. R. Brown and Bernard Harris, 59-85. New York: St. Martins, 1966.

Bauckham, Richard. *Tudor Apocalypse: Sixteenth-Century Apocalypticism, Millennarianism and the English Reformation from John Bale to John Foxe and Thomas Brightman.* Appleford, England: Sutton Courtenay Press, 1978.

Bercovitch, Sacvan. "Love and Strife in Kyd's *Spanish Tragedy*." *SEL* 9 (1969):215-29.

Bergeron, David, *English Civic Pageantry 1558-1642.* Columbia: University of South Carolina Press, 1971.

Bevington, David. *Tudor Drama and Politics: A Critical Approach to Topical Meaning.* Cambridge: Harvard University Press, 1968.

Bowers, Fredson. *Elizabethan Revenge Tragedy 1587-1642.* Princeton: Princeton University Press, 1940.

———. "Kyd's Pedringano: Sources and Parallels." *Harvard Studies and Notes in Philology and Literature* 13 (1931):241-49.

Boyle, Harry. "Elizabeth's Entertainment at Elvetham: War Policy in Pageantry." *SP* 68 (1971):146-66.

Bradner, Leicester. *Musae Anglicanae: A History of Anglo-Latin Poetry 1500-1925.* New York: Modern Language Association of America, 1940.

———. "Poems on the Defeat of the Armada." *JEGP* 43 (1944):447-48.

Breight, Curt. "Realpolitik and Elizabethan Ceremony: The Earl of Hertford's Entertainment of Elizabeth at Elvetham, 1591." *RQ* 45.1 (1992):20-48.

Brenan, Gerald, and Edward Statham. *The House of Howard.* 2 vols. London: Hutchinson and Co., 1907.

Broude, Ronald. "Time, Truth, and Right in *The Spanish Tragedy.*" *SP* 68 (1971): 130–45.

——. " *Vindicta Filia Temporis*: Three English Forerunners of the Elizabethan Revenge Play." *JEGP* 72 (1973): 489–502.

Brown, Raymond. *The Semitic Background of the Term "Mystery" in the New Testament.* Philadelphia: Fortress Press, 1968.

Buffum, Imbrie. *Agrippa d'Aubigné's "Les Tragiques."* New Haven: Yale University Press, 1951.

Bush, Douglas. *English Literature in the Earlier Seventeenth Century.* New York: Oxford University Press, 1945.

Cable, Mary, et al. *El Escorial.* New York: Newsweek, 1971.

Cameron, Keith. *Agrippa d'Aubigné.* Boston: G. K. Hall, 1977.

Chickera, Ernest de. "Divine Justice and Private Revenge in *The Spanish Tragedy.* " *MLR* 57 (1962): 228–32.

Colley, John. "*The Spanish Tragedy* and the Theatre of God's Judgments." *Papers in Language and Literature* 10 (1974): 241–53.

Collins, John J. *The Apocalyptic Vision of the Book of Daniel.* Missoula, Montana: Scholars Press, 1977.

Corbett, Julian S. *Drake and the Tudor Navy.* 2 vols. London: Longmans, Green, and Co., 1898.

Coursen, Herbert. "The Unity of *The Spanish Tragedy.*" *SP* 65 (1968): 768–82.

Crewe, Jonathan. *Hidden Designs: The Critical Profession and Renaissance Literature.* New York and London: Methuen, 1986.

Dickens, A. G. "Elizabethans and St. Bartholomew." In *The Massacre of St. Bartholomew: Reappraisals and Documents.* Edited by Alfred Soman, 52–70. Hague: Martinus Nijhoff, 1974.

Edwards, Philip. "Shakespeare and Kyd." In *Shakespeare, Man of the Theater.* Edited by Kenneth Muir, Jay Halio, and D. J. Palmer, 148–54. Newark, New Jersey: University of Delaware Press, 1983.

——. "Thrusting Elysium into Hell: The Originality of *The Spanish Tragedy.*" In *Elizabethan Theater XI* (1985). Edited by A. L. Magnusson and C. E. McGee, 117–32. Port Credit, Ontario: P. D. Geary, 1991.

Elliott, John, "The Sacrifice of Isaac as Comedy and Tragedy." In *Medieval English Drama: Essays Critical and Contextual.* Edited by Jerome Taylor and Alan H. Nelson, 157–76. Chicago: University of Chicago Press, 1972.

Emmerson, Richard. *Antichrist in the Middle Ages: A Study of Medieval Apocalypticism, Art, and Literature.* Seattle: University of Washington, 1981.

——. "The Prophetic, the Apocalyptic, and the Study of Medieval Literature." In *Poetic Prophecy in Western Literature.* Edited by Jan Wojcik and Raymond-Jean Frontain, 40–54. Rutherford, New Jersey: Fairleigh Dickinson University Press, 1984.

Esler, Robert. "Robert Greene and the Spanish Armada." *ELH* 32 (1965): 314–32.

Farrar, Austin. *The Revelation of St. John The Divine.* Oxford: Clarendon Press, 1964.

Firth, Katharine. *The Apocalyptic Tradition in Reformation Britain 1530–1645.* London: Oxford University Press, 1979.

Fixler, Michael. "The Apocalypse within *Paradise Lost.*" In *New Essays on Paradise Lost.* Edited by Thomas Kranidas, 131–78. Berkeley: University of California Press, 1969.

Fletcher, Angus. *The Prophetic Moment: An Essay on Spenser.* Chicago: University of Chicago Press, 1971.

Freeman, Arthur. *Thomas Kyd, Facts and Problems.* London: Oxford University Press, 1967.

Froude, James. *The Spanish Armada* (1895). Reprinted Lawrence, Kansas: Coronado Press, 1972.

Garber, Marjorie. "'What's Past Is Prologue': Temporality and Prophecy in Shakespeare's History Plays." In *Renaissance Genres: Essays on Theory, History, and Interpretation.* Edited by Barbara Lewalski, 301-31. Cambridge: Harvard University Press, 1986.

Goodstein, Peter. "Hieronimo's Destruction of Babylon." *English Language Notes* 3 (1966): 172–73.

Graziani, René. "Philip II's *Impresa* and Spenser's Souldan." *JWCI* 27 (1964): 322–24.

Hallett, Charles, and Elaine Hallett. *The Revenger's Madness: A Study of Revenge Tragedy Motifs.* Lincoln and London: University of Nebraska Press, 1980.

Heninger, S. K. "The Orgoglio Episode in *The Faerie Queene.*" In *Essential Articles for the Study of Edmund Spenser.* Edited by A. C. Hamilton, 125-38. Hamden, Connecticut: Archon Books, 1972.

Herford, Charles. *Studies in the Literary Relations of England and Germany in the Sixteenth Century.* Cambridge: Cambridge University Press, 1886.

Herrick, Marvin. "Susanna and the Elders in Sixteenth-Century Drama." In *Studies in Honor of T. W. Baldwin.* Edited by Don Cameron Allen, 125-35. Urbana: University of Illinois Press, 1958.

——. *Tragicomedy: Its Origin and Development in Italy, France, and England.* Urbana: University of Illinois Press, 1955.

Hill, Eugene. "Senecan and Vergilian Perspectives in *The Spanish Tragedy.*" *ELR* 15 (1985): 143–65.

Himmelfarb, Martha. *Tours of Hell: An Apocalyptic Form in Jewish and Christian Literature.* Philadelphia: University of Pennsylvania Press, 1983.

Hodges, C. Walter. *The Globe Restored: A Study of the Elizabethan Theatre.* London: Ernest Benn Ltd., 1953.

Hoffmann, Ann. *Lives of the Tudor Age 1485-1603.* New York: Harper and Row Publishers, 1977.

Howarth, David. *The Voyage of the Armada: The Spanish Story.* New York: Penguin Books, 1982.

Hunter, G. K. "Ironies of Justice in *The Spanish Tragedy.*" *Renaissance Drama* 8 (1965): 89–104.

Ide, Richard. "Elizabethan Revenge and the Providential Play-Within-A-Play." *Iowa State Journal of Research* 56 (1981): 91–96.

Iwasaki, Soji. "*Veritas Filia Temporis* and Shakespeare." *ELR* 3 (1973): 249-63.

Jensen, Ejner. "Kyd's *The Spanish Tragedy*: The Play Explains Itself." *JEGP* 64 (1965): 7-16.

Johnson, S. F. "*The Spanish Tragedy,* or Babylon Revisited." In *Essays on Shakespeare and Elizabethan Drama in Honor of Hardin Craig.* Edited by Richard Hosley, 23–36. Columbia: University of Missouri Press, 1962.

Justice, Steven. "Spain, Tragedy, and *The Spanish Tragedy.*" *SEL* 25 (1985):271–88.

Kay, Carol. "Deception through Words: A Reading of *The Spanish Tragedy.*" *SP* 74 (1977):20–38.

Kelly, Donald. "Martyrdom, Myths, and the Massacre: The Background of St. Bartholomew." In *The Massacre of St. Bartholomew: Reappraisals and Documents.* Edited by Alfred Soman, 181–202. Hague, Netherlands: Martinus Nijhoff, 1974.

Kenny, Robert. *Elizabeth's Admiral: The Political Career of Charles Howard, Earl of Nothinghom 1536-1624.* Baltimore: The Johns Hopkins Press, 1970.

Kermode, Frank. *The Genesis of Secrecy: On the Interpretation of Narrative.* Cambridge: Harvard University Press, 1979.

King, John. *English Reformation Literature: The Tudor Origins of the Protestant Tradition.* Princeton: Princeton University Press, 1982.

Knapp, Robert. "*Horestes*: The Uses of Revenge." *ELH* 40 (1973):205–20.

Laird, David. "Hieronimo's Dilemma." *SP* 62 (1965):137–46.

Laughton, John Knox. "Sir Francis Drake." In *Dictionary of National Biography.* Edited by Leslie Stephen and Sidney Lee. London: Oxford University Press, 1921–22. 5:1,331–47.

Leigh, David. "The Doomsday Mystery Play: An Eschatological Morality." *MP* 67 (1970):211–23.

Levin, Michael. "'Vindicta mihi!': Meaning, Morality, and Motivation in *The Spanish Tragedy.*" *SEL* 4 (1964)):307–24.

Loftis, John. *Renaissance Drama in England and Spain: Topical Allusion and History Plays.* Princeton: Princeton University Press, 1987.

Marcus, Leah. *Puzzling Shakespeare: Local Reading and Its Discontents.* Berkeley: University of California Press, 1988.

Mattingly, Garrett. *The Armada.* Boston: Houghton Mifflin, 1959.

McGowan, Margaret. "Introduction." In *Le Balet Comique, by Balthazar de Beaujoyleulx: A Facsimile* (1581). Binghamton, New York: Medieval and Renaissance Texts and Studies, 1982.

McKee, Alexander. *From Merciless Invaders: An Eye-witness Account of the Spanish Armada.* London: Souvenir Press, 1963.

McLane, Paul. *Spenser's Shepheardes Calender: A Study in Elizabethan Allegory.* Notre Dame: Notre Dame University Press, 1961.

McMillin, Scott. "The Book of Seneca in *The Spanish Tragedy.*" *SEL* 15 (1974):201–8.

———. "The Figure of Silence in *The Spanish Tragedy.*" *ELH* 39 (1972):27–48.

Murrin, Michael. "Revelation and Two Seventeenth-Century commentators." In *The Apocalypse in English Renaissance Thought and Literature* . . . . Edited by C. A. Patrides and Joseph Wittreich, 125–46. Ithaca: Cornell University Press, 1984.

Neubecker, Ottfried. *A Guide to Heraldry.* New York: McGraw-Hill, 1979.

Niditch, Susan. *The Symbolic Vision in Biblical Tradition.* Chico, California: Scholars Press, 1980.

Norbrook, David. *Poetry and Politics in The English Renaissance.* London and Boston: Routledge and Kegan Paul, 1984.

Parker, Alexander. *The Allegorical Drama of Calderon: An Introduction to the Autos Sacramentales.* Oxford: Dolphin Book Co., 1968.

Patrides, C. A. "'Something like Prophetick strain': Apocalyptic Configurations in Milton." In *The Apocalypse in English Renaissance Thought and Literature . . . .* Edited by C. A. Patrides and Joseph Wittreich, 207–37. Ithaca: Cornell University Press, 1984.

Prosser, Eleanor. *Hamlet and Revenge* (1967). Rev. ed. Stanford: Stanford University Press, 1971.

Quispel, Gilles. *The Secret Book of Revelation: The Last Book of the Bible.* Translated by Peter Staples. Maidenhead, England: McGraw-Hill, 1979.

Ratliff, John. "Hieronimo Explains Himself." *SP* 54 (1957): 112–18.

The Reader's Encyclopedia of Shakespeare. Edited by Oscar Campbell and Edward Quinn. New York: Thomas Y. Crowell Co., 1966.

Regosin, Richard. *The Poetry of Inspiration: Agrippa d'Aubigné's "Les Tragiques".* Chapel Hill: University of North Carolina Press, 1970.

Ribner, Irving. *The English History Play in the Age of Shakespeare.* Rev. ed. London: Methuen, 1965.

Rice, Eugene. *Saint Jerome in the Renaissance.* Baltimore: The Johns Hopkins University Press, 1985.

Rowan, D. F. "The Staging of *The Spanish Tragedy.*" In *The Elizabethan Theater V.* Edited by G. R. Hibbard, 112–23. Hamden, Connecticut: Shoe String Press 1975.

Rozett, Martha. *The Doctrine of Election and the Emergence of Elizabethan Tragedy.* Princeton: Princeton University Press, 1984.

Sandler, Florence. "*The Faerie Queene*: An Elizabethan Apocalypse." In *The Apocalypse in English Renaissance Thought and Literature . . . .* Edited by C. A. Patrides and Joseph Wittreich, 148–74. Ithaca: Cornell University Press, 1984.

Schelling, Felix. *Elizabethan Drama 1558–1642: A History of the Drama in England from the Accession of Queen Elizabeth to the Closing of the Theaters* (1908). Reprinted New York: Russell and Russell, 1959.

———. *The English Chronicle Play: A Study in the Popular Historical Literature Environing Shakespeare.* New York: MacMillan, 1902.

Siemon, James R. "Dialogical Formalism: Word, Object, and Action: *The Spanish Tragedy.*" *Medieval and Renaissance Drama in England* 5 (1991): 87–115.

Sinfield, Allan. *Literature in Protestant England 1560–1660.* Totowa, New Jersey: Barnes & Noble, 1983.

Spikes, Judith. "The Jacobean History Play and the Myth of the Elect Nation." *Renaissance Drama* 8 (1977): 117–49.

Stein, Charles. "Justice and Revenge in *The Spanish Tragedy.*" *Iowa State Journal of Research* 56 (1981): 97–104.

Stillman, Carol. "Spenser's Elect England: Political and Apocalyptic Dimensions of *The Faerie Queene*." Ph.D. dissertation, University of Pennsylvania, 1979.

Stone, Walter. "Shakespeare and the Sad Augurs." *JEGP* 52 (1953): 457–79.

Street, J. S. *French Sacred Drama from Bèze to Corneille: Dramatic Forms and Their Purposes in the Early Modern Theatre.* Cambridge: Cambridge University Press, 1983.

Strong, Roy. *Splendor at Court: Renaissance Spectacle and the Theater of Power.* Boston, Massachusetts: Houghton Mifflin Co., 1973.

Sutherland, N. M. "Catherine de' Medici: The Legend of the Wicked Italian Queen." *Sixteenth Century Journal* 9 (1978): 45–73.

——. "The Massacre of St. Bartholomew and the Problem of Spain." In *The Massacre of St. Bartholomew: Reappraisals and Documents.* Edited by Alfred Soman, 15–24. Hague, Netherlands: Martinus Nijhoff, 1974.

Tresley, Richard. "Renaissance Commentaries on The Book of Revelation and Their Influence on Spenser's *Faerie Queene* and D'Aubigné's *Les Tragiques*." Ph.D. dissertation, University of Chicago, 1980.

Valentino, Lucille. "Playing for Power: The Meanings of Elizabethan Entertainment." Ph.D. dissertation, Wayne State University, 1983.

Walker, Bryce. *The Armada.* Alexandria, Virginia: Time–Life Books, 1981.

Williamson, Hugh. *Catherine de' Medici.* London: Michael Joseph, 1973.

Wilson, Elkin C. *England's Eliza* (1939). Reprinted New York: Octagon Books, 1966.

Wilson, F. P. *The English Drama 1485–1585.* Edited by George Hunter. Oxford: Oxford University Press, 1969.

Wineke, Donald. "Hieronimo's Garden and the Fall of Babylon: Culture and Anarchy in *The Spanish Tragedy*." In *Aeolian Harps: Essays in Literature in Honor of Maurice Browning Cramer.* Edited by Donna and Douglas Fricke, 65–79. Bowling Green: Bowling Green University Press, 1976.

Wise, L. F., and E. W. Egan. *Kings, Rulers and Statesmen.* New York: Sterling Publishing Co., 1967.

Wittreich, Joseph. "The Poetry of the Rainbow: Milton and Newton among the Prophets." In *Poetic Prophecy in Western Literature.* Edited by Jan Wojcik and Raymond-Jean Frontain, 94–105. Rutherford, New Jersey: Fairleigh Dickinson University Press, 1984.

Woolf, Rosemary. *The English Mystery Plays.* Los Angeles: University of California Press, 1972.

Yates, Frances. *The French Academies of the Sixteenth Century* (1947). Reprinted Nedeln, Liechtenstein: Kraus Reprint, 1968.

——. *The Valois Tapestries.* London: Warburg Institute, 1959.

Index

Note: Index entries for the biblical books of *Daniel* and *Revelation* have been italicized throughout the index to differentiate them from the historical figure of Daniel and the concept of revelation.

A

The Acts of Queen Elizabeth, 130
Ad Thamesin, 130
"An Address to the Captains and Men on the Armada," 155–56
Admiral's Men, 161
An Admonition to . . . England, 124
Adso, Abbot, 51
Afterworld, 67, 117–20
Albion's England, 130, 163–64
Alençon (Anjou), duke of, 110–11
Allegory. *See also* Mystery
    of the Armada defeat, 127–31, 136–38
    as mystery, 13
    shifts of, 92
Allen, Cardinal William, 124
Amintae Gaudia, 130
Analogies, 24–27
Angels, 7–9, 18
Anjou (Alençon), duke of, 110–11
Annus mirabilis, 122
Antichrist
    Catholic church as, 49
    defeat of, 52, 54, 83–84, 92, 123, 140–41
    medieval view of, 51
    and Philip II, 135
    the pope as, 52–54
    Protestant views of, 1–3, 52
    representatives of, 91–92, 95
    Spain as, xiv, 131–32
    triumph of, 91, 120
Apocalypse, 121–41. *See also* Revelation
    dramatizations of, 51
    eschatology in, 78
    imagery of, 135
    medieval views of, 51
    prediction of, 121–22
    Renaissance views of, 51–55

Apocalypse, *continued*
    The Spanish Tragedy as, 56–80
    and St. Bartholomew's day massacre, 114–15
    symbols of, 73–75
    tour, 17–18
Apologists, of *Revelation*, 51
Archdeacon, Daniel, 128
Armada, Spanish, 125–26
    celebrations of, 127
    context of, 130
    defeat of, xv, 127–28, 133, 135, 157–58, 164–65
    maps of, 127
    and nationalism, 133
    poetry about, 127–31
    subtext of, 145–65
    symbols of, 157–58, 164–65
Arthur, mythical king, 87
Aske, James, 129
Assassination, 94
Astrology, 121, 123
Aubigne, Agrippa d', 115–20
Audiences, 117–20, 165–66
Autos-da-fe, 117

B

Babel, Tower of, 31–32, 125–26
Babylon
    and the Armada, 125–26
    and Catholicism, 32, 39
    dynastic unions of, 33
    fall of, 7, 12, 55, 62–63, 70–71, 123, 158
    languages in, 39
    Rome as, 3, 32
    and Soliman and Persida playlet, 29
    Spain as, 3, 28, 32
Babylon, king of, 3–7, 27, 30, 152
Babylonian Captivity, 7, 123

3

Titles Available in
SIXTEENTH CENTURY ESSAYS & STUDIES SERIES
MC 111-L NMSU · Kirksville MO 63501-4211
Tel. 816-785-4665 · Fax 816-785-4181 · ISBN Prefix 0-940474

Ardolino, Frank. *KYD'S SPANISH TRAGEDY.* Vol. 29 of Sixteenth Century Essays & Studies. ISBN 0-940474-31-X., ...cloth $35.00

Brink, Jean R., ed. *PRIVILEGING GENDER IN EARLY MODERN ENGLAND.* Vol. 23 of Sixteenth Century Essays & Studies, 250 pp. incl. Index. ISBN 0-940474-24-8... cloth $35.00

Brunelle, Gayle. *THE NEW WORLD MERCHANTS OF ROUEN: 1559-1630.* Vol. 16 of Sixteenth Century Essays & Studies, 190 pp. Illus., Index. Bib. ISBN 0-940474-17-4.. cloth $35.00

Burnett, Amy. *THE YOKE OF CHRIST: MARTIN BUCER AND CHRISTIAN DISCIPLINE.* Vol. 26 of Sixteenth Century Essays & Studies, approx. 250 pp. Index. ISBN 0-940474-28-X...cloth $35.00

Christensen, Carl C. *PRINCES AND PROPAGANDA: ELECTORAL SAXON ART OF THE REFORMATION.* Vol. 20 of Sixteenth Century Essays & Studies, 149 pp. Index ISBN 0-940474-21-2...cloth $35.00

Coats, Catherine Randall. *SUBVERTING THE SYSTEM: D'AUBIGNE AND CALVINISM.* Vol. 14 of Sixteenth Century Essays & Studies, 136 pp. Index. ISBN 0-940474-03-4.. CLOTH $35.00

Dick, John A.R., and Ann Richardson. *TYNDALE AND THE LAW.* Vol. 25 of Sixteenth Century Essays & Studies 136 pp. Index. ISBN 0-94047426-3... CLOTH $35.00

Donnelly, John Patrick, Robert M. Kingdon, Marvin W. Anderson, eds. A *BIBLIOGRAPHY OF THE WORKS OF PETER MARTYR VERMIGLI.* Vol. 13 of Sixteenth Century Essays & Studies, 136 pp. Index. ISBN 0-940474-14-X ...... cloth $35.00

Eurich, S. Amanda. *THE ECONOMICS OF POWER: THE PRIVATE FINANCES OF THE HOUSE OF FOIX-NAVARRE-ALBRET DURING THE RELIGIOUS WARS.* Vol. 24 of Sixteenth Century Essays & Studies. 250 pp. Index. ISBN 0-940474025-5 ....cloth $35.00

Fix, Andrew C., and Susan C. Karant-Nunn. *GERMANIA ILLUSTRATA: ESSAYS ON EARLY MODERN GERMANY PRESENTED TO GERALD STRAUSS.* Vol. 18 of Sixteenth Century Essays & Studies, 167 pp. Index. Bib. ISBN 0-940474-19-0... cloth $35.00

Friedman, Jerome. *REGNUM, RELIGIO ET RATIO: ESSAYS PRESENTED TO ROBERT M. KINGDON.* Vol 8 of Sixteenth Century Essays & Studies, 186 pp. Bib. ISBN 0-940474-08-5. .... PBK ONLY. $25.00

Geiger, Gail. *FILIPPINO LIPPI'S CARAFA CHAPEL: RENAISSANCE ART IN ROME.* Vol. 5 of Sixteenth Century Essays & Studies, 240 pp. 80 b&w Illus., Index. Bib. ISBN 0-940474-05-0 .... cloth $50.00

Graham, W. Fred, ed. *LATER CALVINISM: INTERNATIONAL PERSPECTIVES.* Vol. 22 of Sixteenth Century Essays & Studies, 564 pp. Index. ISBN 0-940474-23-0 .... cloth $45.00

Hillerbrand, Hans J., ed. *RADICAL TENDENCIES IN THE REFORMATION: DIVERGENT PERSPECTIVES.* Vol. 9 of Sixteenth Century Essays & Studies, 210 pp. Index. Bib. ISBN 0-940474-09-3... Pbk $25.00

Lindberg, Carter, ed. *PIETY, POLITICS, AND ETHICS: REFORMATION STUDIES IN HONOR OF GEORGE W. FORELL.* Vol. 3 of Sixteenth Century Essays & Studies, 210 pp. Index. Bib. ISBN 0-940474-03-4 .... cloth $35.00

Loeschen, John R. *THE DIVINE COMMUNITY: TRINITY, CHURCH, AND ETHICS IN REFORMATION THEOLOGIES.* Vol. 1 of Sixteenth Century Texts and Studies, 238 pp. Index., Bib. ISBN 0-940474-01-8............................cloth $35.00

Martin, A. Lynn. *JESUIT ACCOUNTS OF EPIDEMIC DISEASE IN THE SIXTEENTH CENTURY.* Vol. 28 of Sixteenth Century Essays & Studies. ISBN 0-940474-30-1... cloth $35.00

Mentzer, Raymond A. *SIN AND THE CALVINISTS: MORALS CONTROL AND THE CONSISTORY IN THE REFORMED TRADITION.* Vol. 32 of Sixteenth Century Essays & Studies. ISBN 0-940474-34-4. .... cloth $35.00

Ryding, Erik S. *IN HARMONY FRAMED: MUSICAL HUMANISM, THOMAS CAMPION, AND THE TWO DANIELS.* Vol. 21 of Sixteenth Century Essays & Studies, 136 pp. Index ISBN 0-940474-22-0.. cloth $35.00

Safley, Thomas Max. *LET NO MAN PUT ASUNDER: THE CONTROL OF MARRIAGE IN THE GERMAN SOUTHWEST 1550-1600.* Vol. 2 of Sixteenth Century Essays & Studies, 210 pp. Index. ISBN 0-940474-02-6. .... cloth $35.00

Schilling, Heinz. *CIVIC CALVINISM IN NORTHWESTERN GERMANY AND THE NETHERLANDS, 16TH-19TH CENTURIES.* Vol. 17 of Sixteenth Century Essays & Studies, 167 pp. Index. Bib. ISBN 0-940474-18-2 .... cloth $35.00

Schnucker, R.V., ed. *CALVINIANA: IDEAS AND INFLUENCE OF JEAN CALVIN.* Vol. 10 of Sixteenth Century Essays & Studies 288 pp. Index. Bib. ISBN 0-940474-10-7..cloth $35.00

Sessions, Kyle, and Philip Bebb, eds. *PIETAS ET SOCIETAS: NEW TRENDS IN REFORMATION SOCIAL HISTORY.* Vol. 4 of Sixteenth Century Essays & Studies, 240 pp. Index. ISBN 0-940474-04-0 .... cloth $35.00

Smeeton, Donald. *LOLLARD THEMES IN THE REFORMATION THEOLOGY OF WILLIAM TYNDALE.* Vol. 6 of Sixteenth Century Essays & Studies, 240 pp. Index. Bib. ISBN 0-940474-06-9... cloth $35.00

Spalding, James C., ed. *THE REFORMATION OF THE ECCLESIASTICAL LAWS OF ENGLAND, 1552.* Vol. 19 of Sixteenth Century Essays & Studies, 274 pp. Illus. Index. ISBN 0-940474-20-4. ....cloth $35.00

Thorp, Malcolm R., and Arthur J. Slavin, eds. *POLITICS, RELIGION AND DIPLOMACY IN EARLY MODERN EUROPE.* Vol. 27 of Sixteenth Century Essays & Studies. ISBN 0-940474-29-8. ....cloth $35.00

Tracy, James. *LUTHER AND THE MODERN STATE OF GERMANY.* Vol. 7 of Sixteenth Century Essays & Studies, 108 pp. Index. ISBN 0-940474-07-7. ....cloth $35.00

Vermigli, Peter Martyr. *EARLY WRITINGS: CREED, SCRIPTURE, CHURCH,* ed. Joseph C. McLelland; tr. Mariano Di Gangi; intro. Philip McNair. *The Peter Martyr Library no. 1.* Vol. 30 of Sixteenth Century Essays & Studies. ISBN 0-940474-32-8...cloth $35.00

Vermigli, Peter Martyr. A *DIALOGUE ON THE TWO NATURES IN CHRIST,* ed. and tr. John Patrick Donnelly, S.J. *The Peter Martyr Library no. 2.* Vol. 31 of Sixteenth Century Essays & Studies. ISBN 0-940474-33-6. ... cloth $35.00

Williams, George Huntston. *THE RADICAL REFORMATION.* 3RD ED., enlarged and revised. Vol. 15 of Sixteenth Century Essays & Studies, 1,513 pp., updated Bib., 5 indexes ISBN 0-940474-27-1 ....pb $50

ISBN 0-940474-15-9..cloth $125.00